D1005962

THE FIRST
FALL CLASSIC

ALSO BY MIKE VACCARO

1941: The Greatest Year in Sports

Emperors and Idiots

THE FIRST
FALL CLASSIC

The Red Sox, the Giants, and the Cast of Players,
Pugs, and Politicos Who Reinvented the
World Series in 1912

Mike Vaccaro

Doubleday
New York   London   Toronto
Sydney   Auckland

DOUBLEDAY

Published in the United States by Doubleday, a division
of Random House, Inc., New York, and in Canada
by Random House of Canada Limited, Toronto.

DOUBLEDAY and the DD colophon are registered trademarks
of Random House, Inc.

All photographs are courtesy of the Library of Congress.

Book design by Michael Collica

Library of Congress Cataloging-in-Publication Data
Vaccaro, Mike
The first fall classic : the Red Sox, the Giants, and the cast
of players, pugs, and politicos who reinvented the World Series
in 1912 / by Mike Vaccaro.
p. cm.
1. World Series (Baseball)—History.
2. New York Giants (Baseball team)—History
3. Boston Red Sox (Baseball team)—History. I. Title.
GV878.4. V33 2009
796.357'646—dc22
2009013121

ISBN 978-0-385-52624-1

PRINTED IN THE UNITED STATES OF AMERICA

10 9 8 7 6 5 4 3 2 1

First Edition

For Ann McMahon Vaccaro, my first editor, who provided rides to Little League games, offered the loudest cheers at CYO basketball games, tendered unconditional love when it was needed most, and supplies an unrelenting Irish optimism that sustains in a world too often commanded by pessimists, skeptics, cynics, and doubters.

CONTENTS

Contents

Author's Note

Most of this book—perhaps 80 percent, perhaps more—is the product of reading contemporary news accounts of all the newspapers and periodicals listed in the Acknowledgments section, covering the prime events detailed in this book: the Becker Trial, the presidential campaign of 1912, the assassination attempt of Theodore Roosevelt, and, of course, the 1912 World Series.

Where matters of fact were concerned—the who, the what, the where, why, and how—I made certain that there were at least two sources that concurred. In order to err on the side of accuracy, I omitted all instances where there were differing accounts of basic facts. As for quotes: Everything outside of conversations between characters that appears between quotation marks in this book appeared previously either in one of the cited newspapers or periodicals or in the research materials provided by the National Baseball Hall of Fame Museum. The sole liberties taken involved re-creating conversations that were referred to outside of quotations by the principals involved in those conversations; these I tried to reconstruct as faithfully as possible, given the knowledge gleaned from studying their characters and personalities over the course of fourteen months of research.

I am confident that having applied these standards to every sentence, everything contained in this book is factual and faithful; any errors that do appear are mine and mine alone to answer for.

THE FIRST
FALL CLASSIC

INTRODUCTION

BOSTON— The muckerishness of the fan is exceeding itself in muck this Fall. Boston howled that it was "all fixed," then raved over their team when it won. New York screamed that the Giants were throwing the series. After every game in New York and Boston we were compelled to listen to wild yarns of drinking and dissipation. Such persons really aren't worth answering, but to them one can only say: If they will invent some system by which baseball games can be made crooked without being detected in two innings they can make fortunes . . .

—HUGH S. FULLERTON, *CHICAGO DAILY TRIBUNE*,
OCTOBER 20, 1912

"THE FIRST TIME you see that sign," David Wright said, "it scares the crap out of you, especially if you know a little bit about history."

Wright, the third baseman for the New York Mets, was sitting in front of his locker at Shea Stadium in the spring of 2008, pointing over to where the words of Rule Twenty-one were posted on a far wall of the home team's dressing room. In one form or another, the same words have appeared in every clubhouse in every major-league baseball stadium since 1927, when Rule Twenty-one was officially adopted at the urging of Kenesaw Mountain Landis, the first commissioner of baseball, a man hired in the wake of the most infamous gambling scandal in the history of professional American sport. From the moment a baseball player signs his first pro contract, these words—and the spirit of the words—are drilled, and instilled, and grilled, in a place of permanence and prominence deep within their souls:

"Any player, umpire, or club or league official or employee, who shall bet any sum whatsoever upon any baseball game in connection with which the bettor has not duty to perform, shall be declared ineligible for one year. Any player, umpire, or club or league official or employee, who shall bet any sum whatsoever upon any baseball game in connection with which the bettor has a duty to perform shall be declared permanently ineligible."

"It's hard to conceive of a world in which that kind of stuff is even possible," Wright said, before nodding at another sign listing another set of crimes and consequences. "Now *that*, I guess, seems more relevant to me."

He was pointing at a new set of regulations freshly introduced to baseball clubhouses in recent years, detailing the punishment schedule for any player found using performance-enhancing drugs. For most of its latter history, baseball had turned a blind eye to steroids, HGH, amphetamines, and every other manner of illegal or illicit pharmaceutical (since 2002, it has tried to first minimize and now eliminate entirely steroids' scourge from its landscape, a slow and painstaking process). In its own way, that mirrored how, for most of its earlier history, baseball had turned a deaf ear and a blind eye to the gamblers, bookmakers, shylocks, and fixers who crowded its grandstands.

Wright shook his head, smiled. The average baseball salary in 2008 was $2 million, meaning ballplayers weren't quite the easy marks they were a century earlier, when many of them barely made $4,000 a year. The bookmakers who resided in the game's shadows at the turn of the last century had been replaced by steroid suppliers at the dawn of the new one.

"I guess every generation has its temptations," he said.

Speaking in a different century, inside a different New York City ballpark, describing in many ways an entirely different game, John J. McGraw held court before a small group of New York City newspapermen on the eve of the 1912 World Series, sitting in a dugout at the Polo Grounds, watching his baseball team take batting practice.

"I don't worry about my boys," said McGraw, manager of the National League–champion New York Giants, "and I wouldn't worry about any group of baseball players good enough to win the pennant in their league. You have to be good at the game, and very skilled, that's true. But you'd also better be of sound mind and character. If you are, then nothing else matters. Certainly not something as simple as money."

Then McGraw, whose scatology was legendary in those early years of the twentieth century, smiled, spit a stream of tobacco, and summarized his sentiments in a sentence that made the sportswriters smile.

"Any son of a bitch can make money," he said. "But it takes a *special* son of a bitch to be a world's champion."

Such was the way baseball conducted its business and policed its players in those times that are often described either as "simpler" or "more innocent"; times, we have long been told, when men were men and they played for the love of the game, before the sport was polluted by money and greed and the corrupting peripheral influences endemic to them. True students of baseball have long had a word for that fable: "Nonsense."

McGraw, were he so inclined, might have chosen a different word.

"Bullshit," for instance.

In 1912, when ballplayers played for as little as $1,500 a year and as much as $15,000 a year, they endorsed everything from cigarettes to smokeless tobacco to shoes to whiskey to automobiles and everything else available to consumers flush with disposable income in a relatively prosperous time. They authored books, published newspaper columns, lent their surnames to dram shops and eateries of both high repute and low esteem. They made, on average, anywhere between 5 percent and 200 percent more than the average American worker, traveled in first-class accommodations, lodged at the best hotels, ate gourmet meals mostly on the arm, and if they knew which saloons to visit they could drink to their liver's content without ever once blowing dust off their billfold.

On off days, and in their spare time, they played poker, bridge, rummy, checkers, chess, billiards, and golf, and they didn't exactly play strictly for the love of *those* games, either.

"We were professionals," Fred Snodgrass, a center fielder for McGraw's Giants, would say near the end of his life, looking back fondly from a distance of fifty years. "And professionals get paid."

Not nearly enough, either, if you asked them to tell the truth.

Still, there was a stubborn saliency to McGraw's words. The ballplayers who were *only* in it for the money, and who made no pretense about chasing dollars more than dreams, tended to spend their careers mired in the second division. Hal Chase, for instance, a gifted first baseman who made his major-league debut in 1905 for the New York Highlanders of the American League, was known to consort with gamblers in public, and it was an open, dirty secret that some of his strikeouts and some of his fielding errors were significantly more than the product of baseball probability. He was for sale, and the Highlanders (later the Yankees), Chicago White Sox, Cincinnati Reds, and New York Giants—and, briefly, the Buffalo Blues of the short-lived renegade Federal League—suffered for his proclivities.

No, the men of McGraw's Giants, who in a few days would host the men of Jake Stahl's Boston Red Sox in the first game of the ninth annual World Series, surely wanted to win a championship. They wanted to be able to hang the large "World's Champions" flag that would fly high over the victor's ballpark for all of the 1913 season. They wanted to wear the commemorative clips that generally went to the winners, a permanent symbol of triumph. Back in 1905, after the Giants had captured their first Series title, McGraw had outfitted them in gaudy uniforms that declared them world champions in big block letters, and had provided them with the finest livery and cab service to out-of-town ballgames.

Fine perks, all of them.

But so were these: The $4,000 or so that would go to each member of the winning side (compared to less than $3,000 for the losers), which for some was equal to if not more than their annual income. The vaudeville contracts the winners would be awarded, which could bring in as much as $200 a week depending on the generosity of the impresario, the size of the house, and the breadth of the heroics turned in by the lucky winners.

To say nothing of the potential return on their investment if they'd decided to lay a few dollars down with any of the bookmakers who were as visible at the ballparks as vendors, ushers, and umpires. And if you played for the Giants, you could get yourself at some pretty favorable odds, too: two days before Game One, bookies were pegging the Red Sox as 10-to-8 favorites.

In years to come, all of this would prove to be too much for ballplayers who'd grown tired of watching team owners rake in huge profits from these annual October get-togethers, who'd grown weary fighting with the National Commission, the sport's governing body that never, not once, ruled against the owners in matters of arbitration. Seven years hence, in fact, some of the nation's most prominent gamblers would pull the ultimate coup: They would neatly fold eight members of the Chicago White Sox into their back pockets and fix the World Series, nearly crushing the sport in the bargain.

That, though, was still well in the future. For in 1912, baseball would witness a genuine, beautiful contest quite unlike any that had ever transpired. There would be, that year, a World Series that would put the World Series on the map, and it would take years for another series to come along to match it.

For now, even while those very same prominent gamblers were very much in public view—even as *the* most prominent, a New York hustler named Arnold Rothstein, was entering into a partnership with McGraw opening pool halls across the city—baseball would get lucky, at least in October of 1912. The sport would get two teams, winners of a combined 208 games during the regular season, who may well have been the two finest ballclubs ever assembled to that point. No fewer than five of the men in uniform in that world's series would ultimately find a permanent home in Cooperstown, New York, enshrined in baseball's Hall of Fame.

Most important, during the course of eight games spanning nine days in that marvelous baseball autumn, they would elevate the World Series from a regional October novelty to a national obsession, they would show just how arresting and addictive the game could be (especially when it was played on the level—or, at the least, *mostly* on the level), they would introduce the rest of the nation to the reality of rabid, passionate, unyielding fans willing to go to any length to support their teams. The games would fight for space on the front pages of the nation's newspapers, battling both an assassin's bullet and the most sensational trial of the young century, with the games often carrying the day and earning the "wood."

And they would deliver what remains, nearly a century later, the greatest World Series ever played—so great, in fact, that in all future years, both words would be permanently capitalized. In so many ways, then, the World Series was really born in 1912. What follows is why.

CHAPTER ONE

Spring, Summer, Fall, 1912: A Prelude

NEW YORK—The advance fanfare is over. The English
language has been plucked of its final consonants, and the
last of all figures extant has been twisted out of shape in the
maelstrom of a million arguments. And now, at the end of it,
there is nothing left. Nothing left but the charge of the
Night Brigade against the gates at dawn to-morrow—and
after that the first boding hush as Harry Hooper flies out
from the Red Sox coop and stands face to face with
Mathewson, the veteran, or Tesreau, the debutante . . .

—GRANTLAND RICE, *NEW YORK EVENING MAIL,*
OCTOBER 7, 1912

T HE POOR BASTARDS, they never had a chance, they never even
saw the damned thing coming. It was a beautiful Friday night,
September 27, 1912, a perfect evening to take the sparkling new toy
for a spin, and so twenty-nine-year-old Frank O'Neil and twenty-
year-old William Popp, neighbors from Manhattan's Upper West
Side, had decided to take their freshly souped-up motorcycle for a
breezy ride through the streets of Harlem, and they'd mostly been
ignoring the posted speed limit of nine miles per hour because, let's
face it, who *didn't* disregard that patently absurd and outdated law;

horse-drawn carriages were allowed to zip along at *twelve* miles an hour, for crying out loud.

So there they were, young, free, blissfully sailing down a hill at the foot of 145th Street and St. Nicholas Avenue, when, quite suddenly, their worlds went dark as the night sky above them. A man named Frank Linke, driving a Model T Speedster and actually *obeying* the speed limit, hit them flush with the bumper of his brand-new automobile. O'Neil and Popp went flying over the handlebars of their ruined motorcycle, and now both of them were lying on the street, O'Neil bleeding from his mouth thanks to a bruised liver and damaged gallbladder, Popp groaning thanks to a collarbone now rendered a *collection* of collarbones.

Frank Linke, more horrified than hurt, searched frantically for policemen.

But before he could locate one, he found himself caught in the glare of a set of headlights belonging to a brand-new Cadillac speeding straight for him before screeching to a halt. Out of the car leapt a tall, lanky man wearing a tam-o'-shanter on his head and a brown suit coat over his shoulder, his spit-shined Regal shoes hitting the pavement without missing a stride.

"Put them in my car!" yelled the helpful stranger.

By now, a policeman named Michael Walsh had arrived at the scene, and his first inclination was to shoo the Good Samaritan to the sidewalk . . . except, as the well-dressed visitor's face grew brighter under the glow of the streetlight, Officer Michael Walsh could barely say anything.

"It's . . . it's . . . *you*," the cop said.

Frank Linke, still trembling, squinted at the stranger and his eyes brightened.

"It *is* you," he stammered.

"Yes," said Christy Mathewson, the calmest voice of the three, speaking above Popp's groans and the wails of the neighborhood dogs, "it's me. Now, may I suggest loading these unfortunate gentlemen in my car, so we can get them to the hospital?"

Walsh carefully guided Popp to his feet, loaded him in the front seat of Mathewson's car. Walsh, Linke, and Mathewson laid O'Neil, still unconscious, across the back.

"Hey," Linke said, "how'd you guys do today, Matty?"

"We beat the Braves," Mathewson said. "Seven to six."

"Good luck in the series next week," Walsh, the policeman, interjected. "I'm hearing you guys will be heavy underdogs against the Red Sox."

Mathewson smiled.

"We'll see about that," he said. "Now, can you see to it that none of your brethren stop me on the way to the hospital? They have a knack of pulling me over and giving me speeding tickets."

"No worry," he was told. "Just tell them you know Walsh of the One-Five-Two. And I guess if that doesn't work, show them your cargo."

With that, the most famous athlete in the United States of America gunned his gas pedal, sped off into the night for the thirty-block drive toward Washington Heights Hospital. Walsh looked at Linke, still shaken, then peered over at the Speedster, which had a fair-sized dent in it.

"Too bad about your car," the cop said.

"I met Big Six tonight," Frank Linke said. Maybe the dent would bother him in the morning. For now, he probably couldn't see it for the stars in his eyes.

Of course they recognized Christopher Mathewson—known as "Christy" or "Matty" to the common man; known as "Big Six" to teammate and opponent alike, though no one was ever quite sure why; referred to as "The Christian Gentleman" on the editorial pages of the nation's newspapers, which regularly espoused Mathewson as an ideal role model for both pie-eyed youth and weary citizen alike. Of course they knew the man who had won, to that very moment, 328 games, more than any pitcher who ever lived save for the great Cy Young (and even in 1912, Young's record of 511 career victories had been declared all but unapproachable), the man who had gained lasting fame tossing three shutouts at the Philadelphia Athletics in the 1905 World Series, the man who embodied, along with his pugnacious manager John Joseph McGraw, the very spirit of the New York Giants, the flagship team of the National League, the pride of Manhattan, the obsession of composer George M. Cohan and Mayor William Jay Gaynor and ex–heavyweight champion James J. Corbett, to name three prominent acolytes.

This wasn't a malady unique to New York City, of course, for no matter where you traveled in the cities where major-league baseball was played, baseball players were *always* the most identifiable names and faces, more so than any cop or commissioner, any actor or singer, any pug or politician, any rabbi, priest, or minister. So the denizens of Detroit could spot Ty Cobb or Hughie Jennings from a hundred paces, and the people of Pittsburgh could easily spy Honus Wagner and Claude Hendrix, and the citizens of Chicago were always on the lookout for Joe Tinker and Johnny Evers if they were walking the West Side, home of the National League Cubs, or Ping Bodie and Ed Walsh if they were sauntering along the South Side, ruled by the American League's White Sox.

And in Boston, the self-appointed Hub of the Universe, if you toiled for the Braves at decrepit old South End Grounds or for the Red Sox at gleaming new Fenway Park, you weren't merely a celebrity, you were practically *celestial*. The Braves had a rough go of things in 1912, losing 101 of the 153 games they played, finishing fifty-two games behind the Giants in the National League, but they did feature a future Hall of Famer in twenty-year-old Rabbit Maranville, they did have a perfectly parochially named pitcher named Herbert "Hub" Perdue (who really didn't need an extra nickname since he'd already been elegantly dubbed "The Gallatin Squash"), and they had the requisite player named "Rube" (no fewer than fourteen men with that less-than-flattering sobriquet were scattered throughout the major leagues in 1912), born Floyd Myron Kroh, who pitched six and a third innings that year, allowed eight hits, six runs, and then quietly faded into retirement before anyone could notice he was gone.

It was the Red Sox, however, who captured the imagination of the faithful in New England and placed a lien on their baseball souls, whose 105 victories shattered the single-season record in the twelve-year history of the American League, who featured an array of stars the locals nicknamed "The Speed Boys" and a rabid following of locals who dubbed themselves the "Royal Rooters"; it is debatable which group would earn more fame across that splendid summer of 1912.

The Speed Boys had Tris Speaker in center field, a twenty-four-year-old Texan who would hit .383 that season and .345 for his career, a number surpassed by only five men in the history of the game. Every fourth day (and sometimes more frequently than that), they sent to the pitcher's mound a twenty-two-year-old native of Kansas City named Joe Wood, universally referred to as "Smoky Joe," who that year would enjoy perhaps the finest season any pitcher ever enjoyed, winning thirty-four games, ten by shutout, striking out 258 in 344 innings, and pitching to a microscopic earned run average of 1.91.

But the Royal Rooters had on *their* roster a spirited leader named Michael T. McGreevy, the proprietor of a popular tavern named the Third Base Saloon (on whose storefront a sign maker had misfortunately misspelled the surname, adding an extra *e* before the *y*, a common indignity suffered by so many sons of the Old Country), which was so named because it was, in the parlance of the favored game discussed within its walls, "the last stop on the way home." Nobody called the affable owner Michael, or Mike, or Mick; he was "Nuf Ced," which was the command with which he ended any beery argument—baseball, business, politics, money—that filled his lively inn, always punctuated by a tobacco dart sent to a nearby spittoon. Another prominent voice among the Rooters was the foghorn baritone belonging to forty-nine-year-old John Francis Fitzgerald, the fourth of twelve children born to hardworking survivors of the Irish Potato Famine of 1840 who'd emigrated from Counties Limerick and Cavan. Fitzgerald aspired to be a doctor and even spent a year at Harvard Medical School, but when his parents died young he'd been forced to drop out and take a job as a clerk at the Boston Customs House to support his siblings. Soon enough, Fitzgerald immersed himself in the Democratic political machine that ruled the city's North End, he picked up a catchy nickname—"Honey Fitz," a tribute to his boundless blarney—then got himself elected to Congress in 1894. And in 1906, Honey Fitz became the first Irish-American mayor of this city whose sound track was increasingly being brushed by the brogue. Defeated in his first bid at reelection two years later, by 1910 he was restored to office and as the 1912 baseball season dawned the Red Sox had essentially become a central part of his personal political platform.

"Baseball," Fitzgerald said late in September of 1912, after the Red Sox had wrapped up the pennant and ensured themselves a spot in the World Series, "embodies all that is good about America. And the Red Sox embody all that is good about the great city of Boston. We already know that. Soon enough, so will the rest of the country."

By then, the nation had other sporting icons to worship, if they wished, besides the 400 or so men who filled out the sixteen major league rosters to choose from. That summer, at the Games of the Fifth Olympiad in Stockholm, Sweden, an American Indian named Jim Thorpe, whose Sac and Fox Nation name (Wha-Tho-Huk) translated to "Bright Path," won both the decathlon and the pentathlon, an astonishing feat of sporting mastery. On the medal stand, King Gutsav V declared, "You, sir, are the greatest athlete in the world." To which Thorpe replied: "Thanks, King." Though he was soon honored with a ticker-tape parade down the canyon of heroes along New York's lower Broadway, Thorpe's story would take a sad twist when it was discovered he had been paid about $2 a game for a professional baseball team in Rocky Mount, North Carolina, a few years earlier. This led the International Olympic Committee to revoke his amateur status and strip his medals; it would be some seventy years before they were returned to his family.

If Thorpe had been unofficially declared the world's greatest athlete, another American, Jack Johnson, was undoubtedly its most notorious. It so happened that Johnson was black; he also happened to be the undisputed heavyweight boxing champion of the world, having won the crown on December 26, 1908, when he'd decimated a Canadian named Tommy Burns, punishing him for fourteen rounds in Sydney, Australia, before local police finally stepped into the ring to stop the beating. Johnson's was an unwelcome ascent and the news of his victory was hardly greeted with glee in his native country, where he'd been born in Galveston, Texas, in 1878, to Henry and Tina Johnson, both former slaves, and 1912 marked the fourth unsuccessful year of seven in the worldwide pursuit of a "Great White Hope" that would restore color-coded sanity to the sweet science.

In 1912, life as an African-American was in truth only slightly brighter than it had been forty-nine years earlier, when the Emancipation Proclamation had been ratified, promising a new life and a new path for children of bondage, pledges that had yet to be delivered. Lynchings littered the South while more subtle discrimination prevailed in the North. The Democratic nominee for president, Woodrow Wilson, a son of Virginia and the president of Princeton University, a northern bastion, was an avowed racial supremacist, while even the Republicans—the Party of Lincoln—refused to make civil rights a prominent part of their platform. And even former president Theodore Roosevelt, running on the Progressive Party (or Bull Moose) ticket, refused to tackle racial issues on *his* campaign tour, despite privately railing against prejudice, segregation, and inequality. Johnson, of course, wasn't exactly a unifier. As champion, he spent money wildly and lived flamboyantly, refusing to bend to white discomfort. He married a white woman, Etta Terry Duryea, and when she committed suicide in 1911 he began courting another white woman, Lillian Cameron. And on October 18—two days after the Giants and Red Sox would decide the championship of the baseball season once and for all—Johnson would be arrested in Chicago and charged with "abduction," an arrest prompted by the nineteen-year-old bride-to-be's mother accusing the heavyweight champion of the world of "dereliction" and "kidnapping."

Fans assumed they had no such concerns about the Christian

Gentleman, or any of the other men who'd elevated baseball to such a sacrosanct part of the national culture and whose feats—whether legitimate or hyperbolic—were fed daily to an insatiable public in the ever-growing sports sections of their daily newspapers. For two cents a day, you could learn everything you wanted to know about Big Six, about Muggsy McGraw, about grown men named Rube and Hub and Heinie and various baseball players who weren't only virulent, but virtuous, too.

That was their conviction, anyway, and they would stick to it stubbornly.

The Giants and the Red Sox couldn't possibly have started their journeys toward their epic confrontation in more diverse locations. The Boston players eagerly anticipated the commencement of spring training, for it would mean gathering in Hot Springs, Arkansas, which in 1912 was the Las Vegas of its day, replete with opulent hotels, bathhouses, and restaurants, bountiful casinos and golf courses and a racetrack. The Red Sox could sweat under the scorching sun all morning and long into the afternoon, meticulously preparing themselves for the six-month test at hand, before retiring to an evening full of possibilities for themselves and the three other teams—the Philadelphia Phillies, Pittsburgh Pirates, and Brooklyn Superbas—who shared Hot Springs as a training-camp dateline.

The Giants, meanwhile, had years before abandoned Los Angeles, where McGraw despaired at the distractions that would too often invade his baseball boot camp, and settled in a small Texas hamlet of four thousand residents called Marlin Springs. If you drew an equilateral triangle connecting Dallas, Houston, and San Antonio, Marlin would fall right about in the heart of it, meaning it was close enough for residents of those cities to make weekend pilgrimages to watch the Giants play baseball but far enough away where the temptations lurking in those towns were safely out of the reach of restless ballplayers during the week. The Giants in 1912 were quartered at the Arlington Hotel, a perfectly clean, perfectly respectable lodging house that wasn't soon to be confused with the Waldorf-Astoria. Each morning, the Giants would hike along railroad tracks to the training complex, a good half-mile away, and every afternoon they would retrace their steps back.

In between, McGraw drilled them mercilessly, rode them relentlessly.

"I put my heel down good and hard," said the man known alternately as Little Napoleon and Muggsy (though never to his face).

The Giants who gathered in this dusty paradise came bearing hurt feelings and elevated ambitions. The year before, they'd captured New York's first pennant in six seasons only to be squashed in the Series in six games by the Philadelphia Athletics, managed by Connie Mack, the one man in all of baseball McGraw believed could approach (though never surpass) him in terms of strategy, success, and acumen. Twice the Giants had lost extra-innings heartbreakers at home, in the friendly Polo Grounds, before getting steamrolled 13–2 by the A's at Philadelphia's Shibe Park, where fans rejoiced at the Giants' humiliation. McGraw, an American League émigré, had long denounced the younger league as "inferior," had in fact once helped engineer a boycott of the World Series because he believed it a substandard assemblage of second-rate talent. It was one thing to finish second best in the National League, as the Giants had done three times since 1905; the NL, after all, played the best brand of baseball on the planet.

But to lose to—McGraw's phrase—a "haphazard" league?

It was unthinkable. McGraw, thirty-nine years old, product of a hardscrabble upbringing that was reflected in his baseball philosophy and proud that he was now the highest-paid manager in professional baseball, stewed all winter. In the off-season, he'd led a contingent of Giants on a triumphant tour of Cuba—a country where, years before, as a member of a minor league team from Wellsville, New York, he'd earned the affectionate nickname "El Mono Amarillo" (the Yellow Monkey). They were heavy favorites to repeat in the National League.

None of that made McGraw's disposition any sunnier.

"I don't ever want to feel the way I felt last October, men," he said on the first day of camp. "And I certainly hope you feel the same way. Or else you can find another Goddamned nine to play for."

McGraw, studying his team each day under the oppressive Texas sun, knew he had the horses to breathe life into even his most demanding aspirations. He knew he had good pitching: Mathewson owned the most famous right arm in the sport, left-hander Rube Marquard had won twenty-four games the year before, and there was a big, raw kid in camp from Ironton, Missouri, Jeff Tesreau, whose fastball had caught McGraw's attention and whose spitball had dazzled his imagination. Fred Snodgrass, the catcher–turned–center fielder, was raking the ball all spring, as was Larry Doyle, the second baseman who was McGraw's manager on the field. Even outfielder Red Murray, who'd incurred New York City's wrath by going hitless in twenty-two at-bats in the World Series, looked to be of sound mind and body.

Not all was perfect; Fred Merkle, the first baseman still best known for committing the rock-headed baserunning blunder that had famously cost the Giants a pennant in 1908, was unhappy with his salary and holding out of camp. Merkle, in fact, had actually accompanied the team to New York's Grand Central Station before making a point of refusing to step off the platform and into his waiting sleeper car.

"If McGraw doesn't come across with the necessary money then I refuse to play," Merkle told reporters as he watched the train head west. "I will go back to Toledo immediately and take up my study of law again."

McGraw—who'd gone to the wall for Merkle, who'd defended him publicly and privately for four years despite all the civic slander his mistake invited—bristled at this overt display of disloyalty. But what could he do? "I need the Bonehead's bat in my batting order," he grumped to his coach and closest friend, Wilbert Robinson, over a hand of bridge a few hours later.

Four hundred miles away, the Red Sox were quietly starting to believe that they, too, had something worth getting excited about.

The Sox (then called the Americans) had won the very first World Series ever contested, in 1903, beating Pittsburgh five games to three in a best-of-nine match, and had been hoping to repeat the trick a year later before being rebuffed by McGraw's Giants, the National League champ that refused to play them. Since that triumphant 1904 season—a pennant made all the more satisfying because it came at the expense of New York City, the Pilgrims outlasting the Highlanders on the final weekend of the season—the franchise had fallen on hard times, bottoming out at a frightful 49–105 mark in 1906. Boston had rebounded to win 88 and 81 games in 1909 and 1910, but a regression to 78–75 in 1911 cost manager Patsy Donovan his job. By then, there had also been a shift in the team's corporate leadership, as owner John I. Taylor decided to sell half an interest to a group led by Jimmy McAleer, the manager of the Washington Senators who was really a front for AL president Ban Johnson, who wanted a piece of his league's most lucrative franchise.

To replace Donovan, McAleer placed a call to the president of the Washington Park National Bank in Chicago, to a thirty-two-year-old man who until recently also played a rather elegant first base for the Red Sox. Jake Stahl had retired after the 1910 season to go work for his father-in-law, Henry W. Mahan, and had settled into a comfortable life as an investment specialist. But Mahan was another of Johnson's silent partners, and Stahl was promised a stake in the club as well, and so it was that Stahl found himself in Hot Springs in late February, welcoming a team to whom few gave any hope of challenging the champion Athletics.

"I have lots to do and lots to learn," Stahl said, "and not a lot of time in which to get acclimated." But he liked what he saw, especially his outfield, which he knew had the makings of something special. Speaker was blossoming into a star, anyone could see that, but flanking him to the left was Duffy Lewis, one of the slickest-fielding outfielders Stahl or anyone else had ever seen, and to his right was Harry Hooper, a man who'd recently forced baseball's rule makers to blue-pencil their sacred text. Hooper, it seems, had perfected the art of patty-caking fly balls hit to him in right field, a tactic that was especially useful when a man on third base was thinking of tagging up on a sacrifice fly. Hooper wouldn't actually *catch* the ball until he was a few strides back of the infield, a clever ploy that was now rendered useless; the new rules said a runner could now leave for home the moment an outfielder made contact with the ball.

Stahl himself would play first base. Larry Gardner would play third. Hick Cady and Bill Carrigan would share the catching duties. Wood was a hell of an anchor for his pitching staff, and Stahl figured the rest would shake into place soon enough.

"I make no predictions," he told *The Sporting News* in mid-March. "But I like what I've seen so far."

Such was the optimism springing up all over the southern half of the nation, where slowly baseball teams were kicking off the rust of a long off-season, where the players were trying to melt off the fifteen or twenty extra pounds they accumulated while toiling in winter jobs that almost all of them took to supplement their baseball income. Such was the happy talk heard in New Orleans, where the Cubs and Cleveland Indians trained, and in Waco, which hosted the White Sox, and in Monroe, Louisiana, where the Tigers worked out, and even in St. Louis, whose climate was mild enough that the home-town Browns and Cardinals opted to keep the boys home for their drillings.

Even as the season drew nearer, the hold baseball held on the public at large became even more apparent as stories about the game began cropping up in other parts of the newspaper, as well. On February 28, for instance, a bill that would have given cities in New York the local option of playing Sunday home games was buried in committee in the state legislature, killing the proposal for another year, retaining the "blue laws" that kept ballparks quiet on the Sabbath and deprived the Giants, Yankees, and Dodgers from reaping the weekly windfall Sunday baseball would surely have provided.

Then, on March 11, a congressional investigation of the "baseball trust, the most audacious and autocratic trust in the country," was proposed in a resolution introduced by Representative Thomas Gallagher of Illinois, a measure that would create a special committee of seven representatives to inquire of the Department of Justice "what steps have been taken against the base ball trust as against other illegal combinations" to subpoena witnesses and employ assistants. It accused "the base ball trust of presuming to control the base ball game, its officials announcing daily through the press the dictates of a governing commission, how competition is stifled, territory and games apportioned, prices fixed which millions must pay to witness the sport, how men are enslaved and forced to accept salaries and terms or be forever barred from playing." In trust-busting 1912, when the single biggest issue facing presidential candidates was how they would deal with the nation's "monopoly problem," it seemed only right that baseball—still called "base ball" in many places—should undergo similar scrutiny.

Only baseball didn't quite see it that way.

The Sporting News, which billed itself as "The Baseball Bible" but was, in reality, an unabashed house organ for baseball's owners, raged in an unsigned editorial: "It is not necessary to go into the necessity for contracts, reserve clauses, etc. The ordinary intelligent fan well appreciates the fact that they are regulations required for the conduct of the game. And knowing what is necessary for the game they will have no sympathy for the 'statesman' who seeks for some purposes not yet clear to embarrass the administration of the game. Once the fans of his district get the idea that he means to be serious in his attack on their popular sport he is likely to be more 'put out' than he is described as being at the smiles of base ball leaders. The players whose interests Congressman Gallagher has so much at heart will be the best witnesses for the defense."

The political uprising, not surprisingly, dissolved quietly, and by 1922 baseball would even be granted an antitrust exemption by the U.S. Supreme Court, an immunity that prevails eighty-seven years later. But that didn't prevent other lawmakers from believing that baseball's ubiquitous place in American culture merited some heavy-handed regulation to protect it from that culture's more sinister elements. Later in March, Pennsylvania governor John K. Tener, who had played three years of big-league ball in the 1880s, declared betting a "devil" in the game that "needed to be driven out, at once. If the sport is to be kept clean, local authorities should take steps to prevent pool-selling on the results of games, high scores, and innings.

"In some cities," charged Tener, "so much betting has been going on that the state police have been watching it and if District Attorneys are inclined to act I will back them with all the influence of the state administration."

Still, as the season finally began on Thursday, April 11, everyone seemed to be settled into their proper place: Merkle in the Giants' dugout (after finally agreeing to a modest $500 raise), the Red Sox in their gleaming new palace by the Fens, and bookmakers planted in their familiar grandstand locations in all sixteen major-league parks. It was, indeed, time to play ball.

It didn't take long, once the games began, to determine the class of either league. The Giants lost three of their first four games, but then rattled off wins in their next nine games and nineteen of their next twenty to keep pace with Cincinnati, which had broken from the gate with an equally sizzling start, and when they arrived at brand-new Crosley Field on Saturday, May 18, for the start of a five-game series, the Giants, at 19–4, were a half-game ahead of the 20–6 Reds. The hosts won the first two games, both tight, taut 4–3 affairs, before the Giants roared back to win the next three and seize first place—for good, as it turned out.

In fact, for much of the season, the Giants threatened to make mincemeat out of the National League. After sixty-nine games, their record stood at 56–13, and there has not been a team in the modern era that has approached that kind of scorching start. By the Fourth of July the Giants had a sixteen-game lead on the rest of the league, and not only did that inspire the baseball cognoscenti to wonder if this might not be the finest assemblage of baseball talent ever, it also served them as proof that the sport, as a whole, was on the up-and-up; surely, the argument went, the Giants were killing themselves at the box office by removing the mystery from the pennant race. Of course, Giants fans had long been looked at as a "peculiar" brand of fan, because the Polo Grounds denizens were known to cheer just as lustily for opponents who performed well as for their own home-grown heroes. Besides, Giants owner John T. Brush had already flirted with alienating his fans, eliminating almost all of the twenty-five-cent seats at the Grounds, and switching starting times of week-day games to 4 o'clock from 3:30, the better to lure the prosperous Wall Street crowd uptown. There was a brief outcry, because the later starting time interfered with dinnertime in many blue-collar homes, and an informal poll taken at the turnstiles informed Brush that some 85 percent of his fans wished the starting times moved back. Brush read the results, pondered them, then ignored them.

"Look at the club Brush has," a fan named Seamus Kelly said one July afternoon, waiting outside the Grounds to purchase tickets for a game against the Cubs. "He thinks he can get away with doing any-thing he wants with it. And he's right."

The Giants' dominance was fueled by excellent pitching, though not by the pitcher you might suspect. Mathewson turned in his usu-ally resplendent season—23–12, 2.12 earned run average, thirty-four complete games in forty-three starts—but two odd things occurred. First, for the first time since a six-game sip of coffee as a rookie in 1900 (and for what would be the only time in his whole seventeen-year career), Mathewson failed to record a shutout. More surprising, for much of the year, he wasn't the clear-cut ace of the New York staff. That honor fell to one of baseball's fourteen Rubes—in this case, Richard William Marquard, a city kid from Cleveland who earned his nickname as a minor leaguer in Indi-anapolis thanks to his physical resemblance to another hard-throwing lefty of the day, George Edward "Rube" Waddell. Marquard had been a pet project of McGraw's, the manager paying Indianapolis an unheard-of $11,000 to secure his services for the Giants. The New York sportswriters quickly dubbed Marquard

"The $11,000 Peach," but after three years, after he'd put together an unsightly 9–18 record in forty-three career games, the scribes had gleefully switched that moniker to "The $11,000 Lemon" instead.

But in 1911, Marquard had unexpectedly blossomed into a star, going 24–7 with a 2.50 ERA and emerging as a perfect left-handed sidekick to Mathewson. So delighted was McGraw by his protégé's development that he gave Marquard the honor of pitching the season opener in 1912, an 18–3 romp for the Giants over the Dodgers in Brooklyn's Washington Park. Marquard won his next start, too, at home against the Braves, and his next one, as well, at Philadelphia, and he kept winning, and he kept winning, and by the time the Giants arrived at Chicago's West Side Park on July 8, not only did the team have a gaudy fifteen-game lead in the standings, but Marquard's record sat at an otherworldly 19–0 (and should have been 20–0; on April 20, Marquard had relieved Jeff Tesreau late in a game the Giants trailed 3–2 before rallying for a 4–3 win. The official scorer, for reasons known only to him, nevertheless awarded the victory to Tesreau). Nineteen, twenty, it didn't really matter: No pitcher before or since has approached that number.

The Cubs, of course, took great delight in removing the zero from the right side of Marquard's hyphen that afternoon of July 8, riding the right arm of rookie Jimmy Lavender and stomping the Giants 7–2. What neither team could know was that not only would that game send Marquard into a two-month tailspin (he'd go only 7–11 after the historic start), it would also lead to a most unexpected pennant chase. The Cubs took three out of the four games in that series, spoiled a one-day visit by the Giants ten days later with a 3–1 win, and by July 16 found themselves only nine games out of first place. Suddenly there was a whiff of panic apparent among the faithful in the Polo Grounds, and even a little self-doubt among the Giants themselves, for as much swagger as McGraw and his crew carried around with them, the Cubs were their own personal kryptonite, the New Yorkers having finished second to them in 1906, 1908, and 1910. Would the hex Chicago seemed to hold in even-numbered years continue, even after the Cubs spotted them sixteen games?

Almost. The Cubs whittled the lead to six when the Giants returned to West Side Park on August 15, and when the Cubs took two out of three the newspapers back home responded with due terror. This was the peak of New York's grand newspaper wars, Joseph Pulitzer's *World* and William Randolph Hearst's *American* street-fighting for every reader in New York City (along with twelve other Manhattan-based dailies), and there was no surer way to separate a citizen from his two pennies than to satisfy his baseball jones with huge scare headlines chronicling the collapse of the local nine. And it would get worse: After *another* failed one-day trip to Chicago on August 21 resulted in *another* loss, and after the Giants split a doubleheader in Pittsburgh the next day while the Cubs beat the Braves, the Giants' lead shrunk to only four games, the smallest it had been since May 27.

"They don't seem so unbeatable now!" the Cubs' manager, Frank Chance, crowed in the next day's newspapers, and by Labor Day, September 2, the difference between the clubs was still only four games, with three do-or-die games between them set for the middle of September that everyone in New York had already circled in black ink, knowing how readily the Cubs always feasted on the Giants when they had to.

But then, just as quickly as the Giants had faltered, they righted themselves. They swept a Labor Day doubleheader from the hapless Braves in Boston, pushing the lead back to six. The Cubs—against whom the Giants went 9–13 in 1912 while battering the rest of the league to the tune of 94–35—couldn't keep up. By the time they arrived in New York for that hotly anticipated series the cushion was back up to ten and a half games, so even though Chicago took two out of three (of course), the panic had vanished. The Giants clinched the pennant on September 26 by sweeping two from the always-helpful Braves, and 10,000 rowdy, yet relieved, fans stormed the Polo Grounds to celebrate the coronation.

The Red Sox suffered no such late-summer drama, though they did have to contend with a smoking-hot start from the White Sox, who won twenty-eight of their first forty games. But the Red Sox were fortified by a twenty-one-game home stand that took them through most of May and allowed them to stay within striking distance of first place. When they nipped the Browns in St. Louis, 3–2, on June 10, they improved to 30–18 for the year, .005 percentage points ahead of the White Sox, suffering through their first losing spell of the season. The next day they shut the Browns out, moved into first place all alone, and remained there for the rest of the year. Their lone challenge would come from the defending champion Athletics, who pointed all spring and throughout most of the early summer to the six-game series they would play against the Red Sox across the Fourth of July holiday, in front of large, expectant crowds in Philadelphia. The A's entered the series trailing the Red Sox by six games, but were only four back in the loss column and playing as well as they had in 1911. But Boston took four of those six games, left town eight games ahead, and dropped the A's to fourth place. Philadelphia never recovered, and though the A's did finish in second place with ninety wins, they ended up a distant fifteen games back of the Red Sox, who suffered only two losing streaks of longer than two games all season.

Throughout six months of relentless command, there were two things that stood out above all the other glories that the Red Sox and the Royal Rooters savored. The first was the gleaming state-of-the-art home that John I. Taylor had commissioned for them, a baseball palace unmatched in the American League that from its first hour of life was christened "Fenway Park." On April 9, in front of 5,000 curiosity seekers and a few dozen construction workers eager to tend to the park's final few details, the Red Sox beat the Harvard University baseball team, 2–0, in an exhibition game that officially opened the doors. Nine days later, the Sox were scheduled to open the place for real, against the Highlanders, but rain scotched those plans, which was just as well, for much of the city's attention was focused on another matter of significant local import: the sinking of the unsinkable *Titanic*, which had hit an iceberg on April 14, killing 1,517 people, more than a few of them New Englanders. By now survivors had arrived in New York and tales of grief and loss filled Boston's newspapers; by the time the Red Sox finally beat the High-landers 7–6 in an eleven-inning thriller on April 20, in front of 24,000 witnesses, it was still a proud civic moment, just not the all-consuming event it was otherwise expected to be.

The other was the performance of Howard Ellsworth Wood, nicknamed "Smoky Joe," a hard-throwing twenty-two-year-old born in Kansas City and raised in Ouray, Colorado, "not far," he would later say, "from places with names like Lizard Head Pass and Slumgullion Gulch." His father was a lawyer, but his hometown could easily have been the set of a spaghetti Western, "and every day I'd see these big stagecoaches go by, drawn by six horses, two guards sitting up there with rifles, guarding the gold shipment coming down from the mines." Which makes it all the more interesting, then, that Wood's first professional team would be the Bloomer Girls, an itinerant team of women, and men who dressed as women, similar to the barnstorming House of David teams that would take on all comers in future years wearing long beards as their trademark and Stars of David as their logo. Wood earned $20 for three weeks' work and liked the idea of playing baseball for a living.

As a nineteen-year-old he'd won eleven games for the Red Sox in 1909, and he'd already piled up forty-seven wins heading into 1912, but nobody could have expected what would happen during that golden season.

"He was untouchable," his teammate, Harry Hooper, would recall thirty years later. "It was like magic. Guys who were good hit-ters, rugged ballplayers, would all look like bush leaguers against Joe that year. I never saw anything like it before. I never seen anything like it since. For one season, Joe was—there's no other way to describe it—invincible. He really was."

Wood started forty-three games in 1912, completing thirty-eight of them. In 344 innings he struck out 258 hitters, this at a time when striking out was considered a venial sin, when hitters would choke halfway up their bat rather than walk back to the plate having waved at strike three. Even the great Walter Johnson of the Washington Senators, who was generally acknowledged to own the most intimidating fastball in the world in 1912 (and who actually struck out forty-five more hitters in twenty-five more innings than Wood that season), acknowledged Wood's dominance. Asked that summer which of the two men had the faster fastball, Johnson laughed.

"Can I throw harder than Joe Wood?" Johnson asked. "Listen, my friend, there's no man alive can throw harder than Smoky Joe Wood."

In what would be the signature game of the entire 1912 season, a full house at Fenway Park got to judge for themselves on Friday afternoon, September 6, and there has never been a heavyweight title fight that inspired more hype or hyperbole than this otherwise meaningless game between a first-place team and a second-place team divided by fifteen games in the standings. Back on July 3, in the second game of a doubleheader, Johnson had thrown six breezy innings in a 10–2 pasting of the Highlanders, improving his record on the season to 12–9. Five days later—the same day, in the other league, that Marquard's nineteen-game winning streak finally ended—Wood defeated the St. Louis Browns, upping *his* personal mark to 16–4. And over the next two months, both Johnson and Wood elevated their profession to art, blitzing through the American League with even greater authority than Marquard had done in the National. Johnson was asked to pitch more than Wood, and picked up some wins in relief, and before he finally lost a 3–2 heartbreaker to the Browns on August 28 Johnson had piled up sixteen wins in a row—still a staggering number, and an American League record.

A record that had stood for all of nine days when Johnson and the Senators arrived at Fenway Park on September 6, and one that looked as if it might not last another nine. Because Wood's own streak now stood at thirteen, and he was pitching so well that his roommate, Tris Speaker, gushed, "Logic tells you he has to lose again sometime, but then you watch him pitch and you aren't sure exactly how that's ever going to happen." Wood wasn't originally scheduled to face Johnson; his regular turn in the rotation was to fall on Saturday and Jake Stahl was reluctant to alter his prize pitcher's schedule for anything or anybody. But then Washington manager Clark Griffith—a Boston nemesis dating to his time managing the Highlanders back in '04—piped up in the papers. "We will consider [Wood] a coward if he doesn't pitch against Johnson," Griffith bellowed.

Stahl, a former football player, understood a challenge to duel when he heard one.

"We will pitch Wood," he said, "and we will win the game."

The public bought in, with two fists and armloads of cash. First pitch was scheduled for 3:20 P.M., but by noon the streets around Fenway were choked with humanity. Robert McRoy, the treasurer of the Red Sox, would insist that only 29,000 people were granted admission to the park that day, which still set a record for either league for the biggest crowd ever to see a weekday game. But the real number was closer to 40,000, owing to those who slipped dollar bills into the palms of ushers at the door and those who used more nefarious ways to squeeze into the yard. So thick was the crowd that Wood and Johnson took their warm-ups surrounded on the sidelines by their own personal mobs of admirers.

"That was the only game I ever remember in Fenway Park, or anywhere else, where the fans were sitting practically along the first- and third-base lines," Wood would recall some fifty years later. "Instead of sitting back where the bench usually was, we were sitting on chairs right up against the foul lines and the fans were right behind us. The overflow had been packed between the grandstand and the foul lines as well as in the outfield behind ropes. Fenway Park must have contained twice as many people as its seating capacity that day. I never saw so many people in one place in my life."

More often than not, a pitching duel this hotly anticipated yields something else: a 13–11 slugfest, or a one-sided showcase for one of the hurlers. But this time, both men were equal to their billing. Through five shutout innings, the tension mounting inside Fenway grew palpable, and when Wood zipped through the Senators in the top of the sixth the crowd grew restless: What if nobody scored? Would a 0–0 tie be a fitting result, or the worst possible anticlimax? But then, with two outs, Speaker stroked a Johnson fastball down the left-field line that was ruled a double when the ball was swallowed by the overflow crowd. Duffy Lewis followed with a soft, humpbacked liner to right field, and when it fell safely, the crowd nearly imploded: In came Speaker with the ice-breaking run, and now Wood needed only nine outs to earn a splendid one-day Triple Crown: a win over the great Johnson; his fourteenth in a row; and his thirtieth on the season. The nine outs came quickly, and effortlessly, and he finished with a six-hit shutout in only 108 pitches. Johnson, gallant loser, allowed but five hits.

"In my opinion," Wood said years later, "the greatest pitcher who ever lived was Walter Johnson. If he'd ever had a good team behind him, what records he'd have set."

But Wood had the better team behind him this day, and that team had the better pitcher in front of them. Perhaps fittingly, Wood would extend his streak to sixteen straight before falling to the Tigers in Detroit two weeks after his epic showdown with Johnson. Both men would have to settle for sharing the league record, and they were delighted to do so.

When the Red Sox finally did secure the AL pennant they weren't afforded an on-field celebration the way the Giants were, since they learned of their clinching in a Cleveland hotel dining room on September 18, where they'd repaired after their game with the Indians was washed out. There they received wireless reports of the White Sox beating the A's 9–1 in the first game of a doubleheader in Chicago, which officially eliminated the defending champions and officially elevated the Speed Boys to Boston's first pennant in eight long, frustrating years.

Jake Stahl was upstairs, in his room, when there came a knock on his door and the manager discovered the smiling visage of T. H. Murnane, the esteemed baseball editor of the *Boston Globe*, who'd come to deliver the news personally.

"You get to match wits with McGraw," Murnane informed him.

"Ah, it won't be me against Manager McGraw," said Stahl. "It'll be his boys against my boys, on the field, where it ought to be. These boys worked together as one family, they all had their heart in their work. The more difficult the proposition the stronger they went at their work, so that's why I think we will land the postseason series with New York. They've been working hard since Hot Springs and knew early on they had a chance for the big money. And now they do."

Murnane—more than any player, any manager, any owner—was the biggest, most beloved baseball figure in Boston, a barrel-chested man with a full white mustache who had himself played eight seasons of big-league ball as a utility player from 1872 to 1884 (including two years with the Boston Red Caps of the National League) and whose stories in the *Globe* were hungrily consumed in both morning and afternoon editions by well over a million readers. He could be tough and critical, but he was unabashedly partisan, and in the next day's newspaper he would gush, in prose as purple as a royal sash: "The thrill that electrifies the baseball fan after the victory is won is no new sensation for Boston, but eight years is a long time and the fans of New England are in the proper humor to say, 'Boys, you did your duty well and we fully appreciate the glorious honor that you have brought to our homes to please the old scouts and delight young America.' "

For now, he would just repeat the challenge that soon awaited his friend. To emphasize the point, he opened up the latest edition of *The Sporting News*, which had already begun speculating about a Red Sox–Giants matchup well in advance of the teams actually guaranteeing one, and began reading aloud:

"John J. McGraw looms larger and larger as the real hope of the Champion Giants. In his ten years of Gotham experience, the Little Napoleon has always been about one-third of the team. Now it appears he will have to better this percentage if the National League champions are to annex the 'rubber' of this baseball classic."

Murnane rolled the newspaper back up, stuck it under his arm.

"You against Muggsy, Jake," he said.

"Don't let Muggsy hear you call him that," Stahl said.

The two friends laughed, shook hands, and then Murnane allowed Stahl to return to his thoughts and his preparations. In a few days' time, Muggsy's Giants and Stahl's Speed Boys would gather in New York City for the first of a best-of-seven showdown for the right to call themselves champions and to cash themselves a winner's paycheck that seemed sure to exceed $4,000 per man. Already, the nation's baseball scribes were hard at work predicting in print that this, at last, might be a World Series worthy of their breathless hype and hope, that perhaps it might even take the full seven games to determine the champion—something that had happened only once in the first eight of these autumnal encounters.

What they didn't know—couldn't yet know—was that what lay ahead would include far too much intrigue and interest, passion and paranoia, fight and fury, angst and agitation, to be contained to just seven games.

Or even eight, for that matter . . .

CHAPTER TWO

October 1912: The Run-up

NEW YORK—The very air of New York was vibrant with
suspense last night as lovers of good baseball from all over
America gathered in this city on the eve of the first great
game of the world's series between the New York Giants and
the Boston Red Sox. The hotels were full to overflowing as
though the stage had been set here for some great
convention. The talk in the bars and corridors, the talk in
the theater lobbies and in the streets all turned on the
chances of the two great rival teams . . .

—HARRY CROSS, *NEW YORK TIMES*, OCTOBER 8, 1912

THE LINES BEGAN to form on Sunday night, late, with a chilly
October breeze buffeting the rocky bluff bearing the name of
an old politician named James J. Coogan. The cliffs bordered a
grand baseball basilica named for a game, polo, that would never
once be played within its walls during its entire fifty-three-year existence. This corner of Manhattan was still a virtual countryside in
1912, a world apart from the tenements that crowded the lower portion of the island, a planet apart from the outer boroughs that had
already begun attracting claustrophobic citizens in need of space.
This was the fourth outdoor arena that bore the name "Polo

Grounds" in New York City; the last had burned to the ground hours after the Giants lost to the Phillies on Opening Day 1911, a wooden tinderbox brought to its knees by a lone cigarette thrown from the window of a passing elevated train that landed on a pile of garbage.

This incarnation resembled an overgrown horseshoe, with an ornate façade that ringed the upper deck, invitingly short fences in both left and right field, and an endless pasture leading to center field, where the wall was nearly six hundred feet away from home plate. The Polo Grounds was a magnet for the rich and the powerful as well as the poor and the humble. Broadway actors and Tammany Hall politicians would ride horse-drawn limousines and plunk down $2 to sit within squinting distance of the home-team dugout; barbers and butchers and bartenders would take the El, walk down toward the main gate, and hand over fifty cents for grandstand or bleacher seats. In all, 638,000 people would pour through its turnstiles in 1912, the highest number in all of baseball.

That was the regular season, though. In two days, at 3 o'clock in the afternoon, the underdog Giants would host the heavily favored Red Sox in Game One of the eighth annual World Series, and that meant if you wanted to watch the game you had to get uptown a couple of days early, bring a blanket and a boxed dinner, and whittle away the hours until the box office opened at 8 o'clock Monday morning, some thirty hours before the first pitch of the Series. And you could forget about those half-dollar seats. Spots in the bleachers, the cheapest seats in the house, would sell for $1; the lower-tier grandstand seats, of which there were some 30,000, would go for $2; and the best views, in the 8,400 available upper-tier rows, would set a guy back $3, the equivalent of $65 a century later.

"Hardly leaves a guy any scratch to lay down a wager," said Thomas Brennan, a resident of West Forty-eighth Street, who was the first person to start the queue. But then Brennan laughed and added, "We'll make do, I'm sure."

By dawn, the lines had begun to slither west from the stadium entrance at 155th Street and Eighth Avenue toward Bradhurst

Avenue, and south for thirteen blocks to 142nd Street. And by the time the box office finally opened, it had grown even more, reaching 138th Street to the south and Edgecombe Avenue to the west. By then, the usual casualties of impatience and impertinence had already infiltrated this temporary village. Some in the line complained that all you needed to do was slip a two-dollar bill to a cop and he'd find you a favorable place near the front. One man grumbled to a reporter that he'd gotten in line at 5 A.M. and failed to make any visible progress by 10. "I've actually lost ground," he said. "It's like I'm going backwards. I'll be in the Bronx soon."

The system was simple and effective: Something was passed to the cop—at first, indeed, a $2 bill, but later the price steepened to $5—and the contributor received a timely "bump" into the line. Complainants were dealt with swiftly and mercilessly.

"Shut your mouth," one of New York's Finest retorted to one such dissident, "or you can go to the back of the line."

"Or," added his partner, "you could always go home."

The Giants, who'd watched ticket speculators make a fortune a year before during the 1911 World Series, had sweetened the pot for those policemen not interested in shaking down the folks in line: For every would-be broker they nabbed, they would offer a one-dollar bonus. John Heydler, the secretary-treasurer of the National League, speaking on behalf of the three-man National Commission that ruled over the sport, boasted, "The ticket scalpers will be defeated this year."

To ensure that outcome, the cops rousted anyone who looked even remotely suspicious, such as poor Donald Murphy, who lived in the shadow of the Polo Grounds and was discovered in tears by a columnist for the *New York World*.

"I got here at 2 o'clock in the morning and I've eaten all but one sandwich, which I have wrapped in this newspaper (thankfully, not the *World*). I wouldn't know a speculator if I saw one and I'm a regular patron. My money is as good as anybody's, yet here I am thrown out of line. Worse than that, I'm here to buy two tickets for my boss and now I'll lose my job."

"I vouched for the guy," a man in line said. "But the cop told me, 'Mind your bee's wax if you know what's good for you.'"

The man unfolded his newspaper—the *World*, of course—and pointed to the front page. "In this town," he said, "it's best to listen to the police."

There, on the page, were two prominent stories. One referred to the very line the man was standing on, and the World Series for which the line had formed. The other, bolder, brassier, all but screaming loud enough for everyone in this half-mile line to hear, referred to Lieutenant Charles Becker, who not so long ago had been among the most powerful officers in the NYPD but was now about to be the featured player in what the *World*, the *American*, the *Herald*, the *Mail*, and even the staid *Times* were calling "The Trial of the Century." And even if the century was barely a dozen years old, it was hard to believe there'd *ever* be a story to match this one. The world's series could come the closest; hell, even the stories about Wilson, Roosevelt, and Taft were buried inside.

Back in July, a small-time Jewish bookmaker named Herman "Beansie" Rosenthal had gone to the *World* and spilled his guts all over Page One. Rosenthal and another Lower East Side product named Arnold Rothstein were both protégés of Tammany boss Big Tim Sullivan, but while Rothstein's reputation and bankroll had blossomed (to the point where he was now a silent partner with none other than John J. McGraw in several New York pool halls), Rosenthal's had stagnated, mostly because he couldn't keep his mouth shut. Becker, who headed a special-detail vice detail boldly (and unabashedly) dubbed the Strong Arm Squad, regularly shook down Rosenthal (and dozens of other hoods), and when the bookie finally balked at his methods, Becker shut him down. That's when Rosenthal called the newspaper.

And that's when Becker—allegedly, of course—made a telephone call of his own.

Two days later, as Rosenthal walked out of the Hotel Metropole just off Times Square, a car packed with guns happened by him, took aim, and put Beansie out of business permanently. It didn't take long for the trail to lead back to Becker, who was arrested along with the gunmen and spent much of the summer following his beloved Giants' pursuit of the pennant from the Tombs, the detention center located thirty blocks from the Polo Grounds. Becker would spend the Series commuting back and forth to the courthouse at 52 Chambers Street and sharing a large swatch of the public imagination with those very same Giants, who would be enduring their own kind of public trial.

The Giants understood a couple of things as they readied themselves for the series. First, they were significant underdogs. Almost every major sportswriter had already weighed in, and few expected the Giants to push the Series beyond five games. And while losing the confidence of the sportswriters may have been a blow to the ego, it was losing the faith of the oddsmakers and the bookmakers that *really* hurt. Even composer George M. Cohan, friend of McGraw and regular Polo Grounds patron, sought out Red Sox owner James McAleer to announce, "I have $50,000 to wager on the Speed Boys," which would be the equivalent of a million-dollar bet in 2008. Of course, this wasn't the first time Cohan had transferred his loyalties; a year earlier, he'd bet a similar amount on the Athletics, brought home a bundle, and bragged of his score publicly, a move that put a serious strain on his friendship with all the Giants, especially McGraw (who'd lost the relatively paltry $500 bet he'd placed on his ballclub, a perfectly legal and common practice for the day).

How out in the open was all of this? Even the Christian Gentleman, penning a column for the *New York Herald*, made no pretense about where the real rooting interest lay for a few hundred thousand of his readers.

"All the advance stats and dope have favored the Red Sox in the series but these figures have been compiled by a lot of experts who have based their deductions on past performances, which don't amount to much in baseball," Mathewson wrote. "It's the future that counts. But this inclination toward the Red Sox has affected the betting and made them a ruling favorite at odds all the way from

10-to-6 to 2-to-1. This is not a disappointment to us but rather an encouraging feature of the outlook. In my opinion the club that is the favorite in the world's series is under a big handicap. There's a lot of psychology in it."

Also a lot of money in it, of course, if you bet the underdog and won.

That wasn't the only intrigue, though. From the moment it became apparent that the Red Sox and Giants were destined to meet in the World Series, the most delicious kind of revenge began to seep into the bigger picture throughout New England. For the last time Boston had produced a foe as formidable as these Speed Boys, eight years earlier, they had been denied the chance to defend their 1903 World Series championship because McGraw, and to a larger extent Giants owner John T. Brush, had refused to meet them in the postseason of '04. McGraw, who'd jumped from the National League's St. Louis Cardinals to manage the Baltimore Orioles in the upstart American League in 1901, had leapt back ever more quickly the following year when the Giants inquired after him—an opportunity too much for this product of small-town, upstate New York to resist. Growing up in Truxton, playing minor league ball in Olean and Wellsville, attending classes each winter at St. Bonaventure College, McGraw had harbored dreams of managing the Giants. And so he vaulted, with both feet, and never looked back.

"I know the American League and its methods," he declared in late summer of 1904, arguing against participating in the Series. "I will not consent to a haphazard box-office game with [AL President] Ban Johnson and company. No one, not even my bitterest enemy, ever accused me of being a fool. I have taken the New York club from last to first in three short years. Now that New York has won this honor, I, for one, will not stand to see it tossed away like a rag."

Brush, who was drawn to McGraw's bombast as it mirrored his own, was even firmer in his refusal.

"There is nothing in the constitution of playing rules of the National League which requires its victorious club to submit its championship honors to a contest with a victorious club in a minor league," he said, backing up his manager. "We have gained all the glory there is to be acquired in baseball—winning the National League pennant. Some people say it was understood that the champions of both leagues would play an afterseason series. I never was a party to such an agreement or understanding. I never committed myself definitively."

The outrage was immediate and it was venomous, not only from New England but from the Giants' own fans, who wanted the series, and from Brush's own players, who wanted the extra cash bonanza a postseason series would surely generate. So chastened was Brush, in fact, that only one week after the end of the '04 season—on what should have been the date of Game Six if a World Series had indeed been played—he became a leading advocate in securing a permanent postseason agreement between the leagues. And while both Brush and McGraw took great satisfaction in their 1905 schooling of the American League's Athletics, both men suffered as the ensuing years brought a Cubs dynasty and an indefinite string of hard-luck losses. It's why both were so invested in these Giants.

For Brush, it was an investment that bordered on desperation. On the afternoon of September 11, as Brush left the Polo Grounds in his chauffeur-driven automobile, heading for his home in upstate Pelham Manor, a U.S. Mail truck failed to heed a stop sign at Broadway and 126th Street and plowed into his vehicle. Already in failing health, the sixty-seven-year-old Brush suffered a broken hip and two cracked ribs. The bones didn't knit properly, and coupled with his other ailments he was rendered an invalid; he would have to watch the Giants' home games during the upcoming series from a car parked beyond the right-field playing area. Too ill to attend the pre-series meetings, he nevertheless wanted to put some of his longest-standing affairs in order and invited Ban Johnson to his house. Years earlier, the feud that would reach a climax with that 1904 series snub had begun when Johnson, a sportswriter for the *Cincinnati Commercial Gazette*, regularly took target practice in his column at Brush, who owned the Reds at the time. Johnson, knowing Brush wasn't well, took a taxi upstate.

Seeing his blood enemy, Johnson was shocked, horrified, and saddened.

"Ban," Brush said, "I haven't long to stay here. Let's forgive each other. I think this has been delayed too long."

And with that, the two long-standing adversaries shook hands and 1904 was forgotten, at least in this parlor room in Pelham Manor. Such would not be the case in precincts elsewhere. Red Sox shortstop Heinie Wagner, for one, had harbored a grudge against McGraw, and with good reason, for ten solid years. When McGraw landed in New York on July 17, 1902, he'd demanded total control of all personnel decisions. The Giants were 23–50, thirty-three games out of first place, a pathetic shell of a team, so when his new bosses handed McGraw the roster of his new club, he took a lead pencil and crossed nine names off with a flourish.

"You can begin," McGraw said, "by releasing these fellows here."

Heinie Wagner was one of those fellows, only twenty-one, a local product out of nearby New Rochelle who'd grown up dreaming of being a Giant. It had taken him four long years to return to the major leagues, a journey that took him to such baseball frontiers as the Connecticut League, and now he would be playing shortstop against his old team, and his old manager, and it was a delicious irony in so many ways because Wagner was *precisely* the kind of player McGraw valued most: smart, rugged, hard-nosed, and most important of all a unifier. The Red Sox, for all their success in 1912, were a deeply divided team, the most significant schism falling along religious lines, with the Masons (Protestants like Tris Speaker and Joe Wood) on one side and the KCs (Catholics, such as Wagner, Bill Carrigan, and pitcher Bucky O'Brien) on the other. Sometimes the arguments in the clubhouse grew heated, and sometimes the tension on train trips grew unbearable, but it was Wagner who almost always brought the team back together, however temporarily, preaching the neutral ground of winning.

Wagner had already achieved a small measure of revenge. Three years earlier, the third-place Red Sox and third-place Giants had agreed to square off in a best-of-seven postseason series. It wasn't unusual for teams who shared the same city—the Browns and Cardinals, the White Sox and Cubs, the Giants and the Highlanders—to engage in these exhibitions, local live-action supplements to the World Series, which in 1909 pitted the Pirates and the Tigers. It was a little different for two otherwise unrelated teams to meet, and the wild apathy that greeted the games in both cities underlined that; only 789 people paid for the privilege of watching the fifth and final game in the Polo Grounds, and the players earned precisely $125 a man for their efforts.

"When anyone asked what we were playing for," Giants catcher Chief Meyers recalled sourly on the eve of the '12 series, "we said the championship of the New York, New Haven and Hartford Railroad, since it got most of the money."

Still, it provided the Giants with their first glimpse of both Wood and Speaker, who shined, and the Red Sox' 4–1 victory in the Series allowed Wagner to chortle, "As a lifetime Giants fan, it looks to me like McGraw could use a shortstop. Too bad. I know one he used to have."

The newspapers figured the starting pitchers for Game One of this 1912 World Series had to be Joe Wood for the Sox and Christy Mathewson for the Giants, because what fool would choose anyone *but* the best pitcher of today and the greatest pitcher of all time? Jake Stahl, new to this, wasn't in the mood to play silly games. "Of course it's Wood," he said. "If I chose another man they ought to have my head examined."

McGraw, naturally, *delighted* in playing silly games. Especially with those sonsofbitches from the papers, always looking for a story, for an angle, for a scoop.

"It'll be Mathewson," he announced, watching many of the three hundred gathered sports scribes jotting the name in their notepads. "Or it'll be Marquard," he added, laughing as he saw them all make their revisions. "Or it'll be Tesreau," he said, pleased with himself as the writers dutifully made another amendment. "Or it'll be Hooks Wiltse," he said, and now even the more gullible of writers knew he was toying with them—he had to be, right? "I'll see how the mood strikes me."

McGraw had gone to scout the Red Sox late in the season and had made a very public point of summarizing them as "mostly a one-man team." That rankled the Red Sox, who knew gamesmanship when they saw it. They knew McGraw was trying to send a message to that one man, to Wood, who for all his accomplishments in 1912 was still a kid in many ways, a kid who'd never even *seen* a World Series game before, much less played in one (as almost all the members of the Giants' roster had).

McGraw had no way of knowing that he was late to the party, that no fewer than a dozen of his anonymous neighbors in New York had already tested Wood's nerves by sending him unsigned letters threatening him with consequences as innocent as a thrown tomato to his head and as dire as a bullet to the chest if he opted to take the pitcher's mound for Game One. Were they jokes? Cowards? Cranks? Neither Wood, the Boston police, nor Red Sox management could determine that. All they knew was that all the missives had New York City postmarks. Two were filled with bad spelling, signed illegibly. Another was written in blood-red ink, with a knife and gun drawn at the bottom:

"You will never live to pitch against the Giants in the world's series! We are waiting to get you as soon as you arrive in town!"

Another:

"You better stay in Boston where you are safe among friends."

And a third:

"Look out for us! We're gunning for you!"

"They're just kidding," Wood told James McAleer, who wanted to provide him with a bodyguard, a service this child of the Wild West rejected out of hand. "If someone wants to hurt me, they'll hurt me. They won't announce themselves first."

Nevertheless, McAleer hired a detective agency to shadow the players in New York City, and he altered their usual travel itinerary. Normally, the Sox stayed in one of midtown's opulent hotels, but McAleer suddenly thought it prudent to avoid the glare of the White Light District, so when their Knickerbocker Limited train arrived in New York at around 6 o'clock on the evening of Monday, October 8 (after receiving a rousing lunchtime send-off at Back Bay Station by 6,000 pennant-waving supporters), they were immediately shuttled from Grand Central Station to the Bretton Hall Hotel, on Broadway and Eighty-sixth Street, a relatively quiet segment of the big town, not quite as stocked with shylock and show-girl. They were given a 10 o'clock curfew.

The Royal Rooters, of course, had no such restrictions, and gleefully checked into their own headquarters at the Marlborough Hotel fifty blocks south, right in the middle of the white lights, "right in the heart of enemy territory," Nuf Ced McGreevy said, "the way we like it best." The trips each morning to the Polo Grounds, all the way up at 155th Street and Eighth Avenue, would take a while, but the Rooters were nothing if not inventive when it came to passing the time.

There were three hundred of them, each personally guaranteed tickets for Game One (without having to stand in line) thanks to the efforts of their most visible member.

On September 30, Boston's Mayor Fitzgerald had telegraphed John T. Brush, seeking tickets for himself and his constituents. Brush, knowing that when a politician called seeking a favor he rarely brought his checkbook with him, was reluctant to part with the revenue those seats could generate, but he sent a reply to Boston asking, "What will you do for Giants fans who wish to go to Boston?" To which Honey Fitz immediately replied: "I give you my word that if three hundred seats are not provided for the New York fans by the Boston management I shall refuse a license to play the game." Brush was convinced. The Rooters got their seats.

Fitzgerald, meanwhile, basked in the reflected glow of his favorite team, elated at all the attention the Red Sox' winning ways had afforded him. Back in 1904, he'd come close to purchasing the club but had been headed off, most notably, by Ban Johnson, who was enough of a political operator himself to recognize one who was far more skilled at the job than he. That hadn't stifled Fitzgerald's loyalties, though, either to his team or to the sport. Baseball could solve a lot of ills, he believed, a philosophy especially helpful to him because his eldest daughter, Rose, had begun seeing a lad named Joseph P. Kennedy, a raffish, ambitious young financier whose lone redeeming quality, to Honey Fitz, was that he'd been a star baseball player at Harvard.

Fitzgerald was intent on sitting among his people at the Polo Grounds Tuesday afternoon until he received a telegram just before departing for Boston from Robert Adamson, the secretary for New York's Mayor Gaynor: "The Mayor asks if you will give him the pleasure of sitting in his box to-morrow to witness the defeat of the Red Sox by the Giants."

This was an invitation that no politician of Fitzgerald's stripe could possibly refuse. He answered the message directly: "It will give me great pleasure to be your guest as the Red Sox begin their onward march to the world's championship, and to congratulate you upon the fact that your city, the greatest in the country, possessing the best team in the National League, will have the distinguished honor of adding to the glory of the best city in the *world* and to the laurels of the finest ball team ever organized."

If there was one fly in the ointment for Fitzgerald, it was that for all of his bluster and all of his blarney, he was not the highest-ranking statesman in the Red Sox' stable. That honor belonged to William Howard Taft of 1600 Pennsylvania Avenue, Washington, D.C., currently embroiled in a vicious campaign to retain that address. Employing footwork that not only belied his 350-pound frame but would also make future candidates proud, this son of Ohio made no pretense of his affinity for the Reds before winning the presidency in 1908. In 1910, he became the first chief executive to throw a ceremonial first pitch, handling the honors at the Washington Senators' home opener, and from that day forward, he pledged, he would be a devoted Senators fan . . . until he decided to adopt the 1912 Red Sox "because," he explained in mid-September, "they'll be in the world's series and the Senators will not. And I shall watch them when they play in Boston."

Sound political reasoning. Alas, as would befall untold millions of American men across the next century, Taft's baseball plans would be sabotaged by an irresistible force. Mrs. Taft, it seems, had already accepted an invitation from friends in Vermont and New Hampshire to visit in early October. Taft, it was reported, was hoping his friends would either reconsider or postpone their invitations, but they were stymied by Mrs. Taft, who wanted to make the trip. So the President would have to make alternate arrangements to follow the series— and, in his spare time, the campaign.

The details were set. Both teams had already written out $10,000 checks to the National Commission, security to ensure (it was assumed) that both teams would be playing on the level. The umpires had been selected, and for the first time the World Series would be policed by a four-man crew, rather than the two-umpire setup that was standard for regular-season games; befitting a series of such quality, the men chosen were the four most recognizable, and accomplished, umpires in the land. In fact, in the entire history of baseball only eight umpires have ever been enshrined in the Hall of Fame; two of them would work this series. From the American League came Francis "Silk" O'Loughlin and Billy Evans, from the National League Bill Klem and Cy Rigler.

Klem was tabbed with the duty of calling balls and strikes for Game One, an appropriate honor for a thirty-eight-year-old who was already considered the "father of umpires" and who was seven years into a distinguished thirty-seven-year career that would ultimately lead him to the Hall of Fame, the first-ever arbiter so honored. He was an innovator, the first umpire to use hand signals while calling balls and strikes, the first to use a very primitive form of chest protector to guard against foul tips that could assault umpires like shrapnel if they weren't careful. And he was also completely immersed in the sport that gave him both his livelihood and his fame. "To me," Klem once said, "baseball is not a game, but a religion." Evans, the other man with a future appointment in Cooperstown, was a precocious soul who'd become an umpire at twenty-two, worked his first World Series at twenty-five, and retired young at age forty-three to switch sides and become a general manager, first for baseball's Cleveland Indians, later for football's Cleveland Rams.

Silk O'Loughlin was the most colorful character of the bunch. He earned his nickname as a boy in Rochester, New York, because of his fine hair and who would go on to call a record ten no-hitters in his career, one of which—on July 29, 1911—had been thrown by Smoky Joe Wood. Like Klem, he was an innovator: He was the first to utilize a booming voice to indicate ball or strike, safe or out, rather than merely informing the nearest available player of his judgment, as had previously been the standard practice. His confidence was unmatched, and decades later umpires were still quoting his two most famous observations. To the victim of an unpopular call, O'Loughlin was fond of saying, "I have never missed one in my life and it's too late to start now." And to just about anyone else who would listen, he would remark, "It's the Pope for religion, O'Loughlin for baseball. Both infallible." Rigler, the least-decorated of the quartet, was no less responsible for another bit of baseball legislation; earlier in 1912, while moonlighting as an assistant coach at the University of Virginia, he signed pitcher Eppa Rixley for the Philadelphia Athletics, a move that prompted baseball to ban what had to that point been a common, if quiet, practice: umpires who also served as bird-dog scouts.

McGraw, the most notorious umpire baiter of his generation, was satisfied with the assignments, likely since he knew his presence in the Series had prompted the National Commission to hire the best men available for the jobs, regardless of politics or preference. "These games will be decided on the basepaths, and not by the men wearing ties," McGraw said before Game One. "That is as it should be."

There was one concern for the Red Sox, and it was a significant one. Larry Gardner, their twenty-six-year-old third baseman, had a right pinky that presently looked like a fleshy *z*, an injury he'd suffered in late September, with the pennant well in hand, when he'd dived to try and stop a sharp Donnie Bush ground ball in Detroit. Gardner was easy to overlook in a Boston lineup that included the splendid Speaker as its foundation and also featured Duffy Lewis (a team-high 109 runs batted in) and Harry Hooper (who tied Speaker for the team lead with twelve home runs), but Gardner was second to Speaker with a .315 batting average, third on the team with eighty-six RBIs, led the team with eighteen triples, and on July 2 in New York hit two inside-the-park home runs, a feat accomplished only eight times previously. And while he made thirty-five errors, that was actually well below average at a time when the position of third base truly earned its nickname of "the hot corner"; as a point of comparison, eight different men manned third for the Highlanders in 1912, combining to make *seventy-two* errors. This was not a job for the faint of heart.

Gardner and Hooper lived together that summer of 1912 in Winthrop on Boston's North Shore. Both of them were college men: Gardner had played at the University of Vermont and Hooper at St. Mary's College in Moraga, California, and after each game they would cook shellfish by digging a hole in the sand on the beach in front of their house, throwing in hot rocks, and then covering the hole with seaweed. After his injury, as he returned to the bench, Gardner showed his little finger to Hooper, showed where the bone had fractured so badly it pierced the skin.

"You think you can jam it back into place?" he asked.

"Only if you have some glue on you," Hooper replied.

Gardner had spent the rest of the season recuperating at his home in Enosburg Falls, Vermont, vowing to play in the World Series even though he essentially now had six fingers on his throwing hand. "Nothing that Q and a little tape can't fix," he figured, referring to both Sox trainer Joe Quirk and the most reliable antidote in his tool-box. On October 3, twelve days after the injury, Mathewson and Rube Marquard had stayed behind in Philadelphia after the Giants completed a series with the Phillies so they could get a firsthand look at the Red Sox, who were completing their season with three games against the Athletics. The most notable thing they saw (besides Smoky Joe Wood breezing through the defending champs' batting order in a 17–5 rout) was Gardner, wincing with every swing, taking batting practice under the watchful eye of the Red Sox' team physician, Dr. Richard Cliff. He barely got the ball out of the infield, and was sweating profusely by the time he was done, but reported he was ready to return to duty.

The two Giants pitchers dutifully reported all of this to their teammates when they returned to New York the next day.

"Damn," one of the younger Giants said. "I figured he was out. If they didn't have Gardner, that winner's money would be ours for sure."

Mathewson, who more than anyone else embodied what everyone on the team considered to be "the Giant Way," frowned. Larry Doyle, the pepper-pot second baseman and team captain, who'd enjoyed his finest year in 1912, who would soon be named the Most Valuable Player of the National League and fueled the Giants with the kind of swagger McGraw craved, was a bit more animated.

"If you don't think we can beat the Boston club straight up, then you can get the hell out of this clubhouse and get your ass back to the bushes where it belongs," Doyle fumed.

"That ain't the way we win games around here," veteran Moose McCormick seethed. "Shit, I don't care if they pick up Ty Cobb and Ed Walsh [the American League's best hitter and among its best pitchers, respectively, who played for the Tigers and White Sox, respectively] for the world's series. We'll beat *their* asses, too."

"I want to see Gardner in there with everything he's got," piped in third baseman Buck Herzog. "When we grab the series, we don't want to hear any excuses."

Mathewson, reclaiming the floor, returned a sliver of solemnity to the lecture. "That's the way we are. That's the way it is around here," he said. "We want to beat Boston, but we want to beat Boston's best team. And we want to win that winner's money fair and square."

The winner's money. For Mathewson and the other men gathered in the room, that was the holiest grail, same as it was for the Red Sox. The year before, the Giants and the A's had split $342,264, the winners receiving a record $3,655 per man. That may not seem a lot—and even in 2007 dollars, that translates to roughly $80,000 or so, a fraction of a contemporary World Series check—but that was a good thousand bucks clear of the average salary ballplayers brought home for the whole year in 1912. In 2007, when a future generation of Red Sox would win a World Series, each of them would take home more than $308,000—tip money in a time when the average player income was in excess of $2.6 million. Mathewson could still bitterly recall the 1905 Series, when many of the Athletics and many of the Giants had paired up and agreed to split evenly the $68,436.81 that was allocated to the players' pool regardless of who won the Series. Mathewson was not one of the conspirators that year, when the split was 75–25 in favor of the winners, and he was still outspokenly suspicious of the way the National Commission rewarded World Series participants every year.

For one thing, the players received only a portion of the first four games played in any Series. Baseball owners called that a necessary safeguard; without that cap, there would be nothing preventing players from colluding to play every Series to seven games (or more, if they threw in a few "accidental" ties, too), the better to maximize their profits. Mathewson railed that this was a cynical concession to the lowest common denominator. "Even players who place a bet on themselves now and again have every reason in the world to *win* that bet," he reasoned, failing to factor in the possibility that there would be certain players who might bet *against* themselves, too, depending on the odds. Under existing rules, then, the first four games' receipts would be divided thusly: 60 percent to the players' pool (which would ultimately be split 60 to the winners and 40 to the losers), 30 percent split equally by the two club owners, and 10 percent to the National Commission, an arrangement that sure looked like a legal skim to skeptical players. Any other games would go 100 percent into the pockets of the owners; nobody in that fraternity, apparently, seemed bothered by the fact that temptation could just as easily seduce *them* to artificially extend a World Series by a game or two—especially in a year when the two facilities hosting the games would, for the first time, each exceed 30,000 capacity, fattening substantially the potential bottom line.

Asking such questions wouldn't have done anyone much good, the men who ran baseball agreed. What the public didn't know couldn't hurt them. Or the game.

William Pink wanted to know what kind of self-respecting baseball town would be so tightfisted with its dollars, how any city that thought so highly of itself could think so little of its local nine. Pink was a wholesale liquor dealer from Boston, a member in good standing of the Royal Rooters who'd actually put together the group's travel itinerary, and a man who was itching to spread his money around. In fact, he insisted, the three hundred Rooters among them had close to $100,000 that they wanted to lay down—if only they could find any takers.

"We can't get any bets," he moaned. "Where is all this Giant money we've been hearing about? We run across lots of people willing to argue, but they vanish at the mention of money."

"What odds are you giving?" he was asked.

"Why, it ought to be even money," he said. "If you have any pride in the Giants you shouldn't ask odds. Over in Boston when we try to bet we have to offer 10-to-6 or 10-to-5 to get any takers. But it ought to be different here. One of the troubles is that the newspaper articles have made the Giants fans timid. We are only offering even money now but I guess we'll have to come down to 10-to-9 or 10-to-8 before we can get a bet."

He was right; once the New York bookies—the Supreme Court on such matters—announced their odds at 10-to-8, Pink and everyone else found willing dance partners. By Tuesday morning, when a bright sun dawned on New York City, seeming as excited about that day's World Series Game One as everyone else, it was estimated that more than a million dollars had already been wagered within the city's five boroughs alone. And that was sure to grow quickly, especially once the boys from Wall Street got involved, which would officially occur that morning. Mostly, before now, the moneymen had concerned themselves with placing bets on the presidential election (Wilson was the current betting favorite, at 4-to-1), but shortstops would soon usurp statesmen, at least for the time being. Besides, Taft (the long shot at 15-to-1) had other issues to deal with. Already stuck on a baseball-free vacation, his official car was nearly run off the road of a narrow mountain between Dalton, Massachusetts, and Brattleboro, Vermont, by a truck speeding recklessly right at him. He wasn't having a good month.

Neither were the glut of young boys seized with baseball fever who'd hoped to make an unplanned holiday out of Game One. In fact, so many kids from out of town had made their way to the city from their hometowns that Police Commissioner Rhinelander Waldo put together a special squad at the Polo Grounds to round them up after his office was flooded with dozens of letters from anxious parents seeking aid in tracing missing youngsters. And John Murphy, groundskeeper of the Polo Grounds, found himself having to shoo with a pitchfork fifteen or twenty city kids who'd snuck into the stadium overnight and slept in his toolshed in the hopes of getting a glimpse of the game.

"It was either that or call the Truant Officer on them, because I'm a busy man," explained Murphy, who already had his hands full trying to reinforce the wooden portions of the ballpark's grandstands, which might, for the first time, have to withstand the force of 40,000 people.

The city was electric. Hotels reported guests who'd come from as far away as San Francisco, Los Angeles, and Seattle, all flooding concierges with requests for tickets, some offering to pay as much as $100 for a pair of good seats. And over on Park Row, near the Brooklyn Bridge, where ten of the city's fourteen newspapers were crowded into the same few blocks, newsboys picked up their stash of papers, not sure which front-page story they wanted to hawk louder.

There was the World Series, of course. But things had also taken a turn for the sinister (and the surreal) in the Becker Trial already; "Big Jack" Zelig, who'd started his career as a pickpocket and had grown into one of New York's most flamboyant underworld figures, had been gunned down on a trolley car three days before he was scheduled to testify against the disgraced lieutenant. That was one of many reasons why it had taken three full days and more than three hundred potential candidates to finally identify eleven of the twelve men who would sit on Becker's jury. Being a good citizen could be hazardous to your health, as Big Jack Zelig had discovered during his first and only foray into good citizenship.

A few weeks before, Zelig had been kind enough to share with Hearst's *American* his opinions on the best way to raise children in the modern world. "Make a companion and a chum out of him," he'd said. "Keep him off the streets. Never let him play marbles for keeps. Keep him away from the small dice and the poolrooms."

Anything else?

"Make an athlete out of him," Big Jack suggested. "Go and make a ballplayer out of him. A ballplayer is what he ought to want to be anyway."

So the newsboys listened.

"JINTS AND SOX TODAY AT THE POLO GROUNDS!" they cried. *"JINTS AND SOX START THE SERIES TODAY!"*

CHAPTER THREE

Tuesday, October 8, 1912: Game One

NEW YORK—"Smoky Joe" they call him, although when he made his appearance in the land of the living twenty-three years ago this month, his fond parents thought the world would know him only as Howard Ellsworth Wood. But "Smoky Joe" it was who emerged from that fierce fight up under Coogan's Bluff yesterday afternoon . . .

DAMON RUNYON, *NEW YORK AMERICAN*, OCTOBER 9, 1912

THE POLO GROUNDS was the place to be this morning of October 8, 1912, but it wasn't the *only* place to be if you wanted to follow what would be happening up there later in the day. Already, in three different places across New York City, and in several spots throughout Greater Boston, workmen had begun putting the finishing touches on remote scoreboards that would attract tens of thousands of people, all of them with their gazes fixed on the numbers, lights, and figurines that would replicate the baseball game being played at 155th Street and Eighth Avenue in Upper Manhattan. Already, electricians were working out the bugs between the telegraph lines set up in a lower box along the first-base line and those scoreboards; the papers all boasted that it would take no longer than six seconds for any action uptown to be transmitted downtown, or to

Boston, or to any other city anxiously awaiting updates. Already, three Boston newspapers had set aside telephone lines to be used exclusively for callers who wanted updates from the games. Already, the six afternoon newspapers in New York and the three afternoon papers in Boston had held staff meetings with circulation people, making sure that fresh-off-the-presses extra editions would be in the hands of newsboys within minutes of the final out.

"Telephone 4500 Fort Hill!" screamed the house advertisement in that morning's editions of the *Boston Globe*, and that city's biggest newspaper had already hired two dozen temporary workers to man the switchboards inside its business office so callers could get instant score updates. Outside, the paper would construct its own temporary scoreboard, and another would rise in the middle of Boston Common sponsored by the rival *Herald*.

A century later, it would be virtually impossible to walk a city block without having instant access to scores and pitching changes, to trade rumors and injury reports. Taxicabs have mobile scoreboards affixed to the tops of their roofs. Televisions have a continuous blur of numbers and names crawling across the bottoms of their screens. A click of a button on your cellular phone and you can access video of a home run hit two minutes earlier two time zones away. In 1912, you had to be a little more inventive, a little more creative, except in October. In October, if you walked along the streets of a great city, you were going to hear about the latest development in the World Series whether you wanted to or not. A man would strike out in New York or Boston, Chicago or Detroit, and within six seconds that information would be relayed to a waiting scoreboard somewhere in Cleveland or Pittsburgh or Los Angeles or Cincinnati. There was a reason why baseball called it the "world's series": No matter where you traveled in the nation—the only "world" that mattered to most Americans in 1912, five years before the killing fields of France would permanently expand those boundaries—you found thousands of people hungry for scores, thirsty for baseball information.

Still, nothing compared to the buzz in and around a city when your team was in the series. And so it was that in Times Square, in the hours before noontime, long before the first pitch would be thrown at 3 o'clock uptown, a crowd of several thousand had already gathered outside the offices of the *New York Times*, mindful that to arrive later would mean a poor view and a craned neck. Thousands of others had migrated to Herald Square, outside the building belonging to the *New York Herald*, where its sister paper, the *Evening Telegram*, had built an even bigger, far fancier display board, dubbed a Playograph, replete with color-coded lights and live-action manne-quins to represent, as best as possible, the likenesses of Tris Speaker and Fred Merkle, Smoky Joe Wood and Christy Mathewson. Down on the Lower East Side, where so many other papers were bunched together, another board rose along Park Row, sponsored by Hearst's morning and afternoon papers, the *American* and the *Journal*. And if you fell somewhere in between the privileged few thousand who had actual tickets to the game and the masses who waited impatiently for news nuggets on the newspaper boards, you could spend anywhere from fifty cents to two bucks and pay for a seat inside Madison Square Garden in New York or inside the Arena in Boston, where the information would be fed to you along with frankfurters and other hors d'oeuvres, beers and other beverages, where you could listen to some pregame music, too, if you so desired.

Jack O'Patrick, one of a hundred police officers assigned to keep the peace in Herald Square, shook his head as he reported for duty on Tuesday morning and spotted the gathering throng.

"I've been on the job for seventeen years and this is the first time I've seen so many beat cops reporting for work so early," the resident of Williamsburg, Brooklyn, said as he chewed on a small cigar. "I think they want to get a good spot the same as the other people do, same as the fans. Me? The hell with the Giants and the Red Sox. I'm a Dodgers fan. I'd like to see them both lose. I'm rooting for rain."

The great palace where the grand festivities would take place was in pristine condition when the umpires all arrived to inspect the field around 11 o'clock. There had been a burst of ballpark-building all across the major leagues, a trend that would continue for a few more years and produce some of the most memorable green cathedrals in American lore. Shibe Park (later rechristened Connie Mack Stadium) had started the trend in 1909, rising in less than a year in the heart of a section of Philadelphia known as Brewerytown. It was revolutionary not only because of its careful, elaborate design but also because it was the first baseball field built primarily of steel and concrete; when that wayward cigarette from the passing El felled the wooden Polo Grounds two years later, the imperativeness of such progress was keenly evident. In addition to the rebuilt Polo Grounds (which, shockingly, was ready by June after the Giants spent the first three months of 1911 sharing Hilltop Park with the rival Highlanders), new parks sprouting like cherry blossoms would appear like magic in Boston (Fenway Park), in Detroit (Navin Field, opened on the same day, April 20, 1912), Cincinnati (Crosley Field, which opened nine days earlier), Brooklyn (Ebbets Field, which would open in 1913), and Chicago (which had already welcomed Comiskey Park on the South Side in 1909 and would break ground on Wrigley Field on the North Side by 1913).

Still, there was no place quite like the Polo Grounds, a magnificent project that fulfilled the wishes of John J. McGraw and John T. Brush that their baseball team should play not only in a ballpark, but a basilica. The upper deck was decorated by an ornate and detailed frieze, as was the facing of the lower deck, and a flock of steel eagles stood watch at the roof's very top; the whole presentation was impossible to keep your eyes off of from the moment you first walked into the place. (Yankee Stadium's copper façade would soon enough become the most famous decorative touch in all of American sporting architecture, but there was little mystery about where the designers of Osborne Engineering had taken their inspiration.) The infield was distinctly shaped like a clover, with ornamental dark circles built into the dirt itself. The dimensions were just as unique. To left field, the official measurement was 277 feet, but the second deck extended about twenty feet over the lower grandstand, meaning if you could get a little air under the ball you could get yourself a tidy 250-foot home run (not that McGraw's teams, the ultimate practitioners of "small ball," ever took regular aim at such an inviting target). The outfield sunk, and at the fence it was a good eight feet lower than the infield, meaning that when McGraw looked out from the dugout, he could barely see Fred Snodgrass's neck out in center field. Even the dirt strip connecting the pitcher's mound and home plate, commonplace in ballparks of the era, was distinctive, one stripe of darker dirt (and sometimes two or three) bisecting the wider-than-normal strip.

And all along the outfield fence, and in the walls behind the outfield bleachers, every available inch of wood and concrete was turned over to the local merchants. There were advertisements for Adler Gloves ("Fit For Everybody!") and B.V.D. Underwear ("Be Cool! Loose Fitting!) and the House of Morrison Tailors ("It Fits Well Around the Neck!"), for Bass Ale and Baltimore Whiskey and Peter Doelger Bottled Beer and Ruppert's Knickerbocker Beer, for Fatima Cigars and Philip Morris Cigarettes, for Adams' Pepsin Gum and Schweppes' Dry Ginger Ale and Appollinaris Bottled Water.

When a newspaperman asked Brush one time if there was a segment of his stadium that he wouldn't sell, Brush, a millionaire dozens of times over, had replied, "Gentlemen, we need to find some way to meet the salaries of our baseball players."

Into the quiet breach walked the four arbiters in dark blue suits, white dress shirts, and dark blue bow ties, and it was Silk O'Loughlin who is said to have turned to his three cohorts and said, "Better get 'em all right today, fellows, or there'll be a hundred thousand people who'll say they were here when you got it wrong."

Outside, the men and women on line started to stir. Some had spent the better part of two days in the shadow of Coogan's Bluff, and they waited impatiently for the Polo Grounds' main entrance, facing the Harlem River Speedway, to open. Most of them had their heads buried in newspapers. In the *Press*, an organ of the Bull Moosers, there was an editorial extolling the games, and the game, they were all about to embrace: "With baseball at the top of its popularity and financial prosperity, it is astonishing that the game has been kept so free from the gambling scandal which has ruined horse racing in the United States for this time. Considerable betting does go on in spite of the resolute efforts of baseball authorities to keep their sport free from its blight, though the gambling cannot be indulged on its grounds. The tradition against contact between professional gamblers and players has been stubbornly upheld. Most of the wagers made are of the character indulged by political partisans over election results. If the government of the United States were as efficient, honest, and courageous as the government of American baseball there would be little graft and little complaint of favoritism."

The *World* and the *American*, of course, tried to outscream each other with the latest headlines from the Becker Trial. The *World* scored the bigger coup, getting an exclusive interview with the disgraced lieutenant on his way back to the Tombs, quoting him thusly: "You don't mean to say any decent man is going to give any credit to the testimony of such dirty Jews as that crowd against me are? They can't convict me of anything on the strength of what that bunch swears to." Becker growled, "They're the scum of the earth. Let me tell you this: If they convict me of anything on the evidence given by that crew, then the United States is worse than Russia."

The *American* had to settle for a firsthand account from one of its photographers, who'd brought his camera to Big Jack Zelig's funeral at 286 Broome Street, in the shadow of the Williamsburg Bridge. When he aimed his camera the first time, one of the mourners walked over and tapped him on the shoulder.

"If you click that camera here once, I will get you," the man from the *American* was informed. "Remember this: If I don't get you here now I'll get you if it takes me six months."

The photographer tried to plead his case to a familiar face nearby, a man who also happened to be a detective for the NYPD, who'd heard every word of that oath. "I need to take pictures!" he protested. The cop just shook his head.

"You'd better not," he said. "There may be serious trouble if you do. You'll probably be killed before I had a chance to defend you."

The story ran without pictures.

It was a quarter till noon, fifteen minutes to the opening of the doors, when suddenly the pilgrims in line heard a raucous ruckus drifting in from the south. Many were shocked by the commotion. But the real baseball aficionados in line identified the source of the tumult straightaway.

"Why lookee here," one of them said, "if it ain't the Royal Rooters."

Their sacred journey had begun more than a hundred blocks downtown just about an hour earlier, all three hundred of them gathering along with a thirty-piece brass band at the Elks Club on Forty-fourth Street at 11 o'clock, some nursing hangovers off a boisterous night of imbibing and propositioning, most of them simply high on the opiate of baseball. They came armed wearing buttons, caps, scarves, sweaters, all of it in deep shades of crimson. They held clackers in their hands, the kind of incessant noisemaker that usually got a rise out of whatever city they were invading. Some brought tiny bats to supplement the percussion. Honey Fitz wasn't among them, not yet, because the callings of his office superseded that of his baseball lodge and so he was breakfasting with New York mayor Gaynor, New York's governor John Alden Dix, and Massachusetts's governor Eugene Foss. But Nuf Ced McGreevy was there, and so was Dick Field and John J. Attridge, Johnny Keenan and William Pink, all of them unofficial officers of the court. At 11 sharp, they took to the streets, marching ten blocks to where a motorcade was waiting for them, all the while singing their theme song, "Tessie," a ditty written in 1903 whose annoying melody was surpassed only by its cloying lyrics:

Tessie, you make me feel so badly
Why don't you turn around?

Tessie, you know I love you madly
Babe, my heart weighs about a pound . . .

And even then, most people could stand it except the Rooters sang it incessantly, ten times a game, fifteen times a game, twenty times a game. It was their duty, they believed. Back in 1903, the first World Series had opened in Boston and the visiting Pirates had taken two out of three, then took Game Four in Pittsburgh to seize a commanding 3–1 lead in the best-of-nine series. Then the Rooters—who'd all but commandeered the third-base section of the grandstand at old Exposition Park (seemingly unaffected by the rancid odors that would often waft over from the Allegheny River, on whose banks the park was built)—started singing "Tessie," and the Red Sox won, and they kept winning, and the Rooters kept singing, and when they captured the Series in Game Eight back in Boston, Tessie's immortality was sealed and the legend of the Royal Rooters was hatched.

It wasn't just their rabid intensity that separated the Rooters from other loyal fans scattered throughout other cities, lending their support to other teams. Those fan bases tended to be filled with boaters and neckties, as baseball was still a decidedly male pastime; among the Rooters, it wasn't unusual to see silk stockings and tea hats, for women were more than welcome among their ranks. As they cruised up Broadway this day, their band in tow, a gaggle of the women audaciously carried a banner declaring "Boston Red Sox, World's Champions, 1912." And they toted in their purses the same printed cards that their male counterparts carried in their wallets, passed out back at the Elks Club by McGreevy, stating the Rooters' ambitious goals: "At Baltimore in 1897, Pittsburgh in 1903 and New York in 1904, with the odds against us on the enemy's battlefield, we cheered them on to victory and brought home the flag."

Five songs, replete with lyrics, were included on the cards. And as the motorcade carrying the revelers slowed and dropped the leather-lunged brigade out in the midst of the Giants fans stringing out the queue, they finished off a sixth rendition of "Tessie," plowed their way through "Sweet Adelaide," and then entertained their hosts with some specially written lyrics designed to fill the popular New York tune "Tammany," the ultimate tribute to their favored nine:

Carrigan, Carrigan
Speaker, Lewis, Wood and Stahl
Bradley, Engle, Pape and Hall
Wagner, Gardner, Hooper too
Hit them, hit them, hit them, hit them
Do boys, do.

It is frightening to imagine what a restless pack of New York baseball fans would do if confronted with similar conviviality administered by modern fans of Boston baseball, especially given such a banal libretto. Suffice to suggest they wouldn't do what the people in line at the Polo Grounds did on October 8, 1912.

For they offered up a warm round of applause.

Or maybe they were just in a giving mood. Noon had passed, and slowly all thirty-two entrances at the grounds were lifting their steel gates, and now the crowd eagerly passed through turnstiles, finding their seats, waiting for the first look of baseball players on an October day that easily could have passed for June. The mood in the stands was upbeat, and it was catchy. The previous year, the Giants' giddy captain, Larry Doyle, had remarked to a rookie reporter for the *American* named Damon Runyon, "Damn, it's great to be young and a New York Giant!" Now Giants fans, those lucky enough to have a ticket for this grand occasion, co-opted the expression.

"Damn, it's great to be fifty years old and a Giants fan!" exclaimed William M. Erb, an exiled New Yorker now living in San Francisco who estimated he'd spent close to $500 to cover the basic costs of his sojourn: train travel, lodging, food, cab service from the Hotel Knickerbocker to the Polo Grounds, and, of course, "enough left over to entice the gentleman in the grandstand to engage me in a wager at favorable odds."

While all of this was going on, the players started trickling into the clubhouses, located beyond the outfield fence. Most of the Giants lived in apartments in nearby Washington Heights, although the McGraw and Mathewson clans each owned property farther downtown befitting the heft of their social and financial strata. The Red Sox arrived two-by-two in a procession of cabs from the Bretton, with the exception of McGraw's nemesis Heinie Wagner, who'd stayed with his parents in suburban New Rochelle. It was impossible not to run into players on opposing teams in the cramped quarters of the neighboring dressing rooms, but not one of the forty-five available players on either side dared exchange greetings or even silent pleasantries. Not now. Maybe not even later. The trainers were busy, tending to Larry Gardner's pinky and Duffy Lewis's cold in the visiting room, to Chief Meyers's sore foot in the Giants' room.

McGraw didn't want any of his players bothering with the swarms of newspapermen who'd beaten them to the park, so he handled the duties himself, inviting a few of the scribes into his tiny office where he was pulling on his uniform.

"Are you nervous, John?" Sid Mercer of the *Globe* asked, breaking the ice if not the tension.

"Nervous? Sure I am! Sure we are. I wouldn't give a snap of my finger for a player so stolid in his makeup that he didn't feel the thrill that comes just before a contest such as this one. But when the game begins that nervousness will disappear and the men will give the best that's in them."

Down the narrow corridor, a smaller crop of writers had surrounded Jake Stahl, pestering him for a prediction, until finally he had to say something to get them away from him and off to the press box.

"I don't call this a prediction," he said, "but I just know that flag is going to fly in our field in the Back Bay next year."

"That sounded like a prediction to me, Jake," Murnane of the *Globe* said.

"I'm confident in the boys, Tim," he said. "What else do you expect me to say?"

At exactly 12:45, with the bleachers and most of the grandstand already packed to the gills, the long gate at the bottom of the right-field fence creaked loudly and began to open, parting the Baltimore Whiskey and Peter Doelger ads in half, revealing the hallway leading to the clubhouses, and the loud buzz that had swarmed the Polo Grounds, turning it into a human beehive, disappeared at once . . . and out stepped Dick Hennessey, the Giants' mascot, who was greeted with a loud, disappointed sigh that soon dissolved back to silence. But when McGraw strode purposefully out of the darkness a few seconds later, the solemnity was replaced by a roar that rattled the year-old yard to its brand-new foundation. Mathewson came next, of course, followed by Rube Marquard and Jeff Tesreau, then Snodgrass and Merkle and Doyle the captain, who was the only one who waved at the adoration. The Giants wore brand-new uniforms, but they were of the exact same design as the ones they wore during the season, more gray than white, with pinstripes and the team's distinctive "NY" logo prominently stamped on the front; there was no sign of the imposing all-black uniforms that McGraw had ordered specifically for the Giants' two previous World Series appearances, in 1905 and 1911. Some of the players wore maroon sweaters, too. All of them seemed a little curious at the glee surrounding them, a continuous five-minute spasm interrupted only by the lady with the Royal Rooters who stood up as the manager passed by and unfurled a brand-new sign:

*W*E WERE HERE IN 1904, BUT . . .
REMEMBER THAT, JOHN.

McGraw couldn't help himself when he saw that. He laughed. Then he tipped his cap.

Immediately behind the Giants came the Red Sox, and they were an irresistible sight, walking slowly with gray uniforms and red stockings, each of them wearing striking red blazers. They were greeted with polite applause by most of the gathering throng and with unbridled enthusiasm by the three hundred rooters and thirty trumpeters singing yet another few bars of "Tessie," occasionally throwing into the air their interchangeable straw boaters, all of which featured flaming-red hatbands with "Oh! You Red Sox!" stenciled on them. The Giants were well into their batting practice, and Red Murray drew a few cheers and a loud sarcastic yell when he drilled one of the first pitches he saw about ten rows deep over the left-field fence, off a grooved lob from BP pitcher Louie Drucke.

"Hey, Murray!" came the voice, slicing through the rest of the crowd noise like a foghorn. "You gonna be on the take again this year? You were oh-for-twenty-one last year, Murray, did you have a pile on the A's? You taking the Sox this year too?"

Murray stepped out of the batter's box and walked over to Larry Doyle.

"Pay him no attention," Doyle said.

"That's the same son of a bitch been on my back all damned year," Murray said. "I've wanted to foul off a pitch in his mouth since spring."

"Keep hittin' 'em straight and long," Doyle said. "That'll shut him up."

When the Giants were finished, the Sox hustled to replace them and the first man in the batting cage was Tris Speaker, who took three practice swings and sneered at the pitcher, "Let 'er rip." Then Speaker took one of the most vicious swings anyone could ever remember seeing outside of a real game, and he sent the ball soaring on a breathtaking arc toward right field, over the fence, and over the entire grandstand, the ball finally coming to rest ninety feet beyond the back wall.

There was an audible gasp, then instant silence. It was the longest ball anyone had ever seen hit in this stadium, or in any of the previous three stadiums bearing the name "Polo Grounds."

"Holy smoke," Fred Merkle said, loud enough for McGraw to hear.

"You know how many runs they get for that, Merkle? They get zero runs for that. Next time I catch you admiring their work it'll cost you twenty-five bucks."

Soon enough, the crowd was snapped back into its frenzy, thousands of them plunking down ten cents for a program (a reduction from a quarter the year before, when so many people had complained of price gouging). Harry M. Stevens, the vending magnate, had hired extra workers to keep pushing Coca-Cola, peanuts, chewing gum, "historical sandwiches" and hot dogs, in addition to cigars and cigarettes, and he could barely keep the trays full. The other impresarios doing turn-away business were located far over near third base, in the grandstand. This is where the gamblers had gained a beachhead, and if there was a problem with their presence no one was saying. Not only were they still taking wagers on the Series (at 10-to-8) and the game (even money if Mathewson was starting, 10-to-9 for anyone else), they had also set up a wooden board to accommodate a floating craps game and various brands of poker, silver coins clinking all over the aisles of their little village.

Three o'clock approached, and McGraw sent both Mathewson and Jeff Tesreau out to start warming up. Typical McGraw, many in the crowd hooted. Leave everyone guessing till the final second, even though everyone *knows* it's going to be Mathewson, who looked as resplendent as ever when he peeled off his maroon sweater and started long-tossing. McGraw nervously worked the crowd, shaking hands with all four umpires. Bill Klem, granted the honor of calling balls and strikes for the Series opener, sidled up to McGraw and said, "Let's not give anyone any reason to send you off to watch the rest of the game in the showers, OK, John?" To which McGraw—who for decades would hold the all-time record for most ejections in a career—replied, "Bill, you know how much I admire your work."

"Just admire it quietly today, do we have a deal?" He was smiling, and McGraw smiled back, and before he knew it the Giants' manager was engulfed by photographers, all of them wanting a shot of him shaking hands with Stahl. Soon Stahl was replaced by even heavier hitters: Honey Fitz and Gaynor, and the governors, and the police commissioner. Gaynor led Fitzgerald's hands into McGraw's beefy palm, said, "May I present you, sir, with Boston's chief rooter."

"I hope you've had a pleasant stay, Mr. Mayor," McGraw said, "and that you have an unhappy ride home."

Fitzgerald roared, then let the others take their seats in the VIP box while he trundled out toward deep right field to shake hands with the Rooters and to lend his distinctive baritone to his favorite song, "Sweet Adelaide."

It was Klem who looked at the clock in distant right field, realized they were already seven minutes late starting the proceedings, and summoned both managers to hand him their lineups so he could announce the starting batteries. And when McGraw handed his card to Klem, he fired the first warning shot that this wasn't going to be just another baseball series.

In Herald Square, Jack O'Patrick and the other members of the scoreboard detail knew early on they were in for something different. Over in Times Square, the people were packed even more densely, because just as the folks had flocked to the ballpark early, so too were others now descending on this small segment of town that, not long ago, before the *Times* moved its offices here, had been a nondescript collection of taverns and burlesque halls called Long-acre Square. Half an hour before the game it was already clear that this was going to be the largest gathering in the square's history, and people kept coming even after that pronouncement. New York City, after all, had waited seven long years for a team that they could rally its full force behind; no matter the length of the odds, the town had fallen hard for McGraw's feisty charges as they'd never fallen for any other team. And their swelling numbers proved it. At just past 3 o'clock, a man mounted the stage in front of the scoreboard, raised his arms, and brought the crowd to attention.

"Ladies and gentlemen, I give you the batteries!" he boomed. "For the Red Sox, it will be Cady catching and Wood pitching."

Scattered boos.

"And for the Giants, it will be . . ."

The announcer paused, looked at the piece of paper in his hands, looked at the man who gave it to him, shook his head, cleared his throat again.

"And for the Giants," he said, "it will be Meyers catching and Tesreau pitching."

There was a moment's pause and then . . . another moment's pause. At first, among the 15,000 or so gathered in this small space between the Astor Hotel and Criterion Theater on Broadway and the narrow cross streets of Forty-third and Forty-fourth Streets, there was a dismissal of newfangled technology.

"How can we believe you'll get the scoring right when you can't even get the battery right!" one disgruntled fan yelled at the announcer. Unfortunately for this ill-tempered Giants backer, had he traveled a few blocks away to Herald Square, he would have heard the same announcement, felt the same puzzlement; same with the board over in Newspaper Row, on Frankfort Street, where crowds peering at the *Sun*'s board choked off traffic to the nearby East River bridges. Two hundred and fifty miles away, in Boston's Newspaper Row on Washington Street, there was a mirror reaction: sheer delight at the prospect of sending Smoky Joe out against a rookie rather than the great Mathewson. And at the *Herald*'s scoreboard on Boston Common, a small group of fans nearly revolted: "Don't lie to us!" they protested. "Only a fool would keep Mathewson on the sideline today! Only a fool or a crook on the take!"

Back at the Polo Grounds, where Klem's announcement had caused no small amount of angst among the Giants fans and the gamblers to equal degree, McGraw could hear disenchantment from the faithful, but as he would explain later he was neither fool nor felon; he wanted to keep Mathewson in reserve for Game Two, which would be played in the hostile environs of Fenway Park, no place for a rookie like Tesreau no matter how much affinity McGraw felt for the kid. And so it was. There was still more ceremony to go through: Doyle, the Giants captain, was presented with a new automobile, a Chalmers-Detroit Touring Car, his reward for being named the National League's Most Valuable Player. Then Mayor Gaynor, stroking his beard for good luck, engaged in a full windup before throwing out the ceremonial first pitch, which he merely tossed toward the pitcher's mound. There, Tesreau picked it up, he fired home to Meyers a few times, and Klem delivered the time-honored umpire's blessing: "Play ball!"

And when they did, when this ninth World Series would finally be shifted from debating parlor to baseball diamond, Tesreau very nearly made John J. McGraw look like the wisest man to ever inhabit a dugout. The newspapers had all summer declared Tesreau the best thing to ever come out of Perryville, Missouri, deep in the heart of the Ozarks, whose original settlers were mostly French and thus were still loyal to King Louis while the patriots of Boston and the Tories of New York were engaged in their first true disagreement a century and a half before. In order for his family to keep up with Jeff's progress, his father, Charlie, had to go "into town" to Ironton, a good hour away, to gather up the big-city newspapers from Little Rock, Kansas City, and St. Louis, study box scores, and then engage the locals in telling tales about his son the big-leaguer.

For a time, it seemed that Tesreau the elder would have quite a bit to discuss on his next trip over the hill, for his son kept the mighty Speed Boys off the scoreboard for five innings. Actually, he'd done even more than that: He'd kept the Red Sox *without a hit* for five innings, his spitball all but giggling at the flailing hitters as it splashed past into Meyers's glove. He'd walked Harry Hooper leading off the game, a clear product of nerves that had rendered his pitching fingers virtually numb. Hooper made it all the way around to third on a couple of groundouts to Doyle at second, but Tesreau buckled down, inducing Duffy Lewis to hit a lazy fly ball to Fred Snodgrass in center field. There was one other small bit of trouble in the third, when Wood reached third thanks to a walk, a sacrifice, and a fielder's choice. Up stepped Speaker, who tried unnerving the kid pitcher by taunting him, daring him to challenge with a fastball, but Tesreau was smarter than that, and when ball four fluttered past a frustrated Speaker yelled at him: "That's OK! I'm just as pleased with a walk as a home run, Bush League!" When Lewis again ended the threat with a pop fly to short, Tesreau avoided the temptation of telling Speaker how pleasing *that* was as he left the field.

Before long, the crowd inside the Polo Grounds (and the one that had formed *above* the Polo Grounds, ringing Coogan's Bluff even though the best vantage points yielded views of maybe half the out-field) had been whipped into a fury because the Giants had seized the Series' first lead. With one out in the bottom of the third, left fielder Josh Devore drew a walk, and he scampered to third when Captain Doyle hit a pop-fly double that Lewis, already having a rough Series, lost in the sun. Wood bore down and blew three fast-balls past Snodgrass for the second out, and up stepped Red Murray. Murray was already off to a better start in 1912 than he'd been a year earlier, drawing a walk in the first. Now, with the crowd urging him on, Murray slammed a hard line drive to center, scoring Devore and Doyle, putting the home team up 2–0. The crowd saluted Murray with a huge ovation after the inning as he trotted out to right field and again later on, as he walked back to the dugout; he stared straight ahead both times. His friend Doyle witnessed all of this with genuine bemusement.

"John," the captain asked, "why didn't you tip your lid?"

And with the question, "John" turned as "red" as his nickname suggested he might. "That's the same bunch hollering there that burned me in effigy down on 135th Street because I didn't get a hit in the Series last year," Murray seethed. "I think I recognize some of the guys now. Do you suppose I'd tip my lid to that bunch or any other? If I drop one or fan out the next inning, they will all be after me."

The next day, in the *New York Globe*, Doyle would surmise, "It'll take some time for Red to warm back up to the fans of New York, I'm afraid."

Soon enough, the fans of New York would have other problems. With one out in the sixth, Tesreau's bid for a no-hitter came to a crashing halt when Speaker hit a high and relatively deep fly toward left center field, a ball that felt so routine off his bat that Speaker slammed his weapon into the dirt in anger and frustration. It looked like a far easier play for Devore in left than for Snodgrass in center, to the point where Devore was planted under the ball, waiting to put it away, even as Snodgrass was running at full tilt. Watching this from the mound, Tesreau screamed: "Stay away from him, Snow! Stay away!" But the rule on the Giants was a simple one: If the center fielder believed he could catch the ball, *he* caught the ball. McGraw had been preaching that since his days with the old Baltimore Orioles, and so when Snodgrass screamed "I got it!" Devore, out of habit, stopped short to avoid a collision, and in so doing, he distracted Snodgrass. The ball fell untouched, and Speaker, propelled by his fury, was already standing on third base, no doubt *supremely* pleased by this gift triple. This time Lewis delivered, scoring Speaker on a sacrifice fly to center, and the Giants' lead was officially cut in half.

Back in the dugout, McGraw fumed. For all of his bluster, McGraw was proud of the fact that he'd been a terrific player himself and knew that physical errors happen, they're part of the game, he'd made 413 of them himself across a sixteen-year career. It was the errors that took place between the ears that drove him batty, and even though Snodgrass was his own special project—McGraw had personally shifted him from catcher, seen him blossom into a terrific outfielder—he wasn't about to spare the rod.

"What the hell happened with that mix-up out there?" he raged as Snodgrass jogged back to the dugout. "That was Josh's ball all the way!"

"That's *your* rule," Snodgrass reminded McGraw. "Besides, it's loud out there, and I never heard him call for the ball."

"No, you son of a bitch, *my* rule is that you act like you've played baseball before and use common sense. And listen more carefully out there!"

Then he turned his attention to Tesreau, worried that his rookie would be rattled by allowing a run that should never have scored. "You OK, Jeff?" he asked.

"Never better," came the reply.

But it was plain that Tesreau was shaken, or just tired, or simply overcome at last by the gravity of the game. After buckling Boston's knees for six innings, Tesreau finally succumbed in the seventh, and again his demise was helped along by a little self-sabotage by his teammates. With one out Heinie Wagner singled, and catcher Hick Cady followed with another single, putting runners on first and third, one out, the Sox now capable of scoring the tying run without the benefit of a hit. McGraw chose to play his infield deep with Wood stepping to the plate; even though he was a good-hitting pitcher (and would, in fact, become a full-time hitter in his later years, after that magic right arm wore out), McGraw liked his chances. And, again, he proved prescient: Wood connected with a Tesreau spitter and sent a hard grounder to Doyle at second, a textbook-perfect double-play ball . . . except Doyle slipped on the dry dirt, fell down, and could only get the force at second. Wagner scored the tying run, and it was as if someone had jabbed a knife into a balloon at the Polo Grounds. Dread crept in, and with good reason: Hooper soon lofted a high pop foul that would have given Tesreau a huge second out in trying to wiggle out of the inning, but Meyers struggled picking it up, faltered, and dropped the ball. Given new life, Hooper doubled on the very next pitch, nudging Wood to third, and when second baseman Steve Yerkes, the Sox' lightest-hitting regular, singled to left, it plated Hooper and Wood to give the Sox a 4–2 lead—a two-run advantage that, with Wood on the mound, eight strikeouts in his pocket already, suddenly felt like twenty.

To no one in particular, McGraw muttered at inning's end: "I have some ballplayers who in the fall cannot seem to stay on the ground. They wait until the big series to pull stuff that they would not be guilty of at any other time."

Throughout New York City, thousands of people shared McGraw's gloom as the game finally wound its way to the bottom of the ninth inning. In Times Square, the 25,000 people had been mostly peaceful, if fitfully apprehensive. Inside the Polo Grounds, the only audible noise as Wood completed his warm-up throws came from the Rooters; otherwise the crowd sounded as subdued as 35,730 people could sound gathered in such a confined space.

That would soon change.

Murray led off the inning with a fly ball to right, but then Merkle stroked a clean base hit to left and third baseman Buck Herzog followed with a bloop single to the same spot. That drew some interest. Then Meyers, still angry at himself for muffing the pop-up in the seventh that opened the floodgates for the Red Sox, smoked a vicious line drive toward the gap in right center. Merkle scored easily, and it seemed Herzog would follow right behind him with the tying run, but McGraw, coaching third base, saw that Hooper had made an astonishing play, cutting the ball off and sending it back to the infield in one fluid motion. Herzog was chugging around third at top speed, but suddenly he saw his manager throw up his arms and scream, "No, Buck, no!"

So the score remained 4–3, but now it was the Giants in business, second and third and one out, one well-placed single away from kneecapping the Speed Boys, delivering the most improbable comeback in the short history of the World Series. Now the city was turned upside down. Fire engines positioned near Herald Square unleashed their furious horns as the mannequins on the *Morning Telegram*'s Playograph sped around the bases. The Rooters had stopped singing "Tessie" and started reciting "Hail Mary." Up above, the 3,000 people who'd formed a half-moon around the Grounds on Coogan's Bluff, or standing on the bridge of the Sixth Avenue El, all started screaming, too, a reaction to what they heard from the crowd below since they couldn't *see* a thing on the field. There were others, trying to steal a portion of the day: the twenty people who'd climbed the scaffolding supporting the biscuit ad beyond the center-field bleachers; the water tower in right, where some fifty fans braved the height (and the only "free" vantage point that actually yielded a view of the infield). All of them wanted to be a part of what was happening now, of this unfolding Giants triumph.

McGraw's brain was working on overdrive now. *This* was what he lived for, games where he could actually have impact, where his intellect and his savvy for strategy could prove the difference between winning and losing. He summoned Beals Becker, a reserve outfielder, to pinch-run for the slow-footed Meyers on second base. Instinctively, he started to call out the name of Moose McCormick, a thirty-one-year-old veteran who'd become McGraw's most reliable pinch hitter, then stopped himself: *Damn it all*, he'd already used McCormick in the seventh, two outs and a man on, a hopeless rally but the only one McGraw figured he had a right to expect against Wood.

So Art Fletcher, the shortstop, would hit for himself. Fletcher hit a fine .282 that year, and would hit .277 across thirteen big-league seasons, but he was, by McGraw's own description, "a little nervous, especially in a big spot in a big game."

This was both: big spot, big game, inside the biggest baseball stadium on the planet. Wood, as was his custom, tugged at his pant leg as he took the sign from Cady, then whirled and threw to second, trying to pick off Becker to no avail. He did that a second time. And a third. The tension was nearing an unbearable level, so McGraw walked halfway down the third-base line, Fletcher met him there, and the manager put his arm around him.

"Kid," McGraw said, "just think of how great it's gonna feel in a few minutes when you knock these guys in and these folks are carrying you off the field."

That relaxed Fletcher for about twenty seconds, the time it took Wood to unleash a wicked fastball that Fletcher swung at but fouled back.

"That's it, kid!" a manic McGraw screamed. "You're right on it! This is a Bush League pitcher from a Bush League team! You own this Boston bastard!"

Wood's face was pale from exhaustion, and it took all his energy to tug his pant leg before starting his windup and throwing a curveball that started four feet over Fletcher's head and then danced obediently downward until it passed the plate near his belt buckle. Strike two.

"Be alert out there, Beals, you're gonna have to score this for us!" McGraw yelped. "Buck, you know this Busher is gonna bounce one past his catcher and when he does you're off like a flash! Let's go Arthur, let's go, let's . . ."

Wood went back to the fastball.

"I heard it," Fletcher would later say. "I didn't see it."

Bill Klem did.

"Steeeeee-rike three!" he boomed. "Yer out!"

The crowd exhaled. It was Wood's tenth strikeout of the game, the first one in his career, he would admit, "that I got solely on guts and will. I had nothing left but desire."

Yet his work wasn't done. The Giants still had one more chance, and the crowd started to stir again, waiting to see what McGraw would do now. OK, he'd burned McCormick early, an understandable mistake. Sure, he'd used Beals Becker to run for Meyers (even though a pitcher like Matty or Marquard could have done that) because he wanted a set of legs standing on second with the potential winning run, so Becker's bat (he'd hit a respectable .264 with thirty-two extra-base hits in '12) wasn't available. But Art Wilson's was. Wilson, the backup catcher, hit .289 in 121 at-bats as Meyers's caddy that year, and if he wasn't the perfect choice right now, well, he was the best they had. The fans resurrected a chant they'd used earlier in the day: "Watch Wood, knock Wood! Watch Wood, knock Wood!" Others simply started serenading the Red Sox pitcher, waving at him and yelling, "Good-bye, Joe!"

And then they all turned their gaze to McGraw.

Who did nothing.

Who clapped his hands and yelled, "It's up to you now, Doc!"

That would be Doc Crandall, the pitcher, who'd won thirteen games for the Giants that year, who'd relieved Tesreau in the eighth and turned in two scoreless innings, who was a fine hitter as pitchers go, hitting .313 that year (and .285 for his career), and who was now hitting for himself with the game squarely on the line. The crowd was dizzy with disbelief: This is for *Game One of the World Series* and Muggsy is going to go with a *pitcher*?

"How about a bingle, Doc!" came the cry from the third-base coaching box.

If Wood realized he was facing a pitcher now, he didn't let on. His arm dangled by his side, only a few droplets of gas left in there, he knew, only a few more bullets left in that chamber. Jake Stahl walked over from first base, said, "One more Joe, and you can rest that wing of yours for a few days."

"One more," Wood said.

He started Crandall with a fastball at the knees, strike one. Then he threw two curves, one of which zipped under Crandall's chin, flooring the Giants pitcher. Then another fastball, high and outside, a 3-and-1 count, the din of the crowd building with every succeeding pitch. Stahl walked over again. "It's OK to walk him, Joe," the manager said. "You don't have to be perfect here, remember that."

Wood nodded. Then threw another fastball that nicked the outside corner. Full count. Full house. McGraw screamed himself hoarse in the coaching box, Stahl quietly urged, "One pitch, Joe," at first, and Wood tugged at his pants, gripped the ball between his fingers, rocked, fired his 122nd pitch of the day.

And you could hear the *pop!* of Cady's glove all the way up in the water tower.

"Steeeeeeeeee-rike threeeeeeeeee!" boomed Klem, easily audible in the instantly silenced Polo Grounds.

"Strike three!" came the voice of the announcer in Times Square, amid a hail of groans and some sprinkled boos.

"Strike three!" came the verdict from the man on stage in Boston Common, where close to 50,000 people were now cheering, chanting, hugging one another, and proposing three cheers for Smoky Joe Wood.

Back at the Polo Grounds, the Rooters hadn't waited long to strike up the band, and as they abandoned the premises they unveiled a custom-designed tune strictly for the occasion, sung to the melody of "In the Good Old Summertime":

In the good old summertime
Our good old Boston nine
Beat everything east and west
Now they're first in line

The New Yorks now are after us
Oh me, oh me, oh my!
But we'll do them as we did the rest
In the good old summertime . . .

On the field inside the ballpark, Jake Stahl raced over to his exhausted young pitcher, extended his right arm, felt an almost lifeless right hand shake back.

"I never threw a ball so hard in my life," Smoky Joe Wood told his boss. "Thank God *that's* over."

CHAPTER FOUR

Wednesday, October 9, 1912: Game Two

Boston leads, 1 game to 0

BOSTON—Two great teams—two valiant foes striving with every ounce of energy for mastery in an ever-memorable struggle on Fenway Park yesterday—alike met defeat from an unexpected source when darkness, unwelcome and unsought, sheathed the weapons of the rival factions . . .

—PAUL H. SHANNON, *BOSTON POST*, OCTOBER 10, 1912

IT HAD ALREADY been an interesting year for Ty Cobb.
Just twenty-five years old, the Detroit Tigers outfielder won his fifth batting title in 1912, hitting a robust .409, and coupled with the .420 average he'd piled up the year before he became only the second man in baseball history to hit .400 in consecutive seasons (Ed Delahanty of the Phillies was the first, in 1894 and '95; no one else has ever come close in the near-century since Cobb did it). The Tigers, who'd spent a giddy three-year run as the toast of the American League from 1907 to 1909 (though they'd lost in the World Series every year), had finally taken a serious tumble in the standings, finishing in fourth place with a sickly 69–84 record. Manager Hugh Jennings (once John McGraw's classmate at St. Bonaventure College) had absorbed the brunt of the criticism for that, but Cobb had come in for some withering rebukes, as well. And with good reason.

Cobb had shown up for spring training mad at the world, and he'd briefly quit the team in a huff in early April when, unhappy with the team's lodgings at the Chicago Beach Hotel, he demanded they seek alternate arrangements. When that didn't happen, Cobb jumped the team for two days; when he finally returned, he was welcomed back without even having to pay a fine or apologize to his teammates.

He wouldn't be so fortunate a month later. On May 15, while the Tigers were in the midst of laying an 8–4 beating on the Highlanders at Hilltop Park in upper Manhattan, Cobb suddenly bolted from the playing field and entered the stands to assail a heckling fan named Claude Lueker. Lueker had been riding Cobb for the better part of three innings, and Cobb, never one to turn a cheek or an ear to that kind of thing, responded in kind. For Cobb, however, a product of the post-Reconstruction South, once Lueker amped up the insult exchange by allegedly calling him a "half-nigger," he believed he was left with little choice but to climb into the stands and try to pummel Lueker into oblivion. The fact that Lueker, the victim of an industrial accident, was obviously handicapped (missing one hand and three fingers on the other) didn't faze Cobb a bit.

"Stop!" the fans yelled at him at one point, trying to quell the bizarre scene. "He has no hands!"

"I don't care if he has no feet!" an enraged Cobb responded before he was finally pulled off Lueker—who denied ever making the comment that drew Cobb's ire. The American League responded swiftly, suspending Cobb indefinitely, and this led directly to one of baseball's most ignominious moments. The Tigers—upset by Cobb's behavior but more angered at Ban Johnson's unilateral punishment of their teammate—voted to boycott a game against the Athletics on May 18. And they did: The Tigers had to recruit a temporary band of college and sandlot and semiprofessional players in order to field a team, which fell meekly to the A's 24–2 in one of the most shameful displays in the sport's history. It was Cobb who pleaded with his teammates to return to work, and it was Johnson who shortened "indefinite" to eight games, and while the Tigers were never a factor in the American League their star batsman surely was. And now he was about to thrust himself into the middle of the World Series, too, even though his team had finished the season some thirty-six and a half games behind Boston.

Cobb had agreed to write a syndicated newspaper column off the Series, same as Walter Johnson had, same as the great Cy Young had, same as Hughie Jennings had. But while those articles tended to be detached and measured, full of lauding winners and comforting losers, Cobb's column was . . . well, pure *Cobb*. Before the Series ever started, he angered McGraw and the Giants by hinting that the Giants would have been fortunate to finish fourth in the American League behind Boston, Philadelphia, and Washington. "I don't see this as my opinion," he'd written, "but, rather, a point of fact."

Now, dictating his thoughts to Damon Runyon, Cobb crafted a blistering attack of the way McGraw handled the late stages of the Series' first game.

"The Giants looked dangerous," he wrote. "But Manager McGraw had used one of his best pinch hitters, McCormick, to bat for Tesreau in the seventh and the fatal mistake, I believe, was when he ordered Beals Becker to second to run for Meyers in the ninth. Most any of his substitute players could have scored from second on a hit, but to face a pitcher like Wood on a crisis, was a different proposition. Becker, a very strong hitter, in Fletcher's place, might have wreaked havoc with the hopes of the Red Sox."

When McGraw heard about Cobb's commentary, his face reddened with anger. When he saw the comments of Bill Carrigan, a Red Sox catcher who hadn't even played in Game One, he grew even more agitated.

"After sizing up the first battle between the Sox and the Giants," Carrigan said, "I believe we will win four straight. I do not believe McGraw's men will win even one game. I believe we have their measure and that nothing can stop us now."

"Pure Bush League," McGraw muttered. "You win the world championship on the ballfield, not in the newspapers."

Of course, it would have helped McGraw if he'd taken his own counsel seriously, because he had already sat down with Harry Cross from the *New York Times*, the man who served as McGraw's personal ghostwriter. And while he repeated for Cross what he'd already murmured on the bench, suggesting his players played differently in October than they did the rest of the year, he specifically called out his catcher for dropping the key pop fly in the seventh that extended the inning and ultimately allowed the Red Sox to rally for two runs.

"It should have been an easy play for Chief," McGraw said. "In my opinion, he should have had the ball. Moreover, the two hits that followed I blame more to Meyers's poor judgment than Tesreau's poor pitching."

It was Mathewson who would relay these words to Meyers the next morning, inside the Giants' team headquarters at the Copley Place Hotel, and it was Mathewson who would have to physically restrain Meyers from leaving his room, knocking on McGraw's door, and punching him in the jaw. Which, in a way, was perfect, for it was Mathewson who, a year earlier, had shown just how complicated ballplayers moonlighting as sports columnists could be, because in *his* column he'd ripped Rube Marquard for a pitch he'd thrown Frank Baker in Game Two that the man nicknamed "Home Run" would clobber for a game-winning blast; whatever hard feelings Marquard may have harbored for that morphed into quiet satisfaction the very next day when Mathewson, too, served up a critical home-run pitch to none other than Home Run Baker.

"Maybe," Mathewson surmised, in a column that appeared Wednesday, October 9, the morning of Game Two of this World Series, "it's time to put the pen and paper away and worry just about the bat and the ball."

Maybe. Still, no fewer than fourteen members of the Giants and Red Sox would have deadlines to meet whenever Game Two ended. And all fourteen would get their stories in on time.

There was little time for feeling too good, or too bad, about the way things had gone in Game One. Within ninety minutes of the final out, both teams were back at Grand Central Station, waiting on trains that would take them to Boston for Game Two the very next day. While the players had argued plenty in the past that asking them to travel every day during a World Series was punishing, and that the result—having eighteen exhausted players battling each other every day—diminished the product significantly, player complaints were rarely taken seriously by the National Commission. So in 1911, the Giants and Athletics had alternated days between New York and Philadelphia, a grueling grind interrupted only by the blissful arrival of rainstorms that halted play for a full week between Game Three and Game Four.

Christy Mathewson had been the last Giant to leave the clubhouse after Game One of this series as dusk descended on the Polo Grounds, the burden of what he'd soon have to face suddenly dawning on him. That McGraw was a pip, he said to teammates who were quickly dressing and abandoning him, racing to make taxicabs to Grand Central. He thinks I'm a magic man, thinks I can roll out of bed and shut out a team as good as the Red Sox. There was a time, sure. But he really did it to me this time.

By now, he was speaking to an audience of one, Giants secretary Joseph O'Brien, who looked nervously at the wall clock and realized that if McGraw's star pitcher wasn't on the train, it wasn't the star pitcher who was going to get an earful about it.

"Let's go, Matty," O'Brien said. "You want to get to the station and get aboard and start taking it easy as soon as you can. You have a hard day's work ahead of you."

Mathewson nodded, fixed his necktie, and walked with O'Brien out to the cabstand, the weight of a thousand burdens on his shoulders. Didn't they realize how hard this was? Didn't they know he was thirty-two years old? In the real world, of course, that was a young man's age. Many of his classmates at Bucknell University were only now entering their prime earning years on Wall Street, or as lawyers, doctors, professors, business executives. His arm sure didn't feel thirty-two. It was an arm that had thrown an average of 322 innings a year for the past dozen years, and to put that in perspective, consider this: In 1980, Steve Carlton of the Phillies would throw 304 innings to lead the National League; he was the last man, through 2008, to even approach 300 innings of work, and that is a milestone likely to stand forever in a modern era of pitch counts and five-man rotations and pitchers used to being babied like newborns.

All around him in that postgame clubhouse, Mathewson had heard his teammates crow about how, hell, the Sox might have gotten lucky and taken one off of us, but just wait, they haven't had to face *Matty* yet.

"The old mainstay has had a good, long rest now and I am sure he will uphold his reputation of being the most consistent winner that ever hurled a world series game," Rube Marquard had crowed to reporters. "Matty is right just now, and he will accomplish all that is asked of him."

Said Snodgrass: "We have Matty going tomorrow, boys, so you can start concentrating on what's going to happen in the third game."

Even McGraw, who should have known better, couldn't help chattering.

"I shall pitch Mathewson today and I figure he is almost certain to win this game," McGraw said. "Mathewson is a veteran who pitches as well away from home as he does before a home crowd and is one of the greatest money pitchers the game's seen."

But Mathewson knew that McGraw knew better than that. It was McGraw who had gone to Mathewson with the idea of shutting him down for the rest of the season after the Giants wrapped up the pennant with nearly two weeks to spare, and though there were few things that Mathewson usually found more contemptible than pitchers who shirked their regular duties, he'd agreed to it. The season had been a strain: no shutouts, whispers every time he took the mound that, while he was still the great Mathewson, he was no longer the Great Mathewson, the marvel who'd have clubs beaten before he ever took the slab. Those days, McGraw feared and Mathewson knew, all belonged to yesterday, even if his 23–12 record, 2.12

ERA, and 134–34 strikeout-to-walk ratio were still about as good as pitching got.

So Mathewson settled into his seat on a special train, No. 26, reserved specifically for the Giants and the Red Sox, the National Leaguers sitting in the back, the Americans in the front, and it left Grand Central promptly at 6 o'clock. About an hour into the trip, though, the whole caravan came to a screeching halt: There'd been an accident up ahead and they'd need to wait until the tracks were cleared. Perfect. The train had been only minimally stocked with food since everyone assumed they'd all eat when they got to Boston, so by the time the train got going again, most all the ballplayers were famished; by the time they arrived at the South Street Station in Boston, just past 2:30 on Wednesday morning, they were ravenous. There were a good three hundred or so fans waiting for the Red Sox, who descended to the platform first (led by Wood, smoking a pipe), and of course there was a small four-piece band, and of course they started singing "Tessie."

"I swear," McGraw said to his friend, coach, and bridge partner Wilbert Robinson, "that song is enough to make me want to punch someone."

The Giants soon left the train, wolfed down a dinner/breakfast combination at a local beanery, and were in their beds at the Copley by 3:30—eleven and a half hours before game time. Only they know how well those beans sat overnight.

As soon as the final out of Tuesday's game was announced at the portable scoreboards in downtown Boston, there was a rush to reach Fenway Park, to engage in the same kind of chilly slumber party Giants fans had enjoyed at the Polo Grounds a few nights earlier, all of them swarming the Lansdowne Street side of the park. The first brave soul in line was young James Lehan, a seventeen-year-old from Roxbury who claimed he'd seen "twenty to twenty-five" games in the Sox' new home this year, "although the new place is a little *too* new for me. I rather miss the old Huntington Avenue Grounds. That's what a *real* ball yard is supposed to look like."

As the sun fell, so did the temperature, and so the sight of an ambitious coffee wagon warmed the spirits of the thousand or so people who lined up behind Lehan.

"I'm some kind of cold," he reported, "but I won't mind if I get a chance to see the game. Of course, I will gladly sell my ticket or my place in line if some chap wants to give me real money for it. Otherwise I'll give up my dollar gleefully to watch the game."

It would have behooved Lehan, and anyone else on line, to have packed a heavy winter jacket, because when the sun made its reappearance early in the morning it didn't bring any warmth with it. Still, at first light, the streets around Fenway Park were already thick with humanity, even though a misty rain filled most of the morning hours, to the point that the switchboards of the *Globe*, the *Herald*, and the *Boston Post* were overrun by frantic callers wanting to know if the game was really going to be played.

The umpires wanted to know the same thing, so they showed up extra early, just past 9:30. Cy Rigler had actually suffered an injured knee colliding with Fred Merkle after Game One was over, when Merkle started sprinting for the center-field clubhouse at game's end and inadvertently ran into the unsuspecting umpire. Rigler, however, was assigned to first base and the right-field line, so it wasn't expected to hamper him. It was Silk O'Loughlin's turn to call balls and strikes, and so he carefully chatted with groundskeepers and Red Sox team officials while theatrically keeping his palm pointed toward the sky so photographers could see he was diligently hunting for raindrops.

"The field looks good to go," O'Loughlin told Jerome Kelley, Fenway's head groundskeeper, just before 10 o'clock.

"She's as ready as any field's ever been ready, sir," Kelley replied.

"Well, then. What say we play some ball then?" And with that, the gates were opened and the masses were unleashed on the grandstands and bleachers, ensuring that Fenway Park would be stuffed like a sardine tin for the very first postseason game of its life.

"We hurried into the bleachers and our long vigil began," a Red Sox fan named Kevin Shaughnessy would report to the next edition of *The Sporting News*. "It was then about 10 o'clock. Five hours to wait for the game to start and the worst of it was there wasn't a moment that we did not expect to hear there would be no game because of poor weather. By noon the stands were filled and every woman who passed in front of the center field bleachers received an ovation, and there were quite a few ovations."

Prominent among the fans in attendance was a seventy-something gentleman named Grandpop Nutt, who claimed he'd been at every important Boston game since the National League's Red Caps played at South End Grounds; belying his birth certificate, Grandpop raced to a vacancy in the grandstand and claimed it for his own. The park into which he raced was substantially different from the one the Red Sox had last visited thirteen days earlier, when they'd defeated the Highlanders 15–12 in a slugfest that closed out the home portion of the regular-season schedule. New stands had been erected down the left-field line and in right center, fully enclosing the park for the first time. There would also be temporary stands erected just in front of the left-field wall, into which a batted ball would be declared a ground-rule double. Fifty cents would get you a bleacher seat; if you wanted to be closer to the play, you could spend as much as $5 through the Sox ticket office (which was the preferred method; unlike in New York, forgers had been able to readily duplicate the ducats for the Boston games, and several hundred fans would receive the horrible surprise that day that they carried fakes in their pockets).

Just as there'd been a keen sense of anticipation the day before in New York, there was a tangible, kinetic energy at work inside Fenway, which was completely filled by noon, three full hours before game time. Honey Fitz had already declared the day a civic holiday within the town's borders, so thousands of workmen and school-children freed from their workaday tedium descended on the Fens, and when they discovered no tickets to be had there they jammed both the Common, where upward of 60,000 people would gather by late afternoon, and Newspaper Row, where an additional 30,000 would assemble in an area that could barely accommodate a third of that number comfortably. And there would be other interested parties now, too. Back in New York, the entire Atlantic fleet of the U.S. Navy had come for review in the Hudson River, a staggering display of nautical might that drew thousands of mesmerized onlookers; the sailors, though, were hungry for information about the World Series and so the *New York Herald* had agreed to keep its wireless connection open so the battleship *Wyoming* could get pitch-by-pitch updates, and the *Wyoming* would then relay the news to her sister ships.

Finally, just past one o'clock, the first line of Red Sox took the field, led by Manager Stahl, and they were treated to a long, reverent ovation. Stahl even took the occasion to tweak his more famous, more decorated counterpart, stealing a page from McGraw's book, sending *four* pitchers—Hugh Bedient, Charley Hall, Buck O'Brien, and Ray Collins—out to warm up without once hinting at who his true selection was. When the Giants took the field they were also greeted warmly, although the fans were quick to tease Tesreau. In that morning's Boston papers, various Red Sox had admitted that they'd only begun hitting him when someone on the bench noted the rookie was tipping his pitches: Whenever he lifted the ball to his face and carefully moistened it, the delivery came in high and fast; when he subtly passed the fingers of his right hand as if he were wiping his mouth, that's when the low-breaking spitter was coming.

Tesreau, reading this, had incurred McGraw's sarcasm by wondering aloud why nobody in the National League had picked up that quirk all year. "It's because you didn't have to face the Giants," McGraw sneered, "although that can surely be arranged if you aren't more careful in the future." Sox fans impishly wiped their faces with the backs of their hands as Tesreau walked by, and the pitcher tipped his cap when he saw that, immediately making friends.

Larry Doyle, meanwhile, ever the team captain, made a most intriguing discovery on behalf of his teammates as he was standing alongside the batting cage, waiting to take his practice cuts. Standing next to Buck Herzog and Fred Snodgrass, the Giants' second baseman pointed to an advertising sign hanging on the distant wall in left field (which was not yet green, nor yet an oversized monster) that said, in big black lettering:

THOMAS W. LAWSON OFFERS $250 TO ANY BATTER
WHO HITS THIS SIGN AND $3,000 TO THE FIRST MAN
WHO SMASHES THE SYSTEM'S SLATE.

The slate in question, affixed to the right of the lettering, was about four feet long by three feet wide.

"Hey, fellows," Doyle said. "What do you think about *that*?"

Snodgrass, a right-handed hitter who, like most Giants, prided himself on being able to spray the ball to all fields, said, "I can't speak for anyone else, but I think I just became a dead-pull hitter for the day."

It took Silk O'Loughlin a while to say the two words he loved to utter more than any other. There was more rain: a brief dousing forty minutes before game time that rankled the crowd and brought back horrible memories of 1911, when the Giants and Athletics had spent more time battling storm clouds than each other. There was more ceremony: This time it was Jake Stahl who was given an automobile, by the fans, in grateful recognition for leading the Red Sox back to the World Series after an absence of nine years. There was the spectacle of the Royal Rooters parading around Fenway Park, banners and noisemakers in tow, singing themselves hoarse, finally taking their usual places in the left-field grandstand and their spiritual leader, Mayor Fitzgerald, throwing out the first pitch. There was even a ruckus just before the Sox (behind Collins, who all along was Stahl's choice to pitch despite his gamesmanship) took the field when a gaggle of men from the right-field bleachers made a break for the unoccupied seats in left field that the Rooters hadn't yet claimed; it took a dash from a group of mounted policemen to drag them away, much to the delight of the fever-pitched crowd.

Finally, just as Collins finished his warm-ups, a large ring of photographers snuck onto the field so they could get a closer look at the action through their lenses. But O'Loughlin would have none of it.

"All picture guys, off the field!" Silk screamed. "You stay here, the Red Sox will forfeit, and then you'll have to answer to Mr. Stahl!"

They dispersed.

And O'Loughlin, slipping on his mask, yelled, "Play ball!"

The first Giants batter was Snodgrass, who took a pitch and then swung at the second, and there were two immediate, distinctive sounds that followed: first, a loud crack, the timeless hint that a bat has met a ball squarely and completely. And then Larry Doyle, from the on-deck circle, saying, loud enough for all to hear: "No shit?"

Because Snodgrass's blast was heading—no shit—straight for Thomas W. Lawson's sign, straight for his slate, straight for $250 that Snodgrass was already counting as he trotted down the first-base line . . .

. . . only to watch the ball tumble into a gaggle of hands just in *front* of the sign, maybe ten feet short, maybe five. Snodgrass would have to settle for a ground-rule double and the delighted laughs of his teammates. That's all he would get, as it turned out, because he wound up stranded at third base.

Christy Mathewson then took the mound to great applause from the Fenway faithful. Mathewson had regularly enjoyed his trips to this city in the past, mainly because the pitiable Braves always seemed perfectly willing to add to his gaudy win totals. Now, as he stood tall in the box, he would recall "feeling as comfortable as I ever had on a mound. This was the only place in the world I wanted to be. I could think of nothing greater than pitching this game for the glory of the New York Giants."

And he barely lived to talk about it.

Harry Hooper led off with a hard two-hopper that caromed off Mathewson's glove, rolled out of reach, and rankled Matty because "in my youth I would have snared that with my eyes closed." As great pitchers do, however, he immediately induced a double-play grounder from Steve Yerkes, a happy development that became significantly less so when shortstop Art Fletcher—whom even his teammates called "softly wound," an expression that we would change to "tightly wound" a century later—fumbled it, then booted it away.

"One of the easiest chances in the world for a big leaguer" would be how Mathewson would describe the play for his readers the next morning. "I don't know what it was. Stage fright? Over-anxiety?"

Next up was Tris Speaker, who conceded to the convention of the times by laying down a sacrifice bunt, and who was rewarded for his selflessness with first base when both Mathewson and Herzog converged on the ball and neither thought to actually pick it up off the ground. Bases loaded. None out. Fenway was foaming at the mouth.

Matty wasn't one to yell at a teammate, but he was a Hall of Fame glarer, and now he fixed a withering stare at Herzog, who acknowledged, "My fault, Matty. I owe you one." Funny thing, too: On the very next pitch, a fastball to Duffy Lewis, Herzog made good, snaring a sharp grounder, firing it home, getting the first out. Next, Mathewson induced Larry Gardner to hit the ball right back at him, for what would surely have been an inning-ending (and soul-crushing) double play; but, again, Matty's thirty-two-year-old reflexes betrayed him, the ball merely ticked off his glove, and while Doyle recovered to retire Gardner at first, Yerkes dashed home with the first run. And when Stahl hit a rocket shot between third and short, he brought home Speaker and Lewis, the score was suddenly 3–0, and it seemed Bill Carrigan, who'd predicted a Speed Boy sweep, was as much a prophet as he was a catcher.

But the Giants were a prideful bunch, never more so than when Mathewson was on the mound. "We all would have given up a year of our lives to get that man a win in the world's series," Chief Meyers would remember many decades later. "There's no question we played much better when he was pitching than anyone else."

So it was that the New York bats wobbled to life in the second. Herzog sent a screaming drive toward the cavernous meadow that was (and remains) Fenway Park's right center field, pulling in for a triple, and Meyers followed by nearly decapitating Larry Gardner with a line drive that practically tore through the Red Sox' third baseman before rolling away, allowing Herzog to score the Giants' first run. Two innings later, Red Murray continued his redemption quest by drilling his own three-base hit right to the base of the stockade in center field, scoring two batters later on a sacrifice fly by Herzog to slice the New York deficit to 3–2. Meanwhile, in between those two rallies, the Giants nearly received the break of the Series, and one they would surely have embraced despite all their high-minded talk earlier in the week about wanting to beat the Speed Boys at their best. Leading off the home third, Speaker smacked a hard shot down the first-base line that Merkle knocked down with his chest. Scrambling for the ball, Merkle finally recovered, raced to the bag, and beat Speaker by an eyeblink; Speaker, employing a play that would still give baseball managers migraines a century later, had ill-advisedly slid into first, and when he did that he rolled his ankle something awful. He had to be helped off the field, with Fenway's silence serving as a mournful backdrop.

Speaker would never dream of leaving a World Series game, of course, so he gritted on, and he would find himself with a splendid chance to break the game open—and break Matty's heart in the bargain—in the fifth. With one out Hopper had singled for his third hit of the day, and Yerkes followed by ripping a line drive over Snodgrass's head in center for an RBI triple and a 4–2 lead. Mathewson had been able to write off his first-inning travails to bad luck; as McGraw would say after, "If he'd had a professional team in back of him, he wouldn't have allowed even one run." But now the great pitcher looked shaken, his shoulders slumped, his face ashen. Speaker limped to the plate, but Matty couldn't see that; he only knew, by reputation, that Speaker was never tougher than when there was a man waiting to be driven home. And both men knew that one more run, on Boston's home grounds, could put the game all but out of reach. And here was the worst of it: Speaker met Matty's fastball flush, crushed it on a line, right toward shortstop, and God only knew what high comedy poor Art Fletcher might have in mind.

Only, Fletcher dived, snared the ball, them scampered to his feet and threw back toward third base, where Yerkes had bled a little too far away from the bag. It was a holy-smoke, did-you-see-what-I-saw, bang-bang double play that left Fenway dazed and Speaker confused (and still hobbled), and somehow kept the Giants in the game.

"That," Mathewson would explain, "is why you never show up a teammate. Sure, Fletcher had a bad game. But he made one play that made everything else seem possible for us."

The Christian Gentleman was never averse to showing a little Christian charity. But he needed more than that now if he was to win the fifth World Series game of his career. He needed the Giants to get him some runs. And quick.

In later years, it was the Green Monster that became the most recognizable icon at Fenway Park. Locals referred to it simply as "The Wall," and if you walked right up next to it you could see the pockmarks left behind by thousands of baseballs through the years. Knowing how to play balls off The Wall became a subject of great local debate. Ted Williams became proficient at it, and Carl Yastrzemski mastered it to an almost scientific degree. Even Manny Ramirez, the hard-hitting savant who manned left field in the first decade of the twenty-first century, became an astute practitioner of the various angles, bounces, and caroms so unique to The Wall.

But back when The Wall was merely a wall, the defining aspect of Fenway was also in left field, as it was there that you would find a leg-breaking slope that rose almost ten feet from a spot fifteen feet in front of the warning track to the base of the fence. It was the bane of just about every left fielder who patrolled out there, with the exception of one man.

"Duffy Lewis played the most difficult left field in the league," Harry Hooper would recall many years later. "There was a bank running up to the left field fence and it was difficult to judge the ball running up the bank and almost impossible to throw it going down."

So proficient did Lewis become at perfecting every nuance of the rise that it almost immediately became known as "Duffy's Cliff," and stayed that way until 1934, when a fresh landscaping of the park finally leveled the grounds forever.

"I'd go to the ballpark every morning and have somebody hit the ball again and again out to the wall," Lewis explained. "I experimented with every angle of approach up the cliff until I learned to play the slope correctly. Sometimes it would be tougher coming back down the slope than going back up. With runners on base you had to come down off the cliff throwing."

So it was with more than a trace of confidence that Collins, Stahl, Fred Snodgrass, the 30,148 people in attendance, and Duffy Lewis himself approached the lazy fly ball off Snodgrass's bat that led off the top of the eighth inning. Snodgrass had followed his near-miss of Thomas Lawson's slate with a flyout and a strikeout, and while he'd hit this ball again in the vicinity of the sign, he hadn't gotten all of it. He flipped his bat in disgust and barely half-stepped his way down the line.

Imagine his surprise, and everyone else's, when Lewis got his feet tangled on the patch of Fenway earth named after him and allowed the ball to drop at his feet. The crowd was stunned into a silence so immediate and so complete that the only audible sound came from the third-base coaching box, where McGraw was screaming at Snodgrass for not hustling on the play. "Hope you enjoyed the view on that play, Snow," he crowed, "because if you don't score it's gonna cost you twenty-five bucks!"

Doyle brightened his manager's mood considerably when he singled over second base, pushing Snodgrass up ninety feet, and now the Fenway crowd started to mutter to itself ever so slightly. For the first time in the series the Red Sox' bullpen was busy, Stahl summoning both Charley Hall and Hugh Bedient to start warming up in case Collins couldn't figure a way out of this growing pool of quicksand, but Collins quickly responded by getting Beals Becker (subbing in the lineup this day for Josh Devore) to nearly bounce into a double play, the speedy Becker barely beating Heinie Wagner's relay throw to first. But Red Murray, no longer the "Hitless Wonder" that inspired headline writers across the country a year earlier, jumped all over a Collins fastball and plunked it in the temporary seats in left field for a ground-rule double, silencing the ballpark completely save for a stolen few dozen Giants fans scattered about, slicing the lead to 4–3 as Snodgrass sprinted home, grateful to be able to keep the fine money in his wallet. Stahl, reluctantly, walked over to Collins from first base to deliver bad news.

"Not your fault, Ray," he said. "Ninety-nine times out of a hundred, Duffy catches that ball blind-folded and we're already out of this damned inning."

"A bad break," Collins said, handing over the baseball.

"You gave 'em all hell," Stahl said, patting Collins on the back before flipping the ball to Charley Hall. Hall had spent much of the season sharing the No. 4 slot in the rotation with Collins, behind the peerless Wood, Buck O'Brien, and Hugh Bedient, and he'd enjoyed his finest year as a big-leaguer, 15–8 with a 3.02 ERA. Born in Ventura, California, he entered the world as Carlos Clolo, a son of Mexican immigrants, and while he'd Anglicized his name before entering professional baseball to deflect some of the overt racism aimed at non-Caucasians during that decidedly inelegant epoch of baseball history, he nonetheless acquired two nicknames: "Sea Lion," which he took to gratefully, and "Greaser," which led to more fisticuffs and brouhahas than Hall would care to recollect. "You know what we need," Stahl said, retreating to first. "Now let's do it."

And the Sea Lion damn near did. On his second pitch, Merkle popped one high into the darkening Fenway sky, and Sox catcher Bill Carrigan barely had to backtrack to put the ball away and restore Fenway's regular breathing patterns. And on the first ball Hall tossed Buck Herzog's way, he produced an almost identical picture: a sky-high pop-up, high enough this time that it started to drift, ever so slightly, toward the first-base side of the plate, a little backward, and at first the Fenway faithful started to roar, content that their 4–3 lead was safe for another inning, but as they noticed Carrigan staggering, then stumbling, they switched to a gasp and, lastly, to disgusted disbelief when the ball thumped off the heel of Carrigan's catcher's mitt, fell out, and tapped the grass. The silence was harrowing, broken only by the voice of Bill Carrigan.

"You dumb Irish shit," he screamed at himself.

He would soon have plenty of help heaping fury on himself, because granted a second life Herzog lashed the very next pitch into the temporary right-field stands for a ground-rule double that scored Becker and Murray and gave the Giants a 5–4 lead that had their dugout dizzy with glee. A run up, six outs left, and Christy Mathewson on the mound? Surely the motormen could rev the train's engine up now, if they liked.

And Matty, given a late lead, knew what to do with it. Steve Yerkes was an easy out on a shallow fly ball to Murray in left. Speaker, his ankle howling at him, tapped back to Mathewson, who threw him out easily, Speaker barely able to make it out of the batter's box thanks to his creaky wheel. Up stepped Duffy Lewis, still smarting from his game-changing muff, and he put a charge into a Mathewson fastball, sending it high and deep toward the temporary bleachers in left. Matty kicked the dirt at the mound, angry at himself, but turned in time to see Murray go thundering back toward the wooden temporary fence, take a crow hop, and then vault himself three rows into the stands, in the same vicinity where the ball was descending.

The ball vanished. So did Murray. And neither reappeared for what felt like an hour but was probably only five or six very anxious seconds. Bill Klem, assigned to adjudicate the left side of the outfield, dashed out for a better look, yelling at the fans, "Is he OK? Is he hurt? Did he catch the ball?"

All three questions went unanswered until finally Murray's slightly bruised head, and slightly bloodied face, popped up among the fans. The sight of the still-breathing redhead brought a crashing cheer from the rest of the park; when he lifted both arms, indicating he didn't have the ball on his person, the noise grew earsplitting. The fans in the bleachers, sporting gents all, helped dust Murray off, gave him a hand back over the fence, and saluted him with three cheers for his courage. Klem, still puzzled, had one last query that he needed answered.

"What the heck happened to the ball?" the umpire asked.

Someone pointed to a narrow pathway behind the seats, and then to Murray's bare head. "Same guy who took Red's lid," he said, "also took the ball and ran like the devil."

Satisfied, Klem pointed two fingers high enough for all to see, officially granting Lewis his ground-rule double, then summoned the Giants' dugout to fetch Murray a brand-new brim. Mathewson, unfazed and unflappable as always, quietly applauded his left fielder's effort, then resumed his focus on the matter at hand, on Larry Gardner, whose shattered finger still throbbed and who was still looking for his first hit of the Series after six fruitless at-bats and one sacrifice bunt. Mathewson started him with his famed fadeaway pitch, which Gardner took for a ball, then came back with a fastball, which Gardner hit hard but straight for the Giants' shortstop, Art Fletcher.

"You go, Matty!" McGraw yelled from the dugout.

"The best there ever was," Meyers thought to himself, removing his mask, watching the play develop, shaking his head in awe.

He was soon shaking his head for another reason. Because before anyone could believe what they were seeing, the ball scooted through Fletcher—who never even laid a finger on it—and into left field. Lewis—who'd purposely held up, hoping against hope to screen Fletcher—sprinted home joyfully, amazed that his little piece of gamesmanship had worked to perfection. It was tied, 5–5, and even the stoic Mathewson couldn't help himself; he stared at Fletcher, or at the very least at the hole that had magically appeared in his chest that allowed the ball to scamper untouched.

It was Fletcher's third error of the game, his fourth already of the series, to go with the fifty-two he'd been charged with during the regular season. Fenway's foundation was teetering, the place was so revved up. And the Giants all at once looked like a beaten bunch, especially when Jake Stahl followed with a single, then promptly stole second, giving the Sox two men in scoring position, putting them one hit away from blowing the game open and all but blowing the World Series open, too. But here Mathewson reached back to 1905, throwing four pitches—one high, one low, one close, one wide—that Heinie Wagner swung through, swung through, fouled off, and swung through.

The game was still tied. The Giants were still alive.

Barely.

Back in New York, back in Times Square, an even larger crowd than the one that had gathered the day before filled the air with a nervous hum that turned to a vicious rage when the announcer declared, "Error by Fletcher, New York; run scored by Lewis, Boston; game tied at five runs to five." A few blocks away, a few seconds later, the *Morning Telegram*'s Playograph flashed the same information, with the mannequin standing in for Lewis rounding third and heading home amid a thick stew of catcalls and curses and worse.

"McGraw shouldn't only fire that bum," one disgruntled voice declared. "He should have him shot as a traitor!"

Out in the Atlantic Ocean, on the luxury liner *Oceanic*, the news was relayed to Prince Brancaccio of Rome, who'd spent much of a leisurely few weeks' vacation in New York earlier that summer at the Polo Grounds, learning baseball, adopting the Giants. He'd already secured tickets for Game Three at New York, declaring he was immersing himself in baseball "in order to feel the pulse of the American people." Now he felt his own pulse quicken, wondering if Game Three would now be the Giants' last hurrah.

Back in Boston, the Giants tried to reverse the tide of momentum that now threatened to carry them into the off-season. They loaded the bases on two walks and a base hit, but with two outs Red Murray grounded sharply to Wagner, the Red Sox' shortstop, who rubbed a little more salt in New York's wound by keeping a routine play routine and flipping to second for the force. Mathewson, refusing to succumb, set the Red Sox down one-two-three in the bottom of the ninth. There would be extra-inning baseball in Boston, even as the sun began to disappear beyond the horizon.

The tension was now spilling everywhere. In the federal court-room of Judge William Hough, located right on Broadway in New York City, the rancor of the crowd kept spilling through the windows, drowning out the opening arguments of a case pitting the Pennsylvania Steel Company against the City of New York for $200,000 owed for the building of the Queensboro Bridge. Howard Taylor, counsel for the plaintiff, was trying to question his first witness when another burst of cheering overwhelmed him. Judge Hough ordered the windows shut. When *that* didn't keep the next sea of boos and cheers and chants from invading the room, Hough banged his gavel and threw up his hands.

"I think," Hough said. "we'd better surrender to the Giants. Adjourned."

Across town, on Chambers Street, Justice John W. Goff may have been freed from crowd noise, but he was experiencing his own late-inning meltdown in trying to locate a twelfth and final juror for the Becker Trial, as one talesman after another begged out of the jury box citing one hardship or another. "A remedy must be found for this," Goff warned. "Man after man has taken the stand and sought by subterfuge to be excused. When we can find neither honesty nor patriotism in our citizens we are helpless."

So the Becker Trial would have to wait at least one more day, which was just as well, because it was obvious that there was only one thing consuming the thoughts and passions of the citizens of two great cities right now, and for a wild, wonderful moment, all along the sidewalks of New York, it seemed the Giants really would find a way to restore their fans' belief in their destiny. For Merkle boomed a deep fly over Lewis's head in left, and by the time the ball stopped bouncing he was standing on third base. Three batters later, after Herzog grounded to short against a drawn-in infield and Meyers was intentionally walked, McGraw—still smarting, no doubt, from the avalanche of criticism unleashed that morning by the army of critics in the newspapers—sent up Moose McCormick to pinch-hit for the nearly catatonic Art Fletcher. McCormick, professional hitter that he was, responded with a long fly to left, plenty deep enough to score Merkle and give the Giants the lead. Once again the Giants handed the ball to Mathewson, this time needing only *three* outs to get even.

All across New England, men and schoolboys abandoned their scoreboards, racing home to make dinner, knowing few ever got a second chance against Matty and *nobody* ever got a third. In New York, most of the fans decided dinner would have to wait, too sweet was the prospect of seeing the scoreboard masters plant one more zero under the Boston line for the tenth inning. And Matty wasn't inclined to disappoint, inducing Yerkes to barely tap the ball in front of home plate, which McCormick gobbled up and threw to first. One out. Two to go.

Up shambled Tris Speaker, whose ankle was getting worse, who was fearful he'd broken it, who had prayed for six innings that nobody hit a ball anywhere but right at him in center field, because there was no way he was catching up with anything else. Mathewson threw a fastball that Speaker barely waved at. And then another.

This one, to everyone's astonishment—even Speaker's—exploded off the bat as if it were shot out of a cannon, to dead center field. Beals Becker was off with the crack of the bat, but even that was no help—it sailed over his head by a good fifty feet. And now, as if by magic, the limp vanished from Speaker's gait and he was tearing around first, and roaring around second, and he was just about to touch third with his bad leg when Becker finally retrieved the ball and heaved it back to the infield, and Speaker wasn't sure whether he was being told to hold up or run by the third-base coach, because he was going to run, dammit, run all the way home and all the way around the bases *again* if he had to, there was nobody going to stop him, and . . .

And then somebody stopped him.

It was Buck Herzog, the Giants' third baseman. Following the play all the way, he had no relay responsibilities. But he *did* have an unwritten obligation, one that had roots in the rough-and-tumble world that McGraw used to occupy in Baltimore, where the old Orioles vowed to beat you by any means available, any means possible.

Mostly, they wanted to beat you fair and square. If that didn't work, they cheated. Or, as McGraw himself would write years later: "If nobody saw you doing anything wrong, then you didn't do anything wrong," a tenet that the Franciscans who'd given him his college education may have taken issue with, if not any of his fans.

Herzog didn't tackle Speaker; *that* would have been too obvious. He didn't grab Speaker by his belt loops, which was McGraw's preferred move back in the day. No, as Speaker rounded third, Herzog merely moved a few steps in and to his left, and . . . well, accidents happen. The two men collided. What's a fellow to do?

What Speaker did was scramble back to his feet in an effort to complete his journey, with 30,148 people going positively berserk all around him. But the wasted seconds cost him: As he neared home plate, Tillie Shafer (Fletcher's replacement at short) caught the ball from Becker, wheeled, and gunned it home to Art Wilson (Meyers's replacement at catcher). The throw beat Speaker, and O'Loughlin was ready with his right hand to call him out. But Wilson dropped the ball as Speaker slid past, and O'Loughlin screamed, "Safe!" Speaker, the fury bubbling inside him now, rose from the ground, dusted himself off, stomped on home plate one more time for emphasis (with his bad foot, no less), then ran after Herzog.

"You dirty son of a bitch!" he screamed.

"Get the hell away from me if you know what's good for you!" Herzog yelled back, narrowing the gap between them.

"You crooked bastard! That's a Bush League play and you know it!"

"You oughta know, playing in a Bush League!"

By now Stahl had raced out and grabbed Speaker, and McGraw had done the same thing, pulling Herzog away, and peace was about to be restored when Speaker pointed at McGraw and yelled, "*You* teach them this shit, Muggsy! I hope you're proud."

Bad enough to be labeled a cheater. But who was Tris Speaker to be calling him Muggsy? McGraw forgot about Herzog and started after Speaker himself, before *he* was restrained by Wilbert Robinson.

"What are you gonna say?" McGraw's old friend whispered. "You *do* teach them this shit."

But McGraw did have one more complaint to air; ever the detail man, even as everyone was watching the flight of Speaker's ball, he had been studying Speaker's legs. And what McGraw clearly saw—and what most of the boys in the media would reluctantly confirm later on, since they were all quartered near first base in a makeshift press box—was that Speaker, in his haste, had missed first base by a good two feet. McGraw was trying to get Mathewson to resume play, step off the mound, and throw the ball to first on a protest play, but umpire Cy Rigler halted that posse where it stood. "Runner was safe!" he yelled, and now McGraw was *really* mad.

"You either didn't see the play, missed the play, or you're crooked!" McGraw fumed. "Which one is it?"

"Runner," Rigler repeated, gritting his teeth, trying to forget his own leg pain, "was *safe*."

And that was that. Peace was restored, barely, and Duffy Lewis promptly reinvigorated the crowd by lashing another ball over Becker's head, though this time Beals was able to hold the runner to two bases. Now the winning run was on second, but here was where Mathewson, stunned but still steady, turned back into Mathewson, retiring Gardner and Stahl to end the inning amid shouting and tumult that grew ugly as Herzog ducked into the dugout.

The Series' first genuine to-do had shooed whatever lingering nerves may have been affecting the players, but now it was Silk O'Loughlin's turn to be fidgety. It was nearing 6 o'clock, and darkness was rapidly descending. He watched the Giants get two men on base in the top of the eleventh, then saw McGraw—who could damn well see how dark it was—send both runners to second on steal attempts, and watched both men get caught by five feet apiece. He watched Wagner, Carrigan, and Hugh Bedient—seven, eight, and nine in the batting order, all of *them* also knowing how dark it was—each swing at Mathewson's first pitch in an effort to generate quick lightning, with only Bedient's ball—a sharp two-hopper back to the box that Matty himself snared—generating a rise out of anyone.

And now Silk O'Loughlin looked to the skies, tried to find more daylight where there was none, and reached the only sad conclusion that he could.

"It's too dark for any more baseball today," he proclaimed. "We'll resume with a fresh ballgame tomorrow, at these grounds."

McGraw started to protest, was too tired to do it. Besides, it was too damned dark to keep playing. He saw Mathewson slowly amble into the dugout, remove his cap, and place his glove next to him.

"Hardest game I've ever played," Matty said.

"Damnedest one I've ever seen," McGraw said.

They both nodded, knowing they were both right.

CHAPTER FIVE

Thursday, October 10, 1912: Game Three

Boston leads, 1 game to 0, with 1 tie

> BOSTON—For four seconds yesterday, more than 34,000
> persons held their breath. There were men at third and
> second, with two down, when Forrest Cady, a farmer's son
> with a strong heart and a mighty punch, came to the plate.
> Marquard was appealed to put everything he had on the ball,
> for it meant the game for Boston. The big left-hander took
> his time, measured the Boston man for a fast one, and cut
> loose . . .
>
> —T. H. MURNANE, *BOSTON GLOBE*, OCTOBER 11, 1912

THE REVIEWS, AS they came tumbling off the nation's presses,
were almost universally breathless. "A CLASSIC!" roared the
Los Angeles Times. "Greatest Ball Game in History!" screamed the
Washington Post. And in Boston and New York City, the citizens hungrily grabbed as many newspapers as they could find, perhaps weed-
ing through so many in order to find the one that would disprove
what the others were insisting, that after eleven innings and close to
250 pitches the Red Sox and Giants were *still* unable to reach a resolution regarding Game Two of the World Series. This wasn't
unprecedented; precisely five years and one day earlier, on October
8, 1907, the Cubs had rallied for two runs in the bottom of the ninth

to tie the Tigers in Game One of that World Series at Chicago's West Side Grounds, the tying run scoring when Detroit catcher Boss Schmidt dropped a third strike to Del Howard, allowing Harry Steinfeldt to race home with the squaring run. Three innings later darkness descended, forcing umpire Hank O'Day to rule the proceedings a draw; the Tigers never recovered, dropping the next four games in succession (and eight of the next nine Series games they'd play against the Cubs over the next two years, too).

Not everyone was so pleased with what had taken place this time at Fenway Park, however. There was McGraw, naturally, who'd watched four errors and some generally shabby play sabotage the work of Mathewson, who'd certainly thrown well enough to win even if he hadn't resembled his 1905 vintage. Never shy from airing out his personnel in the local dailies, the manager raged, "While I realize that eleven-inning game was a wonderfully spectacular one from a spectator's point of view, I could not conscientiously call it a well-played ballgame. As a real matter of fact my players have not yet shown the ball of which they are capable. They have slipped up on many chances that they ordinarily would have accepted without an effort."

Interestingly, the one player who escaped the umbrella of his rage was Art Fletcher, the grease-fingered shortstop who'd caused so much of Mathewson's angst and helped allow four of the five unearned runs slapped on Matty's line score. "Fletcher had a bad day. He is a high-strung player and after a hard season work he is a little fine right now. Nevertheless I look for him to do good work the remaining games. I never blame a man for making *physical* errors. I always expect those, they're part of the game. The things I do strongly object to in any players are slow thinking and errors of *judgment.*"

McGraw's professional demeanor wouldn't prevent his hotel room from coming under siege the next morning, when a congregation of "concerned" Giants fans visited him at the Copley Plaza, knocked on the door, welcomed themselves inside, and insisted that Fletcher be replaced by Tillie Shafer as the starting shortstop. It was an impromptu town-hall debate that lasted exactly ninety seconds, or about as long as it took McGraw to respond, "Unless I missed something, this is still my nine, and I shall manage it the way I see fit. And Art Fletcher is still the shortstop of this nine. Now get the hell out of this room and away from this goddamned hotel!" Giants fans were like Giants players: What McGraw told them to do, they did. And so they promptly skedaddled.

It was Doyle, the captain, who gave voice to what many Giants fans were really feeling: "When that game was over I felt like walking on the faces of a couple of Giants with my spiked shoes still on. They were all trying to do their best, but when you're on the field and see chances to win a game kicked away, it riles a guy of my temperament."

The tie didn't diminish the confidence of Bill Carrigan, the most outspoken Boston player, who said, "We still have the jump on 'em, it'll just take one day longer than we expected," although Larry Gardner, the Sox' bruised, bloodied, and beaten-up third baseman, rather presciently conceded, "Whoever loses this series is going to think back all winter to this one and realize what a terrible game this was not to win."

Still, for all the raw nerves and hard feelings that bled through the night, players on both sides awoke on Thursday morning, October 10, unified in one common position: They weren't about to allow the National Commission to screw them—at least not without a fight. The Commission had been founded in 1903, sort of a League of Nations invented to signal the end of hostilities between the American League and the National League (the Giants' defiant 1904 behavior notwithstanding). It was a three-man board, meaning there were six iron fists always ready to defend the interests of the baseball establishment, always eager to smash player complaints and dismiss them as the chortlings of so many spoiled, recalcitrant children. This autumn of 1912 the Commission was composed of Ban Johnson, president of the American League; T. J. Lynch, president of the National League; and August "Garry" Herrmann, president of the Cincinnati Reds, who served as the Commission's president and its nominal head. Herrmann was a lavish entertainer whose gifts as a gadfly far surpassed those at managing his own affairs; when he died in 1932, he left behind an estate totaling exactly ten dollars.

It was the Commission that had set up the grueling schedule for this series that required travel back and forth between the two cities, rather than the traditional two-three-two format (which would have meant two games in New York, three in Boston, and then the final two, if necessary, back in New York with a day off in between site changes). It was the Commission that had immediately declared that Game Two would be replayed in Boston, rather than the Polo Grounds. And it was the Commission, most egregiously as far as the players were concerned, who determined that, even though there was now certain to be at least one extra game played in this Series, the players would not fiscally benefit; they would still share receipts from the first four games of the series, which in this case would now include Games One, Two, and Three, plus the unresolved tie game.

"If we allowed the players to share in an extra game when there was a tie, what assurance would the public have that more ties would not be played?" was the frank (or cynical, depending on your viewpoint) assessment of John Heydler, the secretary-treasurer of the National League. "The object of a world's series is for one team to win as quickly as possible, and, in order to encourage the players to win as quickly as possible, it was thought best when the rules were framed to restrict their portions of the receipts to four games, regardless of whether any of those games are ties."

The implication—that players would turn crooked the moment you opened the door for them to go that way—may not have been unwise, given the preponderance of gamblers at the games, given the transparent relationships bridging many of the game's biggest stars and some of gambling's most notorious names. But it still rankled, and no one was more offended by the inference than Christy Mathewson, chosen by acclimation by players on both sides to fight what they all knew would be a fruitless fight against the Commission to get a portion of a fifth game's receipts placed in the players' pool. There *was* precedent on the players' side—back in '07, the players had been paid for all five games, including the tie—but there was no one named Precedent presently sitting on the National Commission. The men named Johnson, Lynch, and Herrmann who did sit there all held firm to the words written in Rule Ten of the World's Series Agreement, which had been revised *after* that Cubs–Tigers series:

> "The players pool shall be restricted to sixty percent of the receipts of the first four games after the deduction of the commission's ten percent, thereof, *regardless of whether one or more of such games shall result in a tie.*"

An open-and-shut case, the Commission believed.

"When the world's series was first started, the National Commission made a set of rules that gave the players a certain percentage of the receipts of the first four games, including tie playoffs, and there are many of us who think we are entitled to a share of all the games played," Mathewson explained the morning of the soon-to-be-replayed Game Two. "The Commission makes new rules without consulting us or letting us know about their intentions. The Commission's rulings are invariably against the players and we want to be represented whenever our interests—financial or otherwise—are being considered but the time will come when we shall demand to be represented."

It was here that the Christian Gentleman fired a rather ominous warning shot.

"I will not go so far as to say there will be no more world's series unless our rights are more carefully considered and we fail to get representation," he said, "but I will say that the National Commission is liable to find itself left flat without a club to play in some future world's series if they refuse to take up our grievances and give us fair treatment."

To emphasize the players' shared plight, even Smoky Joe Wood lent his voice to the cause after hearing of Mathewson's comments: "It is no more than what was due us that we should share in any play-off games due to a tie. We worked our heads off for eleven innings on Wednesday and all the benefit we derived from the game goes to the club owners and the National Commission. The Red Sox think that is unjust to us as well as the Giants."

The National Commission listened to Mathewson's concerns, weighed his objections, and took a good three minutes before issuing its verdict:

"Four games is the rule," Johnson said. "And four games it will be."

Inside the Giants' clubhouse at Fenway Park, as this was relayed to the disgruntled players, one especially angry veteran grumbled, "They're worried about *us* turning crooked, yet they're the most well-fed thieves in the country."

Soon enough, the Giants and Red Sox would have to turn their contempt back on each other. Soon enough. For now, they both seethed at a common enemy.

The Series had already generated an unprecedented amount of interest, and every day stories surfaced detailing just how impassioned the nation's baseball fans had become. In Oneonta, New York, security officers at a train station stumbled upon the sleepy bodies of Charlie Weighart, eleven, and John Hamilton, thirteen, both of them from Binghamton, both of whom were trying to smuggle themselves to New York "to see the Giants win," both of whom were soon shuttled back home in a truant officer's automobile. Those two adventurous lads simply reflected what had quickly become an obsession among men and women two, three, even five times their age. Ten full-time operators had been hired at the *Boston Globe* to handle the telephones for Game Two, and they were *still* overwhelmed by a flood of inquiries that averaged 150 calls a minute for most of the game, 300 a minute as the game reached extra innings, *12,000* calls in all.

A troublesome tale emerged in Brooklyn, where a pair of workers for A. Schrader's Son, a leading manufacturer of valves, gauges, and pneumatic tire accessories, began discussing the relative merits of the Giants and the Red Sox during a coffee break. George Brown, seventeen, grabbed a small piece of metal and declared that he was Smoky Joe Wood. Frank Groshaus, eighteen, picked up a two-and-a-half-foot file with a wooden handle and announced that he was Red Murray. Brown flung the metal. Groshaus swung with his file, which, fatefully, was not strongly fastened to the handle, flew out, and struck Brown, embedding in his left side. Another employee made the ill-fated decision to pull the file out, and by the time Brown was rushed to Volunteer Hospital there was nothing that could be done for him.

And politics was hardly spared World Series conversation. A day before the Series began, Red Murray had revealed that no fewer than eleven of the Giants had formed their own "Wilson Club," their small effort to boost the campaign of the governor of New Jersey and Democratic nominee for president.

"What I like," Murray said, "is that he plays the game within the foul lines. He has speed and control and he knows the inside game of today. The difference between Governor Wilson and the other candidates is that he uses his inside knowledge for those on the outside, and not simply for the gate receipts."

When that story and those painfully forced baseball metaphors appeared in just about all the New York newspapers, Lafayette B. Gleason, the chairman of New York's Republican State Committee and a staunch Taft man, announced that his response would be to instantly switch his allegiance to the Sox, turnabout being fair play, after all.

"You can't make me believe that any club made up of men who are going to vote the Democratic ticket can win a world's championship," Gleason reasoned. "You might look for Jeff Tesreau to be Democratic because he comes from the Ozark Mountains, where there is more or less a lawless element, but you don't expect to find such men as Marquard, Fletcher, Doyle, and the rest in that party. I like Mathewson because he has not joined the Wilson club but as for Marquard, I said today when he pitched that I hoped his left hand would cleave to the roof of his mouth."

Wilson himself was blithely unaware of the support he'd generated among New York's National League club, as he was busily whipping a Chicago crowd of 100,000 into an anti-Roosevelt frenzy. Theodore Roosevelt, a renowned sportsman if not much of a baseball fan, was himself assailing Wilson before a huge crowd of 70,000 in Duluth, Minnesota. Which left Taft, the "forgotten candidate," and the only one of the three who truly cared about baseball (and who also happened to be the sitting president), to rely on the sailors of the ships filling the Hudson River, who would again be getting updates and relaying them to their commander in chief as quickly as they could.

John Fitzgerald was one politician who needn't worry about how he received his baseball news, because he was going to get it almost as soon as it happened—even though on this day, he'd have to receive it secondhand, through couriers and messengers, since he hadn't expected there to be a game at Fenway and had scheduled a full day of city business to make up for his two-day baseball sabbatical that ended with Wednesday's tie. But while the mayor had made good on his promise to make three hundred tickets available to Giants fans for Game Two (and went the extra yard to guarantee them all seats at the make-up game), he was unable to guarantee them an extra night's lodging in his overrun city, and a lot of those fans who figured they might as well stick around to see a game to conclusion wound up either wandering the streets in search of a bed-and-breakfast, sleeping in Boston Common, finding sympathetic Red Sox fans who agreed to house them for the evening, or simply congregating, as most did, in all-night eateries, guzzling coffee and amusing themselves with song lyrics that may not have been as familiar as the Rooters' standards, but kept them just as awake:

Fifteen men to a looking glass
Never such murderous scenes
We gash and slash our faces to hash
En route to the city of beans

Rarely has a group of strangers been so eager to see a baseball game begin.

Josh Devore would never have registered his complaint with John McGraw directly, of course, or with the papers, because to do that would have been to sign his own exit visa to Pittsburgh or Philadelphia or Cincinnati or some other god-awful baseball outpost. No twenty-four-year-old player, no matter how gifted, would ever be long for New York or for the Giants if he took on baseball's most powerful manager in public. And while Devore was a key part of the Giants' attack—he'd stolen sixty-one bases in 1911, and already had 135 steals in only three full years of service, including four in one inning on June 20, 1912—it wasn't as if he was Christy Mathewson. He was certainly not irreplaceable.

As a youngster in Terre Haute, he'd been a precocious athlete, could run faster and hit baseballs farther than just about anyone else in western Indiana. When his older brother, Bill, read about an opening for an outfielder on the Meridian, Mississippi, club he decided to "place" Josh, who was working in the family general store in Selleyville, Indiana. The manager, Guy Sample, wasn't particularly interested until Bill agreed to deposit expense money in manager Sample's bank account—the cool hundred dollars that ensured he would be placed. But Sample soon discovered he'd received a damn fine ballplayer, and so it was in Meridian where McGraw's bird-dog scouts would find Devore, and by 1910 he'd made it to New York.

But McGraw had benched Devore in Game Two, and Josh had watched every pitch of that 6–6 tie without ever leaving his spot on the bench. The next morning, as he and his roommate, Rube Marquard, arose at the Copley Plaza, Devore wasted little time bending his close friend's ear.

"Look, Roomie, I know I'm not a Ty Cobb against most left-handers, but I do believe I could get a million hits off Collins if McGraw would give me a chance against him," Devore groused.

"Southpaws who are also side-wheelers shouldn't be allowed in the league. But this Collins bird pitches overhand and no pitcher, right or left, can do that to me and get away with it. They're the kind I dote on."

"It was one game," Marquard said. "I'm sure the old man will have you back out there today. He knows I like pitching better when I got you covering your patch of the outfield."

Marquard himself, full of piss and vinegar even on his quietest days, had spent most of the World Series engaged in nonstop chatter with his teammates, his opponents, the press, his manager, the fans. The former peach-turned-lemon-turned-peach had actually spent most of late summer reverting back to sour citrus, turning in two disappointing outings for every solid one. His final numbers for 1912—26–11, 2.57 ERA—looked perfectly gaudy until you considered that nineteen-game winning streak that started the year meant he was only 7–11 from July forward. Still, this was a man who'd begun his professional career bumming his way on a train from Cleveland to Waterloo, Iowa, for a one-shot deal, arrived in time to beat a team from Keokuk, 6–1, then hopped back on the train when the manager reneged on the $5 he'd been promised. He'd seen some things in his day. The World Series didn't exactly have him biting his fingers to the quick, as it did poor Art Fletcher.

"Let me say that I am in better condition right now than ever," Marquard announced to whoever was listening after Wednesday's game, when McGraw officially announced him as the make-up game starter.

"Better than April and May?" one skeptical scribe asked.

"Yes," Marquard said, "even better than the spring, when I won those nineteen straight. The nervous strain in that fight for a world's record told on me for weeks. In fact I never did feel right after that until about ten days ago. Then I worked five innings against the Dodgers over in Brooklyn and never had more stuff on the ball in my life. My fastball had tons of smoke on it and it sailed up to batters as it never did before. It had a hop on it that jumped easily a foot. No team in the world can hit that fast one when I'm on edge. I am better today than ever in my life and I will be shoving them over at these alleged swatters of Boston so fast that they won't be able to see the ball. I had a fine workout during the last two innings today and [coach] Wilbert Robinson, who caught a few of my fastballs, said I never had so much stuff in all my life. 'Hey,' he said, 'don't waste those," I told him, 'Don't worry, Robby, I'll save plenty for the Sox.' "

But the Sox themselves were simply hoping to have enough healthy bodies to take aim at the Giants in what would essentially amount to an official do-over. Jake Stahl understood as much as anyone how fortunate they'd been to escape with even a tie the day before. "You give Matty six runs, sometimes that's enough for him to win six games," the manager said as he pulled on his stirrups and entertained a small group of writers before the game. "And here's the thing: if he'd only had to get us three outs an inning, he'd have had his way with us. But some of those innings the Giants were giving us four and five outs with all the errors and misplays, and my boys, they know what to do with the breaks when we get 'em. Sure, it's tough not to win a game like that. But it sure as hell beats losing the game, right?"

Tim Murnane of the *Globe* asked his friend the question that was on everyone's mind in the press box, in the bursting grandstand outside, and everywhere else where people were deep in debate about this Series: "What about Spoke, Jake?"

"Spoke" was Speaker's nickname. And Spoke, as the writers could plainly see, was hurting in a terrible way, his ankle swollen and purple, his limp painful to watch, the wince on his face palpable as he tried forcing on his stiff black baseball spike.

"I'd need to physically keep him on the bench to keep him out of the game," Stahl said. "Maybe there was a time I could even do it. Not now. He's playing."

Maybe a hundred yards down the hallway, John McGraw echoed Stahl's sentiments. "This is the world's series, boys," he said. "I haven't seen Speaker play much, but what I see he could easily have fit in with my Orioles, where unless you had something *really* wrong with you, you got your ass on the field every day and played like someone was stealing your wallet."

It was Fred Lieb of the *New York Press* who broached the question McGraw knew was coming.

"Mac," he said, "what about . . ."

"Fletcher?" McGraw snapped, cutting off the query. "No one can induce me to make any change in which Fletcher would be taken out of the team. He is one of the greatest young players on the field. I know it, and I'm not going to let my judgment be influenced for a moment anymore than I was changed in my sentiments of Red Murray because he failed to do much in the world's series last year."

Then he gave the writers his very best angry glare.

"Now, if that doesn't sound good to some of the newspaper-critic managers that's too bad, because Fletcher will play the series through. And that's a damned guarantee. Sometimes this is the best job in the world. And sometimes I have to deal with *you*."

There was one other sensitive topic in the baseball news that day as it pertained to the Giants, for the owners of the Highlanders had that morning officially sought permission from McGraw and from John T. Brush to sign a lease and share the Polo Grounds starting in 1913. The team's rent agreement at Hilltop Park had expired and the property had already been sold and dedicated to a new hospital (now known as New York–Presbyterian), and the team was having a difficult time finding a plot on which to build a new park, after a proposed site at Marble Hill, 225th Street and Broadway, fell through. The animosity between the Highlanders and Giants ran deep, and for several reasons. First, of course, was geography, although the Giants were the undisputed kings of New York City, outdrawing the Highlanders by nearly 3-to-1 (and out-victory-ing them by 2-to-1). McGraw had jumped from the Orioles to the Giants back in '02, and then the Orioles had jumped right back at him, landing in New York City as a transferred franchise a year later, taking the name "Highlanders." And while it had been the Red Sox who suffered the brunt of the boycott of the 1904 Series, the true cause was a simple one: Neither McGraw nor Brush wanted any part of playing the Highlanders in any World Series, and right to the final weekend it looked like New York might have an American League champion to go along with the Giants in the National League.

"Will sharing the Polo Grounds be awkward?" Grantland Rice of the *Mail* wanted to know.

"Those animosities are long gone," McGraw insisted, his generosity no doubt fortified by the 50–102 record the Highlanders posted in 1912. "Besides, when our park burned last year, they showed great hospitality to us. They took us in, and treated us neighborly, and we plan on treating them the same exact way. Though they'll likely need a new name now that they won't be playing in the highlands of Manhattan any longer."

"Our headline writers already call them by a different name," said Damon Runyon of the *American*. "They call them the Yankees."

"Yankees, eh?" McGraw said. "Hmmm. I wonder if that name will catch on?"

There was, naturally, more pomp and more ceremony scheduled for this bonus day of Boston baseball, and given the way things had ended the day before, they combined to brew a serious cocktail of anxiety for Billy Evans, the twenty-eight-year-old umpire who would call balls and strikes this day and whose mission, above all else, was to ensure that this game be played to a conclusion. Jake Stahl had gotten his car the day before from grateful Boston boosters and now it was Tris Speaker's turn, the Boston center fielder receiving his ride in recognition of winning the American League's Most Valuable Player Award. With the largest baseball crowd in the history of Boston—34,624—already restlessly wriggling in their seats, Speaker decided the time was right for a crowd-pleasing stunt, and so he approached Larry Doyle, the Giants' captain, who'd been given the exact same car for the exact same reason two days earlier.

"How fast do these things go?" Speaker asked Doyle.

"About as fast as you want 'em to go," Doyle replied.

"Care to join me for a spin?"

Doyle, admittedly a little shaken by this overt display of fraternization in an era when even looking an opponent in the eye was considered a sign of weakness, shook his shoulders, hopped in the passenger's seat, and then held on to his lunch with both hands as Speaker floored the gas pedal and jolted the matching MVPs off onto a brief, speedy joyride that mostly utilized only two of the Chalmers-Detroit Touring Car's four wheels, the tires squealing every bit as loudly as the delighted fans, John McGraw looking on in horror as his captain and second baseman's face turned six shades of green. As a chuckle, the Royal Rooters' band launched into a rendition of "When I Get You Alone Tonight." And when Speaker finally slammed on the brakes, leaving a swath of torn-up sod and an infield dust storm behind him, the crowd roared one last time. Doyle, the color finally returning to his face, shook Speaker's hand and tried to make the most of it.

"He thinks he's a regular Harry Grant," Doyle said, referring to the Boston-area driver who'd competed in both the 1911 and 1912 Indianapolis 500.

Billy Evans wasn't laughing. They were already an hour late getting started, and the sunlight wouldn't last forever. With as much urgency as he would ever use in his career, he pleaded, "Play ball!"

He didn't have to ask Josh Devore twice. Devore's roommate, Marquard, had been right: McGraw *had* penciled his name back onto the lineup card, and he promptly seized the moment, punching a ground ball through the hole between shortstop and third base. Doyle, no doubt still jumpy from his impromptu ride in the park with Speaker, skied lazily to center field for the first out, and Devore, feeling his oats, decided to try to steal second on the first pitch to Fred Snodgrass, hitting third. But Bill Carrigan gunned him out, the ball beating Devore's spikes to the bag by a couple of feet, and as Devore dusted himself off he made a beeline for the opposite side of the dugout from where he knew McGraw was standing. He didn't want a lecture. Got one anyway.

"That's what I want to see, Josh." Devore looked up: McGraw. He bowed his head. "Get your head up!" the manager ordered.

"That was the right thing to do, and you just got caught, that's all. How many times I got to tell you guys: physical mistakes happen. It's when you play with your *head* in your *ass* that I'll jump you."

McGraw turned to the player to Devore's right.

"Ain't that right?"

"Yep," said Art Fletcher, nervously pounding left fist into right hand.

Years later, Devore would marvel about McGraw's ability to be equal parts intimidator and motivator. "He was this gruff, angry guy sometimes, but the reputation was worse than the reality," he said. "How do you think he got so many different kinds of players to play so well for him through the years? Sometimes his strategy would make you scratch your head, and he could yell paint off the walls. But he knew how to handle people. He was a master at that."

His best friend already knew that. When Evans had officially announced the Giants' battery into a megaphone—"Marquard and Meyers for the Giants!"—Marquard had started muttering to himself, specifically about his prized possession. His right arm gave his left arm a reassuring squeeze and he said, "Old lefty, my side partner, do our duty for dear old New York's sake." McGraw saw all this and couldn't keep himself from laughing. He walked over to his pitcher, the erstwhile lemon, patted him gently on the left shoulder. "There's lots of these sons-a-bitches think you're gonna get your head knocked off today, kid," McGraw said. "I ain't one of 'em. Go to it, Rube."

It was all Marquard needed to hear. In later years, Marquard would admittedly become something of a handful. He would try to jump to the Federal League in 1914, a naked act of betrayal that would break McGraw's heart. He would engineer his own trade from New York to Brooklyn in 1915, encouraged to do so by his manager. He married a showgirl, loved the nightlife, divorced the showgirl, later found a second career working a pari-mutuel window at racetracks in both New York and Baltimore, and conceded that his left arm contained far more talent than his 201–177 lifetime record reflected. But for now, at age twenty-five, all he needed was four words from McGraw—*Go to it, Rube*—to make him believe he could throw a baseball two hundred miles an hour if he needed to.

He wouldn't pitch quite that fast this day. But he was awfully damned good. He breezed through the first inning one-two-three, freezing Steve Yerkes on a curveball the Sox second baseman later insisted "broke all the way from Brockton before cutting the plate in two." Through the first six innings, he surrendered only four singles, and only once did a Red Sox runner reach as far as second base, Larry Gardner sacrificing Duffy Lewis in the second, which is where he died when the inning did. The Red Sox tried to throw a little 2008-style baseball at Marquard, taking pitch after pitch, trying to build Marquard's pitch count and wear down his fickle left arm, but Marquard foiled that strategy by throwing strike after strike. Red Murray lent a helping hand in the fifth, making a spectacular, somersaulting grab of a sinking Heinie Wagner drive to left that would have been two bases if it fell, and perhaps four if it slithered past him. Otherwise, Marquard was every bit the pitcher who had shackled the National League for the first three months of the season or, as no less an authority than Walter Johnson would write for the next morning's newspapers, "Every bit the pitcher of his idol, Matty."

Even the hard-to-please, seen-it-all-and-seen-it-twice McGraw, who'd ignored so many calls to exile Marquard to the bullpen, couldn't camouflage his delight. After Marquard briefly flirted with trouble in the seventh, issuing a two-out double to Stahl, he'd immediately coaxed Wagner into an easy fly ball to right and walked off the mound with the most confident gait a pitcher could own. Seeing that, McGraw ambled by his longest-serving foot soldier with wonder in his eyes. "Matty, look at him," McGraw said. "He's *really* got something today. Look at his eyes. He won't let us lose today."

By then, the Giants had even gotten him a couple of runs to work with, grinding to a 2–0 lead over Buck O'Brien, who really *could* break curveballs off from Brockton because that's where he was born. O'Brien had waited a long time to make it to the major leagues, scuffling through various local leagues before finally signing with the Red Sox in 1911, who promptly "loaned" him to the Denver Grizzlies, where he blossomed into a star, winning twenty-six out of thirty-three decisions. Back in Boston the next year as a thirty-year-old rookie, he made the most of the opportunity, going 20–13 with a 2.58 ERA, earning the distinction of starting the very first game in Fenway Park history (though he didn't figure in the decision) and enjoying every fringe benefit, on and off the field, to which big leaguers were even then entitled.

New York opened the scoring in the second inning by scratching a run straight out of the McGraw textbook: leadoff double by the red-hot Red Murray, sacrificed to third by Fred Merkle (since under McGraw, even the heart of the batting order was expected to give itself up when necessary), and driven home on a sacrifice fly to left field by Buck Herzog (much to the consternation of Heinie Wagner, who was certain that Murray left the bag early, an argument in which Bill Klem, umpiring the bases, didn't wish to engage). But the more satisfying inning for McGraw came later, in the top of the fifth. Herzog led off with a double and moved to third on a swinging bunt by Chief Meyers.

That brought Art Fletcher to the plate.

The very first Red Sox hitter that day, Harry Hooper, had inevitably lofted a towering pop fly over the infield, and as Fletcher settled under it each of the 34,624 people crammed inside Fenway Park—minus the three hundred or so Giants fans who were too petrified to even look, let alone utter a sound—had hollered at Fletcher, trying to unnerve him, hoping for an encore of the day before. But Fletcher had squeezed that pop-up easily, and repeated the task on a Yerkes pop-up in the fourth, meaning he'd handled flawlessly the only two balls hit his way so far. Still, as early in the game as it was, that runner on third base could prove to be a critical run. And now, as if sent by silent courier, the same message seemed to be transmitted, kinetically, to and from all Giants fans.

One leather-lunged acolyte at Fenway Park stood up and yelled, "McGraw! Send up McCormick, McGraw!" Back in Times Square, where another enormous crowd had congregated, the announcer actually took the bold step of saying, "Fletcher, hitting for himself," which invited a loud chorus of boos. In Herald Square, after a similar reaction, an old ballplayer named Seth Sigsby, who'd pitched briefly for the Giants in 1893, said he sympathized with Fletcher's plight in a way few members of the angry mob around him could. "There is a psychological connection between the spirits of the team and the humor of the crowd," Sigsby explained. "It takes one day before any of us gets down to cases. That's the reason I never stuck in the big leagues. I blew up my first trial and they wouldn't give me a second. Good thing Fletcher's boss is more understanding than that."

Fletcher's boss never even made a move for a pinch hitter, simply clapped his hands in the third-base coaching box and yelled, "One time, Fletch! One time!" And Fletcher delivered, a hot shot up the middle that made the score 2–0 Giants, sent Fenway into a fitful silence, and turned tens of thousands of fickle Giants fans into longtime Art Fletcher fans. McGraw clapped his hands some more.

Sometimes, this really *was* the best job in the world.

Back in Herald Square, Giants fans nervously communed, waiting for the bottom of the ninth, alternately wanting to leap for joy at the imminent prospect of a tied World Series and cower with fear at how the Red Sox might conspire to break their hearts again. A photographer from the *Herald* tried to snap pictures of these fans, wanted to get reaction to what they were all seeing on the Playograph, yet invariably they all tried to hide their faces, either under a hat or beneath the sleeves of their overcoats.

"That's the influence of the Becker trial," one of the hidden, huddled masses explained. "You don't want anyone to know where you are or what you look like. Either you're afraid your boss will see you out here when you should be working, or you're afraid your wife will see you in the picture standing by that lady."

"My wife," another man said, "is worse than any hanging judge. If she knew I was here there'd be hell to pay."

The Becker trial, as the afternoon papers had already begun to inform the crowds in Herald Square, in Times Square, and on Newspaper Row, had finally seated a full jury and finally had its first explosive moment, as a waiter named Louis Krause, who'd witnessed the murder with his own eyes, officially named three of the men he saw that night: Jacob Seidenshner (also known as "Whitey Lewis"), Harry Horowitz (aka "Gyp the Blood"), and Louis Rosenberg (aka "Lefty Louie), though he couldn't quite say for sure if a fourth gentleman, Frank Cirofici (aka "Dago Frank"), was there.

"It's like this ballgame," a fan named Joseph Murphy (aka "Joseph Murphy"), craning his neck on Park Row, said. "You can't tell the players without a scorecard."

Back in Fenway Park, where a funereal silence had lingered for much of the afternoon, a flicker of hope had sparked in the souls of the faithful in the top of the ninth inning when Speaker, playing on only one good foot, made an almost impossible grab of an Art Fletcher line drive, a play that was especially important because Chief Meyers, on first, had already rumbled around second and was certain to score a third Giants run when the ball stuck in the thin webbing of Speaker's glove. Speaker, who almost seemed as surprised as Meyers, flipped the ball into his bare hand, pegged it back to first base to complete the double play, and dragged himself back to the dugout showered in cheers that followed him all the way to the batter's box, where he led off the bottom of the ninth.

"Three more outs," Marquard muttered, to himself and to his left arm. "You can do this. Three more outs."

Speaker, swinging from his heels, barely missed a Marquard fastball, popping it straight in the air—another baseball seeking the magnet of Art Fletcher's glove. Fletcher had added a couple of routine grounders to his earlier pop-ups, already had that clutch RBI single in his hip pocket, and was a different player altogether from the one who had taken the field two hours earlier. Even as the barkers at the various scoreboards set up throughout Boston and New York tried to maximize the drama, haltingly announcing "*A high . . . pop . . . fly . . . toward shortstop . . .* ," which terrorized those who hadn't actually *seen* Fletcher that day, at Fenway it wasn't nearly that theatrical. Fletcher squeezed his hands a few times when the ball was in the air and then gathered in the pop. One out.

"Two more," Marquard alerted his wing. "Two more."

Marquard, still pumping gas, zipped a fastball to Duffy Lewis that was nearly past the Boston left fielder when it ran into the barrel of his bat, producing a slashing grounder that Merkle, at first base, knocked down beautifully with his chest. He recovered the ball, flipped to Marquard for the second out . . . only, as Marquard felt for the base with his foot, he came up with only dirt. He missed the bag. Lewis was safe. And Fenway Park was suddenly aroused.

"Stupid," Marquard mumbled. "What a terrible break."

McGraw, standing next to Mathewson in the Giants' dugout, didn't like the look on Marquard's face all of a sudden.

"I think he's about to lose his cool," the manager said.

"Leave him be," Matty counseled. "He'll be fine."

That was to be a hard-earned confidence, because left-handed Larry Gardner jumped all over Marquard's next fastball, shooting it just inside the first-base line, just out of Merkle's reach, and now a rising tide of giddiness began to consume the ballpark. Josh Devore, dashing over to retrieve the ball in the right-field corner, reached down, fumbled it once, fumbled it twice, allowing precious seconds to get away from him.

But it was here the Giants caught the break of the Series so far, even if they wouldn't recognize it for a while. Unlike McGraw, who always manned the coaching lines at third, Stahl couldn't always direct traffic from there since he was still an active player. So the Sox employed a rotating cast of players to serve in that role, and as Devore was engaged in his juggling act in right field, it was Heinie Wagner who was on duty coaching third. And whether he didn't get a good look at Devore's follies, or was simply inclined to play it conservatively, he shot both hands in the air, halting Lewis at third and Gardner at second, even though there was no reason in the world to do that. From the dugout, Speaker could see as much, and so out he came, hobbling as fast as he could, yelling in full voice, "Heinie?

Have you lost your god-damned mind?" and waving both his arms, getting the attention of the completely confused Lewis, who hurried home with the Sox' first run of the game. But Gardner, who should have been able to crawl to third, was instead standing on second. It was a critical blunder by Wagner, compounded a few moments later when Stahl sent a smoking line drive back through the middle that Marquard somehow got a glove on. Gardner, wandering too far off second, was in immediate trouble, and though he slid hard into third, his spikes and the dirt flying practically in Herzog's eyes, the Giants' third baseman made the tag—or at least Bill Klem said he did. When Herzog rose out of the dust, he didn't have the ball in his hands, and Gardner tried to convey that to him in the simplest, gentlest way possible.

"He dropped the goddamned ball, Bill!"

"Not as I saw it," Klem replied, and that was that. Two outs.

Marquard, looking like a punch-drunk heavyweight in the fifteenth round, exhorted his left arm one last time. "You got one more out in you, old boy?"

It looked that way. Wagner, who already knew he may have cost the Red Sox the game by mismanaging Gardner, stepped to the plate, and he was probably gripping the bat too hard, swinging too crazily, and he bounced a harmless ground ball straight at Fletcher. Even the Royal Rooters had abandoned jeering Fletcher, whose recovery seemed complete, and the Giants' shortstop easily gathered the ball in his glove, took a crow hop, and fired the ball to first base to end the game.

There was only one problem.

Merkle, one of the best defensive first basemen alive, dropped the ball.

In Fenway Park, there was a moment of disbelieving silence followed by an explosion of unyielding hilarity. All across New York City, six seconds after it happened, announcers on stages in Times Square and Herald Square and Madison Square Garden and Park Row each saw what they needed to say and prepared themselves for the inevitable reaction.

"Error, Merkle!" they each proclaimed.

Merkle? Merkle! The same fellow who'd forgotten to touch second base in a key game against the Cubs back in '08, earning him forever the sobriquet of "Bonehead," easily the least-flattering nickname in baseball history? The self-absorbed player who'd held out on the Giants earlier in the season? *Merkle* had done it to us again? *Merkle* had done it to us again!

Merkle!

In the visiting dugout at Fenway, ironically, McGraw wasn't nearly as unhappy with Merkle as everyone else. *Now* was the time to get mad at Fletcher, who could have flipped the ball to Doyle for a game-ending force but who, for all his frayed nerves, loved showing off his strong arm whenever possible. Doyle had been standing on the base, waiting for the relay that never came. McGraw saw that. *Mental errors.* "Jesus, Fletcher," McGraw muttered. *"That's how you pay me back?"*

Olaf Henriksen, a reserve outfielder who'd pinch-run for Stahl, raced all the way to third on the error. And on Marquard's first pitch to Hick Cady, who'd entered the game as a defensive replacement, Wagner stole second without a throw. So, after a day in which he'd completely dominated the Red Sox, had regained his old swagger, and looked for a time like the best pitcher on the planet, Marquard was now one base hit away from allowing the Speed Boys the all-time miracle comeback in World Series history. His face was as pale as the Red Sox' home white uniforms, and in the dugout McGraw looked no healthier, as the wheels had come off so quickly he hadn't had time to warm anyone in the bullpen. And these weren't even the most pallid people in the park; *that* honor belonged to Billy Evans, who saw dusk descending in a hurry, who already had a hard time distinguishing figures in the outfield, who knew things had to be settled now because there wasn't nearly enough sunlight available for a tenth inning.

"Batter up!" he barked.

But Cady was locked in, and he was ready, and when he saw the fastball leave Marquard's left hand, the 127th ball Rube threw that day, he had no trouble with the encroaching darkness and he picked the ball up right away, high and inviting and out over the plate. He swung, and the ball connected with a sweet crackle that instantly brought both teams out of their dugouts for a look, and only one of those teams seemed to like what they saw.

"That's in the gap for sure!" Speaker yelped, hopping on his good foot.

"Get to the ground fast, ball!" Stahl squealed.

"Shit," McGraw mumbled.

Wilbert Robinson, McGraw's right-hand man, didn't even bother cussing, he simply found the nearest pieces of equipment on the bench and started flinging them around. What a way to lose a game. What a goddamned, crazy, miserable way . . .

But then Robinson stopped: No one else was moving, no one else was stirring. They were all squinting through the gloaming, out toward the right-center-field gap, out to where Josh Devore was blazing a path with his spikes. From the moment the ball was hit, as his heart was sinking, Marquard had seen that, if nothing else, his roommate had gotten a great jump on the ball.

But was it enough?

Most of Fenway Park thought so. The crack of the bat was all many of them needed to see, since they knew they wouldn't be able to see the play clearly when it ended anyway. And so thousands of fans, remarkable as it seems, left the ballpark firmly convinced that the Red Sox had just won a heart-stopping game, 3–2. Those who stayed could see only a speck of a man, Devore, loping after a speck of white.

And really, only Devore saw—or, more precisely, felt—the end result. Because the real miracle here wasn't that he somehow outraced the baseball. The wonder was that the ball missed the glove on his right hand and landed in the *bare palm of his left*. It was an astonishing play. It was an *impossible* play. And Devore, after securing the ball, took off on the dead run straight to the Giants' dugout, straight to the clubhouse, slowing down only to show a gauntlet of umpires—O'Loughlin first, then Rigler, then Klem, lastly a relieved-to-the-point-of-exhaustion Evans—his prize.

"Holy moly!" Marquard shouted. "He got it!"

"I took it over my left shoulder and with my bare hand although I clapped my glove down on it right away and hung on like a bulldog in a tramp," Evans would soon tell the mountain of reporters surrounding him in the deafening furnace of the Giants' clubhouse. "The sight of me with that ball was about as welcome to those people in the bleachers as the appearance of a bill collector Christmas week, I guess."

Marquard came over and hugged him so tight Devore thought his skin was about to burst. "I had to save my big brother," he explained. "I have to take care of him."

Later, in the taxi on the way back to the train station, Devore would confess, "I never came so close to missing anything in my life. And if I had, I couldn't have faced any of these guys. Especially Mr. McGraw."

Instead, he set two towns off into delayed frenzies, one of joy, one of bitterness. In New York, all the fans knew was what the announcer told them: "Cady flies out to Devore in right field. Three outs. Ballgame over. Giants 2, Red Sox 1." They would have to wait until morning to get a fuller account of what they'd just "seen."

In Boston, that reckoning occurred sooner, and with a great deal more shock accompanying it. After the game, Fred Lieb of the *New York Press* had hustled back to his room at the Copley Plaza Hotel to file his story and pack his bags in order to make the overnight writers' train back to New York. Walking into a men's room on the hotel's main lobby, he encountered a Boston fan who yelled, "Boston wins! What a great game for the Sox to pull out! What a ninth inning!"

Lieb was surprised, of course, having just seen the game end with his own eyes.

"But my friend, the Red Sox lost. The Giants won, 2–1."

The man's eyes flashed angrily. "What do you mean, the Red Sox lost? I just came from the game! I was there! The Red Sox beat Marquard in the ninth, 3–2! It was magnificent!"

"Well, I was there too, and I'm telling you you're wrong. I saw it all from the press box. The Giants won, 2–1."

By now, Lieb's new adversary was more than a little angry and more than a little fueled by local spirits. He shot a wad of tobacco into a spittoon and moved closer.

"What are you doing, trying to make a damned fool out of me? I should take a punch at your nose."

Lieb tried to cool things. "Well, before we start punching noses, let's just see what happened. The sports extras of the evening papers should be out by now and we can see just who did win the game."

The men repaired to the main lobby and saw a big-shouldered bruiser carrying a heaping armful of evening newspapers, among them the *Boston American*. And there was the banner headline on the front page:

GIANTS WIN THIRD GAME, TIE SERIES

"Well, I'll be damned," the man said. "What the hell happened?"

"Well, what happened is that Devore caught that last line drive. You didn't see the catch in the light fog and gathering darkness, so you thought Boston won. And you left the park in a hurry without checking. And then you ordered your first brandy."

"I'll be damned," the man repeated, walking away, looking as if he'd seen a ghost, shaking his head the whole way. There were a lot of people who would end this day in precisely the same way.

Chapter Six

Friday, October 11, 1912: Game Four

Series even, 1 win apiece, with 1 tie

New York—Swift spurts of "smoke," low-traveling under a
damp, gray sky, streaked once more under the shadow of
Coogan's Bluff this afternoon. Behind them, turning the Red
Sox Gatling, marksman Joe Wood again pumped a lethal
volley into McGraw's brigade . . .

—R. E. McMillin, *Boston Herald*, October 12, 1912

THE RED Sox, they were in a foul mood.
      Larry Doyle could sense as much on the 6:30 P.M. train that
pulled out of Back Bay Station, the players on both sides plainly
weary from the Series, and wary of each other. On the trip from
New York to Boston two days earlier, various Giants had bumped
into various Red Sox during the journey, a perfectly natural expecta-
tion given the close and crowded quarters, and while it would never
dawn on any of them to share a meal, or even a pleasant conversation, with members of the other team, there had been a flurry of
nodded heads and shaken hands and tipped hats. They were still all
gentlemen, after all, dressed to the nines as they were.

      But that had all been *before*.

      Before the tie game, which still bothered both teams. Before the
National Commission's ruling, the one spasm of unity between the

clubs, which only peeled farther back the already-exposed nerves on both sides. Before Buck Herzog's bump of Tris Speaker at the end of the tie game, an act of gamesmanship for which Speaker swore revenge if it took him the rest of his career. Before Larry Gardner's spikes-high slide into Herzog in the ninth inning of Game Three, which jostled the ball free even if Bill Klem had refused to call it that way for the record. Before Fred Merkle—adding to his terribly busy ninth inning—may or may not have bumped Gardner, Herzog-style, earlier in the inning as he legged out a double, a charge the Boston players insisted was true even as the Giants dismissed it. Before Herzog—a man who didn't mind getting his uniform dirty—had driven his spikes into Sam Yerkes's shins while being thrown out trying to steal in the top of the ninth, a play both teams nearly forgot in the ensuing hubbub until Yerkes peeled off his game pants and saw the bloody tracks left behind.

"The Red Sox acted sulkily on the train," Doyle recalled of the *Gilt Edge Express*, describing the building tension as the cars crawled west. "They don't seem to be in the right frame of mind. There was none of the raillery that there was before the opening games. It's definitely more of a war now. The players on opposing clubs only growl at each other now unless they're trying to get a man's goat, and there's practically no sociability."

Doyle smiled.

"And I think I speak for the rest of the Giants when I say, I would rather have it that way than any other," he said. "You know you're in for a fight then."

Doyle wasn't alone in noticing the feistiness that had already crept into this burgeoning rivalry after only three games. Hugh Fullerton of the *Chicago Tribune*, the most renowned and respected baseball writer in the country, could see it from clear up in the press box, and it delighted him, because he was always suspicious when professional ballplayers respected each other *too* much, worried that there wasn't enough blood and guts on display as there was in years past, that players didn't seem to care as they once did. Not now. Not this year.

"The desperate blocking on the bases, the stopping of runners, is likely to lead to trouble before the series is over," Fullerton wrote for the Friday *Tribune*, and for the hundreds of papers in his syndicate, and you could almost see him rubbing his hands together excitedly as he typed the words. "The Giants are working in the road of base runners on all hits, and the second basemen and shortstops of both teams just dive at every runner. A man cannot reach a bag without having to bunt or chop his way there. They are beginning to show the scars badly. Speaker is limping and very slow; Wagner's legs and hands have been chopped, and Yerkes has taken more cuts than a boxer."

Fullerton wasn't alone in recognizing the rancor that had developed. Heinie Wagner had helped ratchet that after Game Two, insisting bluntly, "Everyone talked about the managers' battle in the days leading up to the series; well, I think it's clear that in both games, Stahl had outgeneraled McGraw masterfully." Asked if he still felt that way after Game Three, Wagner sneered, "Even more so. The Giants are fast and scrappy. But we will win. The harder the fight the faster we go, all season we stiffened when put to the test and now that we recognize the fighting qualities of the Giants we will show our true mettle."

"They're just not as good as half the teams we play in the American League," Gardner said. "That's not bragging and that's not putting them down, it's just the way things are. Anyone looking objectively can see that."

Added Smoky Joe Wood: "They've gotten every break known to man so far, and the Series is still only 1–1. They can't feel good about that."

But the Giants *were* feeling good about themselves, *were* full of piss and vinegar themselves, starting with their manager, the home office for both piss *and* vinegar: "I cannot see why we should not now proceed to clean up," McGraw said. "The Red Sox are not the aggregation that we were led to expect and if we play our game we will surely be able to lay undisputed claim to the championship within the next few days."

Said Merkle: "I for one would rather tackle the Red Sox than the Cubs or Pirates."

But it was Buck Herzog, the agent provocateur on the field, who was equally enjoying himself in trying to goad the Speed Boys once the fellows with the notebooks started asking him for quotes.

"We have them completely on the run that I would not be a bit surprised if we win the series in straight games from here," he said, before throwing a shout-out to the shadows in the grandstands: "In my opinion," he surmised, "we are now a 4-to-5 choice for the series."

Wagner, the chatty Sox shortstop, was his favored target, especially after his bungled assignment in the coaching box.

"Wagner could have won for his club in the ninth inning if he would have coached Lewis and Gardner as one of our own men would have," Herzog said. "It did not require daring base running, just ordinary and intelligent base running and Wagner, brainy as he is on the defensive, was not equal to the occasion. Boston doesn't run the bases anything like as well as we do when we are getting an even break on luck. Wagner's poor coaching proves that, I think."

That was Herzog, underlined, bold-faced, captured in a thumbnail. Born in Baltimore, a city that always knew a thing or two about playing hard baseball and holding hard grudges, he'd already been traded once by McGraw and was destined to be traded twice more from the Giants before his playing career was through, and it is that itinerant résumé that best defines who Herzog was as a player. Perhaps no other player McGraw ever managed more closely resembled Muggsy, which may explain why the two men generally detested each other.

Still, late in his life, Herzog would say of McGraw, "The old man and I had our arguments, I guess because we both liked to win so well. But, when he got into a pinch and needed someone to put fire into his team, I am glad to remember he always was calling back Buck Herzog."

McGraw's epitaph of Herzog was even more succinct, even more appropriate: "I hate his guts," McGraw said, "but I want him on my club."

The Red Sox, as their train rumbled through the night, across Connecticut, past the New York border, finally into the 125th Street Terminal—where all but one of the Giants disembarked—would certainly have agreed, by acclimation, with the *first* half of that statement.

Nobody suffered more than Heinie Wagner, the man who was credited with saving the Red Sox clubhouse from civil war, the big-hearted, good-natured shortstop whose finest season as a major leaguer now threatened to become a footnote to the way he'd mismanaged his duty as a third-base coach, of all things. What Wagner wanted to say to everybody was, *Don't you realize the Speed Boys knew better than to rely on third-base coaches? Why do you suppose they treated the job so haphazardly?* Everyone who saw the 1912 Red Sox agreed that this was the greatest batch of baserunners ever collected on one team, so many of them sharing the rare blend of speed, daring, and instinct. No team went first-to-third better. No team scored more runs going from first to home on a double. What the hardscrabble New Yorker inside Wagner wanted to shout—on the train, at the station, at the hotel, at the ballpark—was this: *Larry Gardner should have known enough to take third.* Gardner was a man who hit *eighteen* triples that year, who scored eighty-eight runs, who was as smart a baserunner as there was in the American League.

Of course, Wagner wouldn't say that. He couldn't. And so he suffered in silence. He seethed. He was already angry at himself for allowing his ancient feud with McGraw to get the better of his tongue; while he had to smile at how angry the old bastard would get when he saw the quote about Stahl "outgeneraling" him, he knew it was bad form to give a man like McGraw extra motivation to burn you, extra fuel with which to scald you. That wasn't Wagner's way; he was a conciliator, a reconciler, not a rabble-rouser, and so in many ways was Buck Herzog's diametric opposite. Six years later, all of those people skills would reach a fateful, noble climax when it would be Wagner who was asked to reach out to Babe Ruth, then the Red Sox' prime star, to return to the team after he'd jumped it over some or other dispute in early July, threatening to stay away forever. Ruth was a hardheaded ox, and he wouldn't have listened to anybody else. But he listened to Wagner. "I'll come back because of you," the Babe said softly.

With the train making its way south from 125th Street toward Grand Central, Wagner sidled up next to Stahl, who was trying to catch a nap using a newspaper to shade his eyes.

"I'll make it up to the club, Skip," he said.

"You don't owe the club a damn thing," Stahl replied. "We're fine. Look at who we're pitching tomorrow."

That did make Wagner feel better, because in all the games he'd played in his peripatetic career, he'd never felt the same way he felt playing in back of Smoky Joe Wood. Back when he'd had his seventeen-game cup of coffee with the pre-McGraw Giants of 1902, he'd played with Christy Mathewson, but that was different; Matty was still only twenty-one, he was still finding himself as a pitcher. As a minor leaguer, there was always some new kid with a big arm ready to conquer the world, and invariably they wound up with sore shoulders or small hearts, with reputations far greater than their results. But not Wood. This kid was different.

"This kid," Wagner told Stahl, "is something like we've never seen before."

The Giants had tried to diminish what they'd seen in Game One, when Wood not only had fanned eleven of them, he'd struck out the final two batters of the game with the tying and winning runs in scoring position, with a raucous Polo Grounds ready to pounce at the first opportunity, and he'd done it without any tricks, without any mirrors. He'd beaten them with his fastball. They *knew* it was coming. And *still* never had a prayer.

And *still* they weren't ready to give the kid full credit. Wagner had seen their comments sprinkled throughout the last few days, and they almost made him giggle.

"He went with his fastball," Mathewson sniffed, "because he couldn't get his curve over for anything." *If you still had that fastball, Matty, you'd go with it too . . .*

"Wood depends too much on speed," Chief Meyers, the New York catcher, said. "That is bound to sap his reserve energy and his recuperative powers. Wood showed us nothing like the speed [Chief] Bender displayed against Matty in the opening game last year. He is not so hard a pitcher to beat." *Then by all means, beat him if you can. . . .*

"He's a fine, fine pitcher," McGraw half-conceded, "but he's still got a lot of things he has to work on." *Any suggestions you have, Mug-gsy, we're all ears. . . .*

Even Bill Klem, who'd seen every one of Wood's pitches up close in Game One, couldn't find it in his heart to praise poor Joe: "Wood didn't have half the smoke on his balls that Bender had on his last year." *What do you expect from a National League man?*

Typical of Wood, he was unfazed by all of it.

"Don't worry," he told Speaker, who spent the entire five-hour trip to New York with his foot elevated and his pain splashed plainly on his pale face. "Those boys'll get another crack at me. Maybe two more. They'll get their turn."

The *Gilt Edge Express* finally pulled into Grand Central Station, which was where the Red Sox were to get off before catching cabs back uptown to Bretton Hall. At first, they all had to laugh, wearily, because there were three hundred Giants fans on the platform and they all started cheering wildly.

"Rubes," Bill Carrigan chortled. "They don't know the difference between the team they root for and the one they're supposed to hate."

Oh, but they did. Because as twenty-three Red Sox walked off the train, they all noticed that they were joined by one straggling Giant, puffing on an enormous cigar, tipping his bowler hat toward the adoring crowd with a practiced flourish. Rube Marquard had waited a long time for a day like this, and a night like this. What was the point in ending it so prematurely with something as annoying as sleep? He enjoyed every one of the two hundred steps he took toward the cabstand, and when one of the fans started screaming, "Speech!" Rube just smiled and winked.

"I'm afraid," he said, "that I'm all talked out."

Only a rube would believe *that* for even a second.

This time, the man everyone wanted to talk to was named John W. Dowd. He had spent Thursday afternoon watching every pitch in Times Square, and the second the final out was announced—as far as he knew, a routine fly ball to Josh Devore—Dowd had sprinted to the nearest subway station and begun the journey all the way uptown. Sure enough, he was the first man in line at the Polo Grounds, although he was quickly joined by a few dozen others, then a few hundred others, then a few thousand more. The whole cross section of a New York baseball crowd was firmly in line as midnight came and went, the obsessive baseball fan and the curiosity-seeking out-of-towner; the wide-eyed schoolboys with one eye peeled for truant officers and the sleepy-eyed bookmakers with *their* eyes on the lookout for policemen seeking the odd sawbuck or two to look the other way. These merchants expected a swift business today, because with the Series even at a game apiece the betting line had evened out, too. Red Sox fans could suddenly bet even money on their boys to win the Series, after facing odds as steep as 10-to-6 after Game One, and that was a splendid turn of events for the men keeping track of the money.

Still, as enthusiastic as the crowd may have been, may have wanted to be, the marvelous weather that had made Game One such a pleasurable outing no matter where your rooting interests lay had evaporated without warning. By midnight, the mercury had dipped below fifty and showed no signs of slowing down, and sometime around two in the morning it started to rain, a steady barrage of showers and mist and biting, bracing wind, forcing the people in line to enter into unspoken gentleman's agreements so they could all seek shelter under the nearby elevated roads during the worst of it without surrendering their hard-earned places in line. When morning arrived, so much rain had already fallen that some in line figured there was no way baseball could be played, and they gave up and went home. Little did they know, however, that late in the season the Giants had installed an ultra-modern, ultra-rainproof tarpaulin so their grounds crew could protect the infield to maximum efficiency. If the rain could give them a break for just a few more hours, they might even be able to make the soggy outfield playable. By 10 o'clock, with the soaked crowd growing restless, Giants secretary O'Brien appeared and announced, "Every effort will still be made to start the game on time." For the thousands who'd stubbornly stayed in the line, that provided their first cheer of the day, before they'd even walked inside the gate.

Ninety minutes later, the umpires arrived led by Cy Rigler, the last of the quartet to be assigned home-plate duty. Whether it was a celestial commentary or just coincidence, the moment they showed up at the Speedway Entrance the skies darkened again, and that didn't escape the folks in line.

"Even God wants to kill the ump!" someone shouted, eliciting a cheerful roar.

But the umpires weren't laughing. Bill Klem had worked the 1911 Series, when what seemed like an isolated thunderstorm had blown in after Game Three and then stuck around for a full week, robbing the show of its momentum, its drama, and ultimately its box-office appeal; the decisive sixth game filled Shibe Park to only two-thirds its capacity. Klem knew that while keeping the grounds dry was not part of an umpire's supreme powers, it was certainly well within their purview to sweat every minute an ominous cloud lurked overhead. So Klem and O'Loughlin, the two senior members of the crew, took slow, vigilant jaunts around the bases, careful to look for soft pockets of dirt that could easily break an ankle and slick patches of grass that could make a spinning baseball do all manner of odd tricks. They studied the sod grimly. In the outfield, the Seventh Regiment band was practicing for its pregame performance, several of the musicians seeing their shoes sink completely into the turf.

"It's bad," a French horn player named Hans Bauman reported to the fans in line as he left, shifting his horn from left hand to right, pushing his hat up his forehead. "It will probably take two hours of sunshine to dry it up. I just wish the sun would come."

It was O'Loughlin who finally walked inside, to the Giants' corporate offices, picked up a telephone, and called over to the Waldorf-Astoria, where the National Commission was keeping its New York headquarters. August Herrmann, who'd been waiting impatiently for news from uptown, took the call.

"Well?" he asked. "What's the verdict?"

"The grounds are very heavy," O'Loughlin reported. "If any more rain falls I don't know if we can play. But John Murphy, the groundskeeper, says if it stays dry the field will be ready. He says that for now they're fine."

O'Loughlin peeked out the window of O'Brien's office, saw dark clouds, no rain.

"Me?" he surmised. "I'd say it's fifty-fifty we can get nine innings in."

"OK," Herrmann said. "Hold the line." In the background, O'Loughlin could hear chatter, could make out the unmistakable voice of Ban Johnson, could hear him warn that if they didn't get this game in, who knew when they could, it's the craziness of playing baseball in the fall, it's a summer game that should be played in the sunshine, more chatter, more debate, and then Herrmann was back on the line.

"We're on," he said. And hung up. It was 11:48, a little less than two and a half hours before first pitch. O'Loughlin called Red Sox headquarters at the Bretton, discovered they were already on their way. The Giants had already started to arrive, one by one, from their apartments in their surrounding neighborhoods. Twelve minutes later, the ticket windows officially opened, signaling there would be baseball today after all, and you never heard such a relieved cheer from 10,000 soaking, sopping baseball fans, some 36,502 of whom would make their way into the Polo Grounds that day with tickets, another 5,000 or 6,000 of whom would duke an usher to let them sneak in, a crowd that would officially be the third largest in the history of this stadium (and, thus, the history of the sport) but unofficially shattered that record to smithereens.

The game may have been on. But now the World Series—tied at one win apiece—was, most assuredly, *on*.

Lena Marquard couldn't understand what all the commotion could possibly be about. She was spending her Friday morning the way she spent all of her Friday mornings, concocting a batch of grape juice in the kitchen of her home at 3180 W. 46th Street in Cleveland. She frowned as she watched to see if the ingredients would jell properly, and was startled when there was a loud banging on the front door, and even more surprised when she opened it and was immediately blinded by the harsh flash of a photographer's bulb. Why, there must have been twenty people on her porch.

"What do you want?" she asked angrily. "I am not interested in salesmen!"

"We are not salesmen!" one of the mob helpfully corrected her. "We're from the newspapers. We want to talk to you about your son!"

"What has that boy done now?"

The newsmen looked at each other. It was well known that Rube's father, Ferdinand, had been most displeased with his son's decision to bypass his education and make his living among the dirty-fingered lot of baseball players. But Rube had always said he had a wonderful relationship with his mother. Surely, she followed his career?

"Um, ma'am, he won a world's series game yesterday."

Lena waved them in, because she couldn't stand to be away from her grapes for too long, lest she waste her morning efforts. When they reached the kitchen she said, "He won the game all by himself?"

"Well, he pitched," the man from the *Plain Dealer* said. "The Giants won. And he was the winning pitcher."

Mrs. Marquard shrugged her shoulders. *What's that supposed to mean to me?*

"Some people think he's a hero this morning," said the man from the *Press*.

Finally, a laugh from Mrs. Marquard, and the boys with their pens made sure to note every last chuckle.

"A hero? Ha! Rube, he ain't such a wonder," she said. "What do I care about ballgames? Why are they making such a fuss about that boy? He ain't such a wonder. He ought to win, right? That's why they pay him!"

The scribbling scribes weren't sure how to react to that.

"But, Mrs. Marquard," asked the fellow from the *Daily News*, "don't you want to hear more about the game, more about your son's pitching?"

She was back with her grapes, and she waved her hands for emphasis, and everyone could see they were a deep shade of purple.

"He'll tell me when he tells me," she said. "We got to eat this winter, ain't we? I got chores to do. Can't worry about some silly baseball game."

She shook her head.

"A hero! Imagine that."

A few hundred miles to the east, at just about the same moment, the hero in question was walking onto the field at the Polo Grounds and drinking in every last droplet of adulation he could. It turned out he wasn't nearly as talked-out as he'd claimed he was at Grand Central the night before. He kept talking up and down Broadway until a wee small hour of Friday morning. He'd awoken, headed to work, and talked to the fans in line. When the newsfolk approached, he was more than happy to talk to them, too.

"All I want," he told them, "is just one-ninth of the credit for winning that one yesterday. But I can't help claiming something, and that's the prediction that I would win my game. As it turned out, it came out just as I said it would, didn't it, boys?"

He cackled, picked up a baseball, started having a catch with Art Wilson, the backup catcher.

"Tell you what, though, boys," he said. "When we win today, you don't have to give me even one-hundredth of the credit. Do we have a deal?"

McGraw was back to playing games, warming up both Christy Mathewson and Jeff Tesreau, but this time the Sox weren't falling for any of his trickery; clearly Mathewson would benefit—as would the Giants—from his taking an extra day's rest. The Speed Boys were anxious to see if Tesreau really had learned any lessons from having tipped his pitches in Game One, as he swore he had. Even then, they believed, it wouldn't matter.

"He's a rookie," Larry Gardner said flatly. "He did well to pitch the way he did in the first contest. The Giants can't expect him to do that again. We certainly don't."

Jake Stahl, of course, saw no need to match McGraw, not when he was sending to the mound a man in search of his thirty-sixth win of the season. Joe Wood was eager to pitch, eager to show the Giants he was more than just a fastball wonder, but he had also started to ponder if his prized arm would ever feel normal this day. The biting chill had forced almost all the players on both sides to take to the field and warm up in heavy mackinaw jackets, and some of them wore thick wool sweaters underneath that, and long-sleeved shirts under their heavy flannel uniforms. With that many layers, it was hard to get a ball higher than your chin, much less throw warm-up pitches, so Wood didn't have the luxury of warmth swaddling his arm. Still, whenever he felt too badly about the stiffness lingering around his shoulder and his elbow, Wood would take a look across the field at his best friend, Speaker, whose ankle howled twice as loudly in the raw weather, who'd actually admitted to him that morning, "Joe, if I can't run I can't play. It kills me to say it. But I can't lose the series for the boys just because I want to play."

So Wood made a deal with him.

"Play," he said, "and I'll make sure they don't hit the ball anywhere near you."

That made the rough-hewn Texan roar. What it must be like, Speaker thought, to be young and invincible, and think you can control things that only God can . . .

Suddenly, unexpectedly, there rose a roar from the overflow crowd, and it caused the players to stop what they were doing, look around, see the source of the commotion. Was President Taft in the house? Colonel Roosevelt? Governor Wilson? Charles Becker?

No, it was better than that. The players slowly understood, once they saw their own shadows. The sun had arrived. And as it did, as if by magic, so did thousands of reserve-seat ticket holders who'd kept the expensive seats mostly empty so far. Now that they'd pulled their lace curtains back and seen favorable weather, they hurried to the Polo Grounds, making the day complete.

Cy Rigler, who before he was done would umpire more World Series games than anyone in history besides Bill Klem, was eager to get the game started on time, lest they start fooling too badly with fickle weather patterns. He grabbed a bullhorn, announced the batteries, and shortly after 2:15 in the afternoon, with the sun still standing sentry in the middle of a temporarily clear sky, he called the parties to action.

"Play ball!" he cried.

Conspicuous by their absence from the Polo Grounds were the Royal Rooters, almost all of whom had stayed home in anticipation of a busy Saturday, which would not only include Game Five of the World Series but the Columbus Day Parade, as well, an event that, in immigrant-heavy Boston, was an even bigger secular holiday than New Year's Eve (though, depending on what part of town you were in, not quite as popular as St. Patrick's Day).

The loudest Rooter of all, John Fitzgerald, didn't let the lack of his physical proximity to the games worry him any. A few minutes before the first pitch would be thrown in New York, Fitzgerald arrived at Washington Street, Boston's Newspaper Row, climbed onto a stage, and whooped the twenty thousand fans gathered there into a fever-pitched frenzy. Standing directly in front of the *Globe* building, he lifted his left hand, called for three cheers for the Red Sox, and the crowd enthusiastically responded.

"Now then, boys," Honey Fitz continued, "three cheers for Smoky Joe Wood, the peerless pitcher who will take the hill for us today in Gotham!"

"*HIP, HIP, HOORAY!*"

"Three cheers for a Red Sox victory tomorrow, back here in the greatest city in the world!"

"*HIP, HIP, HOORAY!*"

"Three cheers for the *Globe!*"

Those cheers were a little more muted, which was just the way Honey Fitz intended them to be; it was, after all, the Taylor family, publishers of the paper, who'd gained control of the Red Sox when Ban Johnson engineered its sale away from Fitzgerald many years before.

In New York, it hadn't seemed possible for there to be more interest in the Series than there'd already been, yet this Friday dawned with numerous empty office cubicles and dozens of addled truant officers, summoned to deal with classrooms that looked for the day like the middle of summer. Not only were there well over 40,000 people crammed into the Polo Grounds, there were a good thousand more who'd taken to the old perch on Coogan's Bluff, just to say they were *around* the game. Back in the old version of the park, the one that burned in 1911, you could actually follow the game from up there, but the new horseshoe shape kept everything a mystery, just the way John T. Brush wanted it, the better to lure those folks down to his stadium ticket windows.

At Herald Square, where 20,000 people had already swarmed and where an additional 20,000 would spend at least a portion of their afternoon, a chant rose up immediately after the announcer called out the batteries:

Old Joe Wood!
He's no good!
Oh yes, I guess
That he's no good!

It was a merry, festive occasion for most. A brass band set up in the second floor of a music shop across the street from the board. The *Herald* and the *Telegram* had hired cabaret dancers to perform in between innings. The whole hullabaloo attracted more than just the hard-core baseball fans, and sometimes it accounted for some hard feelings.

Such as the man and his wife who showed up near the Thirty-fifth Street side of the Playograph maybe half an hour after the first pitch, too late to get a prime spot. The man stood on his toes to see the score.

"It's 1–0," he reported to his wife, who couldn't have been less interested if he'd given a score from a cricket game in Jersey City. "Giants are down."

"I can't see a thing," his wife said. "Where are the dancers?"

"That's OK," the man said. "I can see. I'll tell you every play."

"Sure you will. You haven't spoken to me since we got within sight of the board. You haven't even noticed I'm here except to slam me on the back and push my hat over to one side."

"Well," the man said, "I want to see the game. It's important."

"All right, then. Lets get on a streetcar and go out to the Grounds. We can get a seat there and actually, you know, *see the game!*"

The man turned, his faced flushed with frustration.

"Listen here," he said. "Do you know *anything* about baseball? Do you think I'd be *here* if there was a vacant seat *up there?* Come now and don't worry me."

She tried being a good sport. She enjoyed the dancers. She enjoyed the band. She laughed at how much everyone around her seemed so completely obsessed by the little plastic figurines on the board, and all the fancy lights for balls, strikes, outs, and errors,

whatever on earth any of that meant. But she soon reached a breaking point, in the middle of the seventh inning, when a sign was
raised ordering, "Everybody Stretch!" and she watched everyone
around her responding to the sign like trained circus animals.

And that was that. "I won't do it and I won't be made to do it!" she
railed, gathering her hat, her purse, and her overcoat. "I don't feel
like stretching, and I won't do it for all your old Giants and Cubs and
Red Stockings. I'm going home."

And she did. She left. Her husband? He stayed.

"She never could understand me," he muttered to a fascinated
Herald reporter, who'd watched them the whole afternoon. "She'd
rather read a novel than watch the game. No wonder we lose when
the women folk ain't loyal."

The Giants, in truth, had far more to worry about than any perceived disloyalty among their distaff fans. They had to concern
themselves with Smoky Joe Wood; worse, they had to contend with
a Smoky Joe Wood with something to prove, a Smoky Joe Wood
with a chip on his shoulder, a Smoky Joe Wood who didn't have near
the fastball he'd had in Game One, who had to rely more and more
on his curveball, who would surrender nine hits in nine innings, yet
who managed to turn rigid and unyielding the moment he sniffed
trouble.

"You can have any pitcher you want to have," Harry Hooper
would say some six decades later. "But for me, if I could have one
pitcher in history on my team, it would be Smoky Joe Wood from
1912, because in that year he was the finest pitcher who ever lived,
the gamest, the grittiest, the most unbelievable pitcher you ever
saw."

Tesreau was almost as good, and just as had been the case in Game
One, that was almost enough for the Giants. Almost. He'd wiggled
his way out of trouble in the first inning when, after allowing the
first two men to reach base, he'd induced the hobbled Tris Speaker
to hit into a backbreaking double play (and both Speaker and Stahl

would be roasted later on for not sacrificing there, a reflection of just how trained people were in 1912 to the ways of small ball), and then was saved a run when Art Fletcher, of all people, made an eye-popping stop of a hard Duffy Lewis grounder. In the bottom of the inning, as Josh Devore bent over to grab a handful of dirt before leading off for the Giants, the Polo Grounds broke into a sponta-neous version of "For He's a Jolly Good Fellow"; the morning papers had brought all of them up to speed on just how remarkable a catch he'd made the day before, and even though Devore fanned on three pitches they serenaded him again on his way back to the dugout.

Their collective mood wouldn't stay very festive for very long. Larry Gardner led off the bottom of the second with a vicious drive that sailed over Red Murray's head in right field and headed for the heart of the horseshoe, allowing Gardner to take third base standing up, and for one of the first times in his remarkable rookie campaign, Tesreau looked shaken. There was a good reason for that, too: Lead-ing off the game, Hooper had drilled a ball right back through the box that Tesreau, instinctively, had tried to knock down with his hand—his pitching hand, his money hand—and instead the ball had ripped the nail right off the middle finger. He told no one, because men were men in 1912 and didn't ask for Band-Aids. But it affected his usual pinpoint control, a problem that manifested itself right away, when a spitter to Stahl bounded crazily away from Meyers, allowing Gardner to trot home with the icebreaking run.

"I knew I would have to throw shutout ball, or close to it, to beat Wood on a day like this—dull, with a slight mist hanging over the grounds," Tesreau would later lament. "It is a day made for his speed, not for my finesse. In my anxiety to keep the ball away from the center of the plate on Stahl I turned loose a wild pitch and Gard-ner scored. I was solely responsible for the first run. I accept that."

The Red Sox added a run to make it 2–0 in the fourth when Hick Cady, denied the hero's laurels a day earlier, drove in Stahl with a sharp two-out single. With Smoky Joe Wood on the mound, 2–0 could well have been 20–0, and the quiet of the Polo Grounds reflected that hopelessness. But those who'd seen every game knew that the match couldn't possibly continue without something for the papers to chatter about.

Not that they would need it, necessarily. Downtown, on Chambers Street, the most electrifying moment yet at the Becker trial had already occurred early in the afternoon, and rewrite men at all fourteen New York papers were already spinning the tale. It seems a small-time hood named Morris Luban had been called by the prosecution, been sworn in, and under oath testified that two weeks before the sensational murder, he'd heard Charles Becker tell Jack Rose, a fellow underground associate, "If you don't croak Rosenthal, I'll do it myself."

The judge then asked Luban, "Did you see who fired the gun?"

Luban pointed. It wasn't enough for the judge. "Touch him," he said.

And so Luban, visibly quivering, frightened out of his mind, left the witness stand, walked over to where Frank Cirofici—Dago Frank—was sitting. Luban touched him on the shoulder, said, "I saw this man shoot, your honor."

The gallery gasped, the judge called for a recess, reporters raced for the telephones in the hallway. The news quickly spread uptown, buzzing around the Polo Grounds, the only buzz in the building thus far.

That, not surprisingly, was about to change.

Heinie Wagner wanted so badly to make amends for what he'd done, or what he hadn't done, and figured the best way to do that was to have a big day against the kid pitcher, Tesreau, collect two or three hits, knock in a bunch of runs, and that would be that. But that hadn't happened. He'd flied to center in the second, grounded out to first in the fourth, and while his team had a 2–0 lead with their ace on the mound as they took the field in the bottom of the fifth, he couldn't shake the feeling that he was being carried to glory on the shoulders of his teammates, along only for the ride.

All these thoughts crowded his brain as Fred Merkle stepped to the plate to a spattering of boos, Giants fans growing impatient with Merkle's growing résumé of ill-timed missteps. By now, Wood had struck out five Giants but he'd all but abandoned his fastball, which was anything but smoky this time around. Feeding Merkle a big, sweeping curve, Merkle tapped out a slow roller to the left of the mound, where the still-soaked grass ate it up and killed its momentum. Merkle, running hard out of the box, figured he had a sure infield hit, and so did the rest of the Polo Grounds, but suddenly in swooped Heinie Wagner, his spikes sloshing in the turf, his bare hand reaching down for the soaked ball, firing it as he launched his body parallel to the ground before falling with a dramatic splash. Somehow, there was plenty of mustard on the throw. Somehow, the ball popped Stahl's mitt at first an eyeblink before Merkle's foot slammed into the base. O'Loughlin bellowed "Out!" and Merkle, in disbelief, slammed his cap to the ground.

"Watch yourself, Merkle!" O'Loughlin warned.

"I'm not mad at you, Silk," he said. "How the *hell* did he make that play?"

Everyone wondered the same thing. Wood helped his shortstop to his feet and sent him back to his post with a simple "Thanks." He then allowed a sharp single to Herzog (already Buck's seventh hit of the Series), which would have been far more problematic if not for Wagner's acrobatics. Wood settled down, struck out Chief Meyers, then figured to have little trouble with Art Fletcher, who may have cured his defensive hiccups but was still the lightest hitter in the New York lineup. Some in the stands murmured for a pinch hitter, but it was far too early for that and, besides, when Wood offered up a not-so-fast fastball, Fletcher clobbered it, and the ball appeared destined for left center field and the Giants appeared set up for first and third, two out, with Moose McCormick taking a walk toward the bat rack.

Only, the ball never reached its destination, because Wagner had quickly broken toward second, he'd dived headlong into the muddy basepath, speared the ball, spit dirt out of his mouth, and slingshot a perfect strike to Stahl that beat Fletcher by half a step. Fletcher, like Merkle before him, threw his cap in the air, but by now O'Loughlin perfectly understood his frustration and didn't say a word.

Wagner, his uniform filthy now, accepted backslaps and attaboys from every one of his teammates, especially Wood, who understood his shortstop had definitely kept at least one run off the board and had prevented the possibility of a big inning. But even that wasn't as satisfying as when he peered into the Giant's dugout, where he saw John McGraw staring back at him, shaking his head, muttering something to Wilbert Robinson, something Robinson later revealed went something like this:

"*That* guy," McGraw had growled, "ain't *that* good."

The Giant's manager was beyond aggravated now. He'd ordered his players to take every one of Wood's first pitches, a strategy that backfired when Wood threw first-pitch strikes to sixteen of the first seventeen men he faced. So in the bottom of the sixth, McGraw reversed himself, telling Jeff Tesreau, "Look for the fast one on the first pitch and smoke it." And Tesreau, who'd hit only .146 that season, did just that, singling to left. Devore, also obeying, did likewise, and the Giants were set up, first and second, none out. But then Doyle and Snodgrass, swinging at the first pitch, popped to third and grounded into a fielder's choice, and even though Red Murray let one go by before he grounded out to second, Wood had somehow allowed the Giants to start a rally and then extinguished that rally by using only six pitches. Even the great McGraw couldn't solve Smoky Joe Wood.

But, damn it all, he would keep trying.

So in the bottom of the seventh, with the crowd restless and the Giants' bench antsy and McGraw getting more and more ornery after Merkle led off with a meek strikeout, everyone was finally rousted back to attention when the scorching-hot Buck Herzog smoked a line drive to left for a single, and now McGraw was back at his hands-clapping, foot-stomping best, calling Wood a bush leaguer, exhorting Chief Meyers to keep the rally going.

At first it looked like he might, because he lofted a deep fly ball toward dead center field. Plenty of room out there for a ball to roam. Especially with a one-legged center fielder out there.

For six and a third innings, Wood had kept his promise to his roommate. He'd struck out seven. He'd gotten five groundouts, induced one outfield fly, one infield pop-up, picked one runner off first, even made sure that the six hits the Giants had already collected went either to right field or left field, keeping his roommate perfectly idle. His crazy plan had worked, until now. And while Speaker still tried to ignore the ankle—even attempting to steal after drawing a walk in the fifth, not the best idea he'd ever had—it was impossible for anyone else with eyes to disregard. Especially now. Meyers's drive wasn't exactly routine, but a healthy Speaker would have had no trouble getting to it. The wounded Speaker had nothing *but* trouble getting there, lumbering, limping, finally settling under the ball, which had helpfully stayed in the air a long time, finally squeezing it. A grateful Wood tipped his cap to his center fielder, stepped back on the mound, and went to work against Fletcher.

And then Fletcher went to work against *Wood*. McGraw's advice still held, and when Wood threw a first-pitch fastball Fletcher swung and got great wood on the ball, spanking it down the right-field line for a double that scored Herzog, sliced the Giants' deficit in half to 2–1, and suddenly the Polo Grounds was alive with energy and noise and possibility. Out of nowhere, the Giants had risen up to scuff the invincible Smoky Joe, and as that news was relayed from one precinct to another, from one scoreboard stand to another, it seemed the entire island of Manhattan was bedeviled by baseball. As the news of Fletcher's double arrived on the New York Stock Exchange floor, then on its wire, all of Wall Street shut down instantaneously. Downtown, uptown, New York, New England, New World: This game suddenly meant everything to everyone.

None more so than the man in the third-base coaching box. Now, McGraw knew, he had to seize the moment. He sent Tesreau back to the bench. He summoned McCormick to pinch-hit. The sight of big Moose cradling his bat sent another jolt through the grandstands,

Fred Snodgrass, pictured in the Giants' distinctive all-black uniforms at the 1911 World Series against Philadelphia, was a particular favorite of John J. McGraw's.

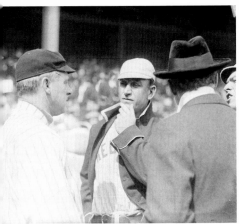

New York Giants skipper John McGraw (left) was considered the premier strategist of his era as well as a hotheaded umpire baiter. Meanwhile, in Boston, Jake Stahl (center) was coaxed out of retirement and a cushy bank job to manage the greatest assemblage of talent he'd ever seen.

For one season, Smoky Joe Wood was the most dominant pitcher in the game.

James McAleer, owner of the Red Sox, was at first immensely popular with Boston fans ... until they caught wind of his apparent wish to extend the Series at all costs.

Children called Christy Mathewson "The Christian Gentleman," and adults called him "Big Six." By 1912, he was already acknowledged to be among the two or three greatest to ever throw a baseball.

Tris Speaker had wanted to play center field for the New York Giants but had been dismissed by McGraw as not good enough to make his club, a decision McGraw would rue for the rest of his career.

The right-field bleachers at the Polo Grounds some two hours before the start of Game One of the 1912 World Series.

The Royal Rooters, the most fanatical group of fans in all of baseball, were led by Mayor Fitzgerald and saloon owner Nuf Ced McGreevy (at left, waving a megaphone).

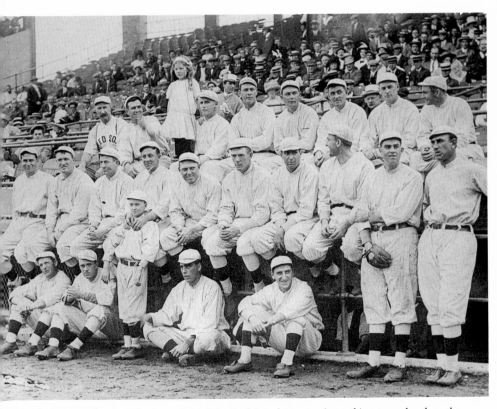

While there were always entire segments of the Red Sox that weren't speaking to each other, they mostly forgot their differences between the white lines.

The Giants swagger onto the field at the Polo Grounds prior to Game One, to the delight of their fans. Though they hadn't won a title since 1905, the Giants carried themselves as perennial champions, much to the chagrin of opposing teams and fans.

The crowds at the 1912 World Series were unprecedented both in their enthusiasm and their sheer numbers, as evidenced by this line at the Polo Grounds.

The *New York Herald* was one of the first newspapers to provide wireless play-by-play coverage of World Series games, beginning in 1911. By 1912, ten of the fourteen daily newspapers in New York City, and four Boston papers, provided similar services, drawing mammoth crowds.

The four stalwarts of the Red Sox lineup (left to right): Duffy Lewis, Larry Gardner, Tris Speaker, and Heinie Wagner.

Giants owner John T. Brush had become one of the World Series' fiercest advocates after leading the charge to cancel the event in 1904.

Throughout the so-called "Trial of the Century" of New York Police Department Lieutenant Charles Becker (left)—a devoted Giants fan—the jury heard more and more stories of his ties with underworld figures such as "Lefty Louie" Rosenberg and "Gyp the Blood" Horowitz (above, seated, with their NYPD captors).

As prosecutor in the Becker trials, Charles Whitman sealed his political career and paved his way to the governor's chair, in which he sits on the morning of his inauguration in 1915.

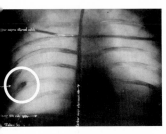

Theodore Roosevelt was shot in the chest by a saloon owner named John Shrank on October 14, 1912, on his way to deliver a speech at the Milwaukee Auditorium. Despite the fact that his would-be assassin's bullet was still lodged in his chest—as clearly visible in his X-ray—Roosevelt refused to seek medical attention until he was done delivering his speech.

Roosevelt recovered quickly from his wound and returned to his home in Oyster Bay, N.Y.

President William Howard Taft (left) was a noted sportsman and followed the 1912 World Series closely—possibly to the detriment of his re-election campaign.

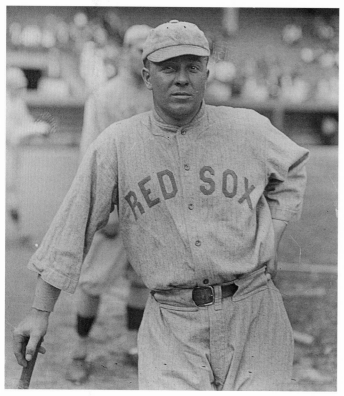

Christy Mathewson admitted he knew very little, if anything, about the Red Sox reserve Olaf Henricksen (left), but by the time Henricksen's at-bat was over Mathewson knew he would never forget the only major league player ever born in Denmark.

The press boxes at the Polo Grounds (above) and Fenway Park filled to overflowing with such familiar bylines as Damon Runyon, Hugh Fullerton, Grantland Rice, and Tim Murnane, and the telegraph booths were busy transmitting pitch-by-pitch updates all over the country.

Few players channeled McGraw on the field as completely as Buck Herzog (above), who nearly caused several brouhahas during the 1912 World Series.

and it sparked a visit to the mound from Stahl, who had a simple reminder for his pitcher.

"You're the best there is," he said. "Don't forget that."

McCormick had earned his nickname for his wondrous eight-foot stride, a gait that was especially impressive when he made his way into a batter's box. Like Mathewson, he was a graduate of Bucknell, and he would later coach at both his alma mater and at West Point. Periodically he would take sabbaticals from baseball to work as an engineer in the steel industry, so he was an unusual choice to be a favorite of McGraw's, but Muggsy had signed him once and reacquired him once, and in 1912 he'd hit safely in eleven of the thirty pinch-hit opportunities he was given. That .367 average made him just as popular with Giants fans, who otherwise remembered him as the unfortunate soul who'd been on third base and whose game-winning run hadn't counted during the famous Merkle Boner Game of 1908. They were used to Moose delivering when it mattered.

And he delivered here.

The big lefty dragged his enormous, forty-eight-ounce bat behind him, kicked the dirt out of his spikes (though how much dirt could have accumulated in them as he sat for seven innings in the dugout, no one could quite say), removed a thick wad of chewing gum from his mouth and placed it on the button of his cap, took one practice swing. And then drilled a hard line drive toward the hole between first and second, which Yerkes was able to knock down, an infield single that would keep the rally alive and bring up the top of the order and further demoralize Wood, who was leaking gas by the gallon now, who was shrinking before everyone's very eyes, who was . . .

WHAT THE HELL?!?!

Have you ever heard the sound of an entire baseball stadium recoiling in horror? If you were sitting in the Polo Grounds this eleventh day of October 1912, right around 3:30 in the afternoon, the sun a distant memory, the chill hanging low and heavy, then that is *exactly* what you heard—that, and the desperate silence of a promising rally murdered in cold blood. Because the first thing all 36,502 people in the stands had clearly seen, together, was that the ball hadn't dribbled that far away from Steve Yerkes. Unfortunately, the one man who *had* to see that, John J. McGraw, would swear he saw something else, would insist he had seen the ball trickle farther away, and so now he was doing the *next* thing all those people saw, which was to frantically wave Art Fletcher home, a heroic gesture in his mind, a suicidal one among those with a better view.

Fletcher, obedient soldier to the end, put his head down and dutifully began his trek home even though everyone else in the park— the most important one being Red Sox catcher Hick Cady—had seen Yerkes recover, gather the ball, and fire to the plate, a perfect strike that landed in Cady's mitt with Fletcher at least twelve or fifteen feet away. It was the easiest call Cy Rigler would have to make in his twenty-nine years as an umpire. Fletcher, knowing he was dead, did what every McGraw-trained baseball player was taught to do: He tried to jostle the ball free, his only hope. But Fletcher, who weighed 170 pounds soaking wet, was never going to live to tell about trying to barrel through Cady, who was built like a brick wall. So Fletcher tried doing the dirty work with his spikes, and those cleats wound up digging into Cady's chest protector, and Cady took exception to that and told Fletcher so by flicking him off his legs and spiking the baseball about three feet from his head.

"You can't beat us playing ball so you try this horseshit?" Cady screamed at Fletcher. "I should pound you into the dirt!"

"You sons-a-bitches are the god-damnedest dirtiest bastards I ever played against!" screamed Tris Speaker, hopping mad and hopping off the field toward McGraw, shaking his finger at the Giants' manager, waving his fist, none of it mattering because as angry as anyone might have been at him, or his players, there was no one anywhere on earth who was angrier with anyone than McGraw was at himself. He'd seen untold thousands of baseball games in his time, and he could recognize the passing of an opportunity when he saw one. The Giants would briefly threaten in the eighth, getting the tying run to third on a single and an error, but Wood blunted the rally by retiring Merkle with his eighth and final strikeout. And when the Sox added an insurance run in the ninth off Red Ames, it seemed to take all the fight out of the home team, which meekly went down one-two-three in the bottom of the ninth.

The Sox stormed off the field surrounded by stony silence, 3–1 winners in this game, 2–1 leaders in this series, believing, as their manager would soon crow, "That game right there, boys, means the Series for us. Watch us win tomorrow and drive another nail in the championship flag. We will be back here for one game next week to clinch the title. End of story."

Still, as jubilant as Stahl was, he couldn't quite match the giddiness of his shortstop, who had to believe the karmic gods were smiling on him this day, not only allowing his glove to provide a measure of redemption but spooking his archenemy into one of the great managerial blunders in World Series history.

"Proper coaching," Heinie Wagner crowed, "would have held Fletcher at third in that situation. But he was foolishly urged to try for home. And he didn't have a chance of getting there. Foolish coaching, indeed."

By now, Wagner didn't care if McGraw read that or not. After all, what could he say?

CHAPTER SEVEN

Saturday, October 12, 1912: Game Five

Boston leads, 2 games to 1, with 1 tie

> BOSTON—Four hundred and twenty years ago yesterday, Mr.
> Columbus discovered America and yesterday afternoon, Mr.
> McGraw and some other millions of more or less transient
> New Yorkers discovered to their astonishment that the
> Boston Americans possess more than one pitcher . . .
>
> —HUGH S. FULLERTON, *CHICAGO TRIBUNE*, OCTOBER 13, 1912

IN JULY OF 1908, an eighteen-year-old kid named Hugh Carpenter Bedient, while trying to figure out what he wanted to do with the rest of his life, blissfully marked the days and nights of that summer by playing semiprofessional baseball for the Falconer Independents. Falconer is a suburb of Jamestown, New York, crammed into the southwestern corner of the state, seventy miles south of Buffalo and fifty miles east of Erie, Pennsylvania. The Independents played a busy schedule against teams from both sides of the border, and already Bedient had proven to be one of the more gifted pitchers in the league, a hard-throwing right-hander who also featured a sharp-breaking curve and a "drop" (similar to the famous "fadeaway" employed by Christy Mathewson, better known today as a screwball), and earlier that month he'd struck out seventeen men in a nine-inning game against Youngsville, Pennsylvania, winning 7–3.

That superb performance whet the appetite for many baseball-hungry locals who had already been looking forward to a three-game interstate series between Falconer and Corry, the other top team in the league. And neither team disappointed. The New York team won the first game, played at Falconer, 2–1, and a few days later in the rematch at Corry, the teams played fifteen innings to a draw. The third and final game, set for July 27, was such a hotly anticipated affair that the ballclubs themselves were only a part of the parochial battleground. The *Jamestown Evening Journal* announced, "A hair-raising game next Saturday in Corry will require a large number of locals to travel with the team to support them," while the *Corry Journal*, on game day, warned of "a frenzied, excited mass of people who will greet the invaders." And when the day arrived, it was every bit as frenzied as advertised. As the Jamestown paper reported: "The Corry fans had some money to bet and backed the home boys believing that the visitors would be overcome. All bets offered were covered, although a few backed up, and a large amount of money changed hands on the game." They were also covered, unbeknownst to the newspaper, by the fact that Corry had imported three outfield ringers from a team in Erie to square off against Bedient and try to salvage the last of the three games.

Corry did touch Bedient for a run in the bottom of the seventh inning. Falconer responded by scratching in the tying run in the top of the eighth. That was the end of the scoring for a good long while, but it wasn't the end of the playing. On and on the two teams battled, into the twelfth, into the seventeenth, into the twentieth. Finally, in the top of the twenty-third, in front of an exhausted gathering of more than 5,000 people, Falconer nudged across two go-ahead runs when the Corry third baseman, his judgment no doubt fried by the sun and the long day, threw wildly home with the bases loaded. The Corry pitcher, Charles Bickford, had performed heroic work, striking out sixteen men, walking only two, scattering thirteen hits, and allowing only the one earned run.

And not one soul left the ballpark in Corry that afternoon talking about poor Charles Bickford. Because when Hugh Bedient got the lead that day, he quickly slammed the door shut on the home team by striking out the side in the bottom of the twenty-third.

For his fortieth, forty-first, and forty-second strikeouts of the day.

Immediately, word of this world-record feat—at least, people suspected, it had to be a world record, because no one would try and make up such a fantastic tale, and no one yet had—was sent out on the national newswires, picked up in hundreds of towns, read by millions of readers. Sight unseen, no fewer than nineteen professional organizations descended on Falconer, helping to solve the riddle of how Bedient would spend at least the immediate segment of the rest of his life. He'd settled on Fall River, a team in the New England League, gone 13–9 in 1910, been purchased by the Red Sox, farmed out to Providence, loaned to Jersey City after struggling with good minor-league hitters, rediscovered his form, was bought back by the Red Sox, and in 1912 he'd stormed upon the American League at age twenty-two, winning twenty games, losing but nine, allowing just under three runs per nine innings. Almost seventy years later, the Society for American Baseball Research would retroactively name him the AL Rookie of the Year, an award that didn't yet exist in 1912, and he would win the honor in a landslide. He was that good, that young.

Late in the evening of October 11, 1912, Bedient was sitting on the Red Sox train, keeping to himself, watching the small towns and factories of Connecticut and Massachusetts rumble past his window. All around him, his teammates were bitching and complaining about the Giants, about their spike-first tactics and their haughty attitudes. No one was more furious than Speaker, although Carrigan was just as steamed. Bedient smiled: No two men better represented the subtle, smoldering divide on this team than Speaker, the Southern Baptist from Hubbard, Texas, and Carrigan, the Irish Catholic from Lewiston, Maine, and yet here they were, sharing the same side of an argument for a change, united in their loathing of McGraw and the National League. Wisely, both clubs had decided to take separate trains back to Boston, preventing any of the on-field bad blood from spilling into dining cars.

To make matters worse, the Sox already had survived a harrowing trip together earlier in the day, when frustrated fans along Eighth Avenue had spotted the procession of taxis containing Boston players. At first, the fans good-naturedly booed them, and the Speed Boys just waved back. But then a more sinister element took over, and a few of them started throwing mud, stones, and overripe fruit at the vehicles. Buck O'Brien had actually been hit in the side of the head with one of the rocks, and he was still oozing blood. A few of the players' wives had splattered fruit now covering their designer hats.

"New Yorkers are savages," Smoky Joe Wood sneered.

"Not all of us are," insisted Heinie Wagner, the son of New Rochelle.

Every day, it seemed, the feelings between the teams grew more and more bitter. And none of them did anything to camouflage the contempt.

"The opposing players do not talk to one another anymore except to snarl their remarks," Christy Mathewson had written for his Saturday-morning column, drawing back the curtains of alleged sportsmanship and letting the world know about the bile boiling in the Series. "At the least provocation there is a flare-up. And I suspect we haven't seen the last of the harsh words exchanged between us."

Hugh Bedient had grown up the way millions of others of his generation had, not only idolizing Mathewson as a pitcher but practically worshipping him as a person. Periodically, Mathewson's tips on pitching would appear in the *Sporting News,* and inevitably those issues would be the first to disappear from the newsstands in Falconer. Bedient would study the *Evening Journal* box scores whenever Matty pitched, visualizing what it would be like to pitch in the World Series, what it would be like to be on one of those enormous baseball fields about which he'd read so often but never seen. Well, tomorrow he would know all about that, all right. In Game Five of this series, he would square off with Mathewson, and there wasn't a soul anywhere who believed the day would end well for him. How could it? The Sox had already beaten Matty once; even they knew it would be an awful task to try to replicate. Plus, the Sox were playing with house money: Already up 2–1 in the series, with Smoky Joe Wood set to go at least one more time, they could afford to pitch the kid, let him get his feet wet. Why waste one of the veteran arms against Matty? That would make no sense.

James McAleer, the Red Sox' owner, had ended his uncharacteristic silence by pumping up Bedient to New York writers unfamiliar with his work, telling them, "This boy is going to show the Giants something like they've never seen before. He is in fine trim. He has everything. I never saw a youngster just breaking into the big leagues with so much stuff, not even Mathewson or Walter Johnson. Bedient, in my opinion, will beat the Giants hands down."

Jake Stahl just rolled his eyes when he heard that hyperbole. Typical McAleer, sticking his head—and his lip—where it didn't belong, still thinking he was a player even though he was barely a .250 lifetime hitter in thirteen years in the majors, still thinking he was a manager even though he was nearly a hundred games under .500 in eleven years as a skipper, and had never led a team to a first-place finish. Stahl had been lucky most of the year, avoiding the lengthy losing streak that would inevitably have brought McAleer around the club more. Now he approached Bedient.

"Kid," he said, "remember one thing tomorrow."

"What's that, Jake?"

"You got the best damned baseball team in the world behind you, and we'll all be looking out for you. You don't have to beat the Giants all by yourself."

Bedient, one of the few pitchers ever born who actually knew what it was like to beat a team by himself, shook his head. "I know that, Jake. I'm looking forward to it."

Stahl shook his head, saw how calm and collected his rookie pitcher was, thought to himself: Son of a bitch, it looks like he really is.

Giants fans were the ones in a foul mood now, no matter where you looked, whether it was the fruit-throwing hoodlums on Eighth

Avenue or down-in-the-dumps kids who hung their heads all night after the Game Four loss, whether it was John J. McGraw, still furious at his coaching gaffe, or Christy Mathewson, who understood that an entire city now depended on him to reach back and pitch like it was 1905 again or risk nudging the Giants to the brink of elimination.

In Ironton, Missouri, Charlie Tesreau slowly and sadly read the *Kansas City Star,* the *Arkansas Gazette,* and the *St. Louis Globe,* all of the correspondents coming to the same conclusion, that while young Jeff had fought gamely and pitched admirably, he hadn't been able to shut down the Sox completely on a day when that's what was necessary to beat Smoky Joe Wood. Back home a few hours later reporters found him sitting on his porch, whittling a stick of wood and smoking a corncob pipe. He'd sent his youngest son out in search of the papers first thing, because "I just had a sense my boy had done something awfully special yesterday," but insisted he was still proud of him.

"He'll get them fellers yet," Charlie said. "I know what a pitcher my boy Jeff is and there ain't nobody can beat him when he's right. When the real money's on the line, Jeff'll know how to get it in his pocket, you watch."

By now, the players knew exactly how much real money they were playing for, since after the fourth game the receipts were totaled and the players' portion of the profits were added up to $147,571.70, meaning that the winning team would divide $88,543.02 and the losers would share $59,028.68. That was by far the richest player pool in the history of the World Series, eclipsing 1911 by some $20,000, and that was a point the National Commission quickly put out in front of the public in order to combat whatever lingering gripes the players might have. And those were significant: There were some Giants and some Red Sox who'd wanted to at least have a conversation about a job action before Game Five to make their grievances public. But those feelings had died down as the rancor between the clubs rose, partly because they really wanted to beat each other, partly because they knew they could never match the Commission's public relations machine.

And that was significant. A Commission-friendly writer, Sid Mercer of the *New York Globe*, scolded the players in print before Game Five, warning, "One of these days the world's series will go to smash, and that day will come just as soon as the commercial end is played above the sentimental end, a day which will come sooner than expected if the players keep their selfish behavior going."

And James McAleer, suddenly very visible and very, very chatty, had this to say about the situation:

"This talk about giving the players a share in five instead of four games is absurd. The players went into this with their eyes open. They knew its conditions as they were drawn up. I should think that the players would realize that they have been most liberally treated and leave well enough alone."

Needless to say, when his players were made aware of their owner's contempt-laden commentary, they were none too pleased. "There are a lot of long memories in here," one Sox player whispered to Tim Murnane of the *Globe*.

For McGraw's sake, it was probably best that he had a short memory, because by the time Saturday morning broke and he descended to the Copley Plaza lobby for breakfast, he'd already forgiven himself for needlessly killing the Giants' key rally the day before, reasoning, "It was all about the weather. On a dry day, that ball gets by Yerkes easily and Fletcher can walk home. But the wet grounds slowed the ball up enough for Yerkes to stop it." McGraw conveniently failed to explain how, exactly, it was that he'd suddenly forgotten about the rainstorms that had practically drowned his field, and none of the writers cared to engage him so early in the morning. They rolled their eyes when McGraw told them, "I don't care to reveal who my pitcher today will be," all of them knowing that if McGraw *didn't* throw Mathewson, John T. Brush would rise from his sickbed and fire his manager personally. But the scribes did find it interesting when McGraw turned his attention to the Red Sox, who, like them or not, were certainly sitting in the catbird's seat. McGraw, not surprisingly, disagreed.

"I believe that my team can beat any pitcher that Boston has with the exception of Wood, and I think that the next time we have *him* we will beat him, too. Wood has been pretty lucky to get away with the two games that he has won, and we see the Red Sox as having only one man who can beat us, anyway."

There it was. He'd said it. *A one-man team.* For weeks, the newsmen had been goading McGraw, guiding him, leading him, looking for him to say exactly that. Now that he had, they dutifully sought out selected Red Sox when they all arrived at Fenway Park later that morning. Mostly, the Sox were used to McGraw's bluster, and mostly they laughed it off. All except Heinie Wagner.

"I'll take our one-man team over their twenty-man team," Wagner said.

In fact, he already had, as had everyone else on the Red Sox team. And at quite agreeable odds, too.

In truth, the only team that was having a rougher go of things than the Giants as this Columbus Day dawned was the squad of highpowered Republicans whose mission it was to keep William Howard Taft in the White House. The party had suffered through a devastating summer, selecting Taft over Theodore Roosevelt at its convention in Chicago and then watching helplessly as Roosevelt joined the nascent Progressive Party, redubbing it the "Bull Moose," and surging ahead of Taft in almost every poll conducted since the middle of the summer. Harsh reality was starting to settle in; it would have been hard enough to reelect Taft with a unified party behind him, but with Roosevelt siphoning off millions of would-be GOP votes, Taft's backers were merely hoping the sitting president wouldn't be humiliated, that he wouldn't get shut out in the electoral college or finish—horror of horrors—fourth behind Socialist candidate Eugene V. Debs.

Of course, the one person least bothered by all of this hullabaloo was Taft himself, a man who never much desired the presidency, who in fact had always aspired to the Supreme Court instead, who found following the popular Roosevelt an impossible burden and the fishbowl of the Executive Mansion a suffocating bore. Many were the days that Taft would take refuge at local golf courses throughout southern Maryland and northern Virginia, and despite his 350-pound girth he would gladly prefer walking nine holes to sitting in his office for nine hours. It also seemed, to his round of critics, that he spent most of his time watching baseball games, and while that was a slight exaggeration it was true that he threw out the first pitch at fourteen major-league games during his four years in office: seven in Washington (although he was forced to miss the 1912 opener because he was poring over the grim news coming in from *Titanic* survivors), three in St. Louis, two in Pittsburgh, and one apiece in Chicago and his beloved Cincinnati.

It is probably an urban legend that it was Taft who unwittingly invented the seventh-inning stretch by rising late one game at Washington's American League Park to uncoil his massive frame from the park's small, restrictive, wooden seats; what is a matter of public record is his statement that "any man who would choose a day's work over a day of baseball is a fool not worthy of friendship."

Taft finally won a small victory from his wife this Saturday, after spending most of a week having to make due with dribs and drabs of baseball news thanks to Mrs. Taft's refusal to rearrange their schedule early in the week to accommodate his wish to watch a game at Fenway Park. After a few days' leisure in New England followed by his official review of the naval fleet back in New York, the Tafts were back on vacation (much to the chagrin of anxious campaign officials), floating on the *Mayflower,* the presidential yacht, in the waters off Newport, Rhode Island. The boat was scheduled to be passing in the vicinity of Beverly and Nashon Point at about the time Game Five would be played, and so he arranged that every detail of the game would be relayed to him via U.S. Navy ships posted at the Torpedo Station.

His chief rivals would continue to beat each other up this day, Governor Wilson attending a Knights of Columbus gathering at the Astor Hotel in New York (his remarks coming in a whisper, thanks to campaign-induced laryngitis), Colonel Roosevelt railing in

Chicago that if Wilson were elected the nation's monopolies would find him "a most delightful and harmless companion."

What Taft probably found most amusing about all of this was that even if his chances of reelection were decidedly slim, it seemed most of the country favored his own priorities, because voting registration had commenced at the same time the World Series had, and it was down some 30 percent from 1908. The *New York Times* was far more appalled about this than the President, scolding its readers, "Men of voting age who could get away from their daily labors devoted their leisure to seeing the Giants get walloped a second time by the Boston Americans, or to watching the scores of the game in the bulletin boards and on the tickers. We put the matter plainly to the baseball managers: Is it fair thus to interfere with the welfare of the country?".

Then the *Times* answered its own question.

"The country must be governed, and we cannot change the Constitution just to accommodate the world's series. Hereafter baseball days and registration days must not conflict. Let that be understood."

Taft surely read that sentence with a smile and a hearty chuckle, knowing that soon enough neither upholding the Constitution nor overseeing the government was likely to be his problem any longer.

The day didn't begin auspiciously for the Giants. As they were gathering in the lobby at the Copley Plaza, a patron on one of the upper floors dropped a cigar out an open window and immediately set four of the hotel's awnings ablaze. Chief Meyers, a cigar smoker himself—"It's good medicine," he explained—helped direct the firemen when they arrived, and was so fascinated by their work that he had to be dragged away so he could tend to his own job.

Nor did it proceed well for one of their fiercest rooters. John Wilson, who'd seen Games One and Four at the Polo Grounds, had decided to take in a road game as well, and as an automobile enthusiast he decided to take his brand-new, six-cylinder Stutz for a nice long ride. But as he was headed for Mattapan Square, maybe ten miles outside Boston and less than a mile from a police station, he was halted by two thugs in golf caps who jumped out of nearby roadside bushes. One of them pushed a revolver under his nose.

"Empty your pockets," he snarled. "Wallet. Watch. Jewels. Cash. Everything. Hurry, make it snappy."

Wilson was traveling light. He dropped a few coins from his pocket.

"That's all?"

"All I have otherwise," he said, "is this," and he removed a single ticket to Game Five from his glove compartment. "I'd rather keep it if you don't mind."

The crooks looked at each other.

"I hate baseball," one of them said, pushing Wilson out of the way, hopping into the Stutz, and speeding away. Wilson walked the mile to the police office and filed a report; the cops were nice enough to give him a ride to Fenway Park.

"I hope they find the car," he said from his seat behind the Giants' dugout. "I need a ride home."

Around him was already the most boisterous crowd of the series, so many of the 34,683 having already taken part in parades, parties, or other such festive gatherings celebrating Columbus Day. Street kids had been prowling the avenues around the park, peddling salted peanuts and hot coffee, the beverage of choice on a morning that dawned with frost on the Fenway grass rather than dew. Some of the more entrepreneurial among them arrived bearing pieces of cloth, cardboard, and old linens, selling them to the weary dwellers of lines on Ipswich and Lansdowne Streets for anywhere from a quarter to fifty cents, throwing in a newspaper-stuffed pillow for another two bits.

At seven o'clock they produced the day's first loud roar when a lieutenant groundskeeper showed up for work, bringing with him a bright red pennant with Red Sox stenciled in white, and he carefully opened the door of the ticket shed on Ipswich Street, raised the banner to the top, and officially signaled that Fenway was open for business at last. By 7:30, streetcars started arriving and they wouldn't stop for hours, dropping the folks off and flooding the area every five minutes. By 8 the gates finally opened, and by 10, fully four hours before game time, most all of the seats were already filled, a sight that made James McAleer gasp and at least one of his players grumble.

"If only this could be a best of twenty-one," McAleer sighed, cash registers jangling in his mind's eye.

"Look at this place," Duffy Lewis said to Harry Hooper as they walked on the field, the first of the Sox to do so, greeted by cheers and songs and general merriment. "You mean to tell me we don't deserve a piece of this gate? You think these people are here to see McAleer, McGraw, and Johnson?"

The people were already causing more of a commotion than the four previous crowds put together. Already, the swollen mass in center field had knocked the fence down once, requiring police attention, and it was being pushed near the bursting point again. Soon enough, they would be roused to the brink of rebellion thanks to a stunningly audacious display by, of all people, Fred Snodgrass. Snodgrass had already incurred his manager's wrath once, and invited his teammates' mistrust, when in Game One he had allowed Jeff Tesreau's no-hitter to go up in smoke by misplaying what should have been a routine Tris Speaker fly ball into a triple. He'd also scuffled at the plate, amassing only three hits in sixteen at-bats, and had yet to drive in a run.

While the Red Sox were taking their batting-practice swings, Snodgrass and a few other Giants were wandering around the outfield, taking a few wind sprints, shagging some flies, flipping some of the more battered balls into the stands to grateful souvenir-seeking fans. The crowd was in a fine mood and so were most of the other Giants, despite their predicament in the Series. Snodgrass, though, had come to the park in a dark mood, and when Red Sox fans started riding him about his minuscule .188 batting average, Snodgrass shot right back at them, which all but guaranteed that the Sox fans would be relentless the rest of the day. And they were.

"They call you 'Snow' because your bat's so cold?" one yelled.

At that, a ball came flying into the outfield, just past Snodgrass, and a few men jumped over the vulnerable center-field fence, racing to get the ball. But they had to pass Snodgrass first, and the Giant inexplicably lowered his shoulder and tackled one of them, a shocking blow that set the other fellow scampering for the safety of the stands. But Snodgrass wasn't through. He reached down, picked up the ball in question, and fired it at the trespasser just as he was climbing back into the bleachers, barely missing the man's back, to say nothing of his backside. It hit the fence with a dull thud. Snodgrass laughed as the crowd began to boo, and curse him by name, and by now they were cursing out the rest of the Giants too, and before Snodgrass could continue the debate Larry Doyle came running over, grabbed him by the front of the jersey, and pulled him away.

"What the hell is the matter with you, Snow?" the captain screamed, inches away from Snodgrass's nose. "It isn't hard enough to beat these bastards without inciting a riot? You want to get us bloody killed?"

"They were getting on me, Cap . . ."

"*Getting on you?* Is this your first day in the big leagues, Snow? This is the world's series for *professional* baseball for crissakes. Act like a pro, or I'll tell Mac to find someone who will!"

McGraw himself, sitting in the dugout, didn't yet know why the ballpark was starting to sound venomous, but he had his own problems. Sitting next to Wilbert Robinson, he pointed to a man standing with a gaggle of Royal Rooters, yukking it up and having a jolly good time.

"You know who that is, Robbie?" McGraw asked.

"Who's that, Mac?"

"That's Abe Attell, the featherweight. He was champion until a few months ago. Lost to some fellow named Kilbane. Twenty rounds. Abe's people put some junk in his gloves to make Kilbane go blind, and it didn't take."

"I guess he didn't punch him enough in the face, eh?"

McGraw folded his arms. He knew Attell well through a mutual friendship with Arnold Rothstein, the fastest-rising gambler in New York, with whom McGraw had gone into the pool-hall business.

"Abe's mad at me now," McGraw said. "Yesterday, at the Polo Grounds, this kid comes over to me, tells me someone wants to say hello, I tell the kid to go stuff himself, I'm getting ready for a game. Kid says, 'Come on, Mac, he wants to say hello, is all.' And I tell the kid, 'That's Mr. McGraw to you and to whoever your guy is.' Well, the guy was Abe. Right there, he walks over to the grandstand and puts a grand down on Wood and the Sox, can you believe that?"

"Pretty smart, as it turns out, wasn't it?"

McGraw mumbled something Robinson couldn't quite understand, refolded his arms. "First Cohan makes a killing betting against me, and now this ham-and-egg bum? I mean, shit, if you can't trust your gambler friends, who the hell can you trust?"

McGraw was ready for the game to begin, ready for some redemption, ready to see his team try to square the series at two games all, ready to make Abe Attell, who had already placed another thousand on the Sox, squirm a little. So was Silk O'Loughlin, the first ump to get a second go-round calling balls and strikes. Right on time, right at the stroke of two o'clock, with the clouds lying low over Fenway Park and a chill lying thick in the air, O'Loughlin announced the batteries—Bedient and Cady, Mathewson and Meyers—and cleared his throat.

"Play ball!" he cried through the soupy mist.

The people who gathered around the scoreboard in Times Square and the Playograph in Herald Square were a little more subdued than they'd been, even if there were more of them thanks to its being Saturday afternoon. Giants fans, who only seven years before thought of their team as a bulletproof baseball machine, had grown into a melancholy lot, still rabid for their team but also certain that, at any time, the other shoe was sure to drop on their heads. How to explain the bizarre way the Giants had lost the pennant in 1908, with Merkle forgetting to touch second? How else to explain how the

Giants had been flattened by the Athletics a year earlier thanks to a barrage of home runs (of all things!) off the bat of Frank Baker? How else to explain the way Mathewson suffered through a tie in Game Two of this very series?

"The Giants are a wonderful team," a thirty-year-old clerk named Paul Frazier said at Times Square. "But they are just about the unluckiest team around. And Matty is the king of the bad break. He always pitches just well enough to lose, it seems."

The faraway faithful started their sighing and their grumbling early, as the announcers fed them troubling information right away through their bullhorns in the bottom of the first inning:

"Hooper singles to right field!"

"Speaker singles to left field, Hooper to second!"

Already the crowd was licking its wounds. Such was the lot, and the fate, of Giants fans. Mathewson would get out of the jam, inducing a groundout from Duffy Lewis and striking out Larry Gardner, but that didn't mollify the already disconsolate crowd, stirring where they stood.

"We had our chance," Frazier explained. "We already blew it."

For a long time, that seemed to be a self-fulfilling prophecy. For as down in the mouth as a lot of New Yorkers were, that's how optimistic Red Sox fans were, sparked by the Royal Rooters who seemed intent on singing as many choruses of "Tessie" as it would take to get the job done right. While Mathewson wiggled out of a little more trouble in the second inning, Hugh Bedient looked as comfortable on a World Series mound as if he were in his bedroom back in Falconer, allowing only a couple of walks and mesmerizing the Giants with his drop, a pitch that acted, in essence, like a curveball in reverse, darting down and away from left-handers and down and in against righties. Perhaps it was only right that the first Giant to figure the pitch out was Mathewson, whose own "fadeaway" pitch had acted similarly for years, flummoxing hundreds of hitters. Matty stroked a single to center in the top of the third, New York's first safety, and was pushed to second on a walk to Josh Devore but was stranded right there. You could almost hear the sighs emanating east from Manhattan.

But only for a few moments, because Fenway Park would soon be overtaken by a rollicking, roaring wave of glee. Mathewson tried to fool Harry Hooper with what was essentially a changeup, a version of his fastball that was much, much slower, but Hooper wasn't fooled a bit, blasting a high drive to center field that Fred Snodgrass misjudged, to almost everyone's great delight. Snodgrass took two steps in before realizing it was actually flying over his head, and by the time he recovered it was too late and Hooper was flying around the bases, and the ball was now stuck in a tiny hole in the extreme corner of the bleachers, and by the time Snodgrass could pluck it free Hooper was standing on third with a triple. McGraw was incensed, jumping all over O'Loughlin.

"How is that not a ground-rule double, Silk?" McGraw screeched.

"Mac, you were here same as me every time we've gone over the ground rules," the umpire said. "There's nothing in there about the ball getting stuck in that hole."

"It's common sense, Silk!" McGraw raged.

"Take it up with the Commission," O'Loughlin said. "For now, the runner is safe at third base."

McGraw said he would do just that, not that it would help his man Mathewson any right now. But Steve Yerkes made that a moot point anyway, driving Matty's very next pitch to the gap in left center, a clean double for sure that became a triple instead when Snodgrass failed to get his body in front of the ball and it rolled behind him. Red Sox fans couldn't believe their great fortune: a rally *and* Snodgrass was pissing up his leg; what a parlay! In half a heartbeat, the Red Sox had a 1–0 lead and the Royal Rooters were already hoarse with satisfaction. Mathewson, knowing that it was now up to him to do everything in his power to keep Yerkes planted on third base, took a deep breath, steeled himself, and glared in for a sign. Glaring back was Tris Speaker, his ankle only moderately better, a man who lived for these very types of situations, who despite his physical limitations was still hitting .294 for the Series and was still the last man any pitcher wanted to see when he absolutely, positively needed an out. This was, after all, *Tris Speaker.*

But this was also *Christy Mathewson.*

Twenty-four years later, in 1936, the first-ever class would be inducted into the newly created Baseball Hall of Fame in Cooperstown, New York. Five names were on that inaugural list. Mathewson's was one of them. In 1937, the second group would be selected, and there would be eight names on *that* list; Speaker's was one of *those.* By any measure, this was one of the great moments in baseball history (even if nobody at the time could possibly have known that), one of the twelve times Mathewson would face Speaker in this World Series, the only twelve times that 363 career wins would ever take measure of 3,514 career hits. History in a snapshot.

Mathewson won this one, snapping off a fadeaway that Speaker got on top off, rolling it on the ground to second base. Larry Doyle was playing in, but that didn't stop Yerkes from running toward home, a reckless move that was surely about to change the course of the game, and Mathewson's first great obstacle was about to be cleared.

Only, the baseball bounded right through Larry Doyle's legs.

It took a second for anyone in Fenway Park to realize what they'd just seen. Doyle was having his problems at the plate in the Series, but he was never one to take those woes to the field with him. Later, in consoling Doyle, Mathewson would tell him, "There isn't a player in either league I'd rather have behind me when I needed to get an out." But that didn't help any now. Neither did the stand-up way Doyle would accept responsibility later on, saying, "There's no use apologizing for it because the ball was hit squarely at me and I ought to have fielded it easily. The prisoner pleads guilty."

The facts were the facts: The Red Sox now led 2–0, Fenway was in a frothy fury, and while Red Murray recovered the ball and gunned out Speaker, trying to stretch into second base, the Giants were suddenly in the kind of hole from which Series-losing teams almost never recover.

Mathewson walked off the mound massaging his right arm, a sight that petrified McGraw. "It's nothing," Matty said. "Stiffness. Get me some runs, and I'll be fine."

But that would be no easy task. Because as the Giants were about to find out the hard way—and much to the delight of the Red Sox— the Speed Boys were more than just one arm, more than just one man. Hugh Bedient, it turned out, hadn't won those twenty games in a raffle, or in a lottery. He might not have owned the blow-away stuff that Smoky Joe Wood did at his best, but who did? He was good enough to fool the American League all year. And on this day, he was more than good enough to reduce the Giants' bats to saw-dust.

Watching this kid who didn't yet look old enough to shave have his way with the proud Giants batting order, McGraw could contain his rage no longer. As the Giants trotted back to the dugout at the end of the sixth inning, they'd managed only two scratch singles and three walks off Bedient. They'd been virtually noncompetitive, a sin McGraw never could tolerate in any of his teams.

So he gathered his team around him. And went off on them.

"Suddenly it seems any guy with speed and a little control to put the ball where he wants it can beat you fellows now!" he roared. "It's a disgrace! You disgust me! And you embarrass the whole National League!"

He turned away from them, stalked off to the coaching box, leaving Larry Doyle to hammer the message home.

"Don't get hacked off at the old man," the captain said. "He's right."

Merkle tried to nudge the boys back into McGraw's good graces the best way he could, by lofting a long fly into the temporary stands beyond Duffy's Cliff in left for a ground-rule double, and suddenly the Giants looked alive for the first time all day. Buck Herzog, who'd hit a scalding .571 over the Series' first four games, was next, but he was experiencing his first difficult day and popped up lazily to short-stop, slamming his bat down in disgust as he saw Wagner squeeze it. Then, when Chief Meyers lofted a routine fly ball to Speaker in center, it seemed the Giants were prepared to squander their best scoring chance of the day, but McGraw still had his favorite weapon in reserve. And while Moose McCormick didn't get a base hit, he did send a bullet to third base that ate Gardner up, allowing Merkle to score on the error, drawing the Giants to within 2–1.

They were back in business.

And then they weren't.

Just as quickly as the New York offense sprung to life, it withered again. Bedient was that good. He struck out Devore and Snodgrass in the eighth. He retired Murray, Merkle, and Herzog one-two-three in the ninth, a lay-down that was so inevitable that McGraw never even bothered to move from his spot on the bench, figuring the way the Giants were hitting—or not hitting—it would be silly to occupy the third-base coaching box, and he was right. It wasn't just the results that were shocking, it was the ease with which the kid did it.

"I wonder," Heinie Wagner would ask, through a smile so wide you could fit the whole Fenway outfield in it, "if Mr. McGraw still thinks that we are a one-man team?"

The final out, a weak grounder from Herzog that Yerkes fielded and flipped over to Stahl, unleashed the wildest baseball celebration anyone had ever seen in Boston. Even nine years earlier, when the Pilgrims had won the very first World Series with a Game Eight win over the Pirates at the old Huntington Avenue Grounds, there'd been only 7,455 people in attendance that day. Now, every one of the 34,683 who'd entered the gate were still shoehorned inside, and they all wanted to get a piece of their heroes, wanted to climb onto the field, commune with the park and the team and the fact that everyone now stood only nine innings away from the world's championship. Not everyone got there, but the Royal Rooters all did, and two brass bands did, and the singing and the laughter filled the brand-new ballpark for a full hour after the final out.

In the postgame commotion, hardly anyone noticed Christy Mathewson, who'd quietly stepped out of the dugout to shake hands with Herzog after making the final out, then quietly retreated to the bench to retrieve his mackinaw jacket, fold up his glove, and make the long journey back to the clubhouse and then to the train station.

In his own way, Mathewson was despondent, and it was obvious why. Because as brilliant as Bedient was—and he would never be greater, it would be the highlight of a career that would last for only three more seasons and thirty-nine more victories—Mathewson had, in many ways, been even better. Those two early runs wound up dooming him. But from the moment Speaker slid into second base with the first out of the third inning—the play that started out as Doyle's fateful error—Mathewson faced eighteen Red Sox. And he retired all eighteen.

"It doesn't look like I'll ever win a world's series game again," Mathewson said later on, his demeanor stoic even as his shoulders slumped with evident disappointment. "I threw my arm out eight times there today, and there were a couple of innings when I felt like just leaving it in the box and coming on in without it. The old arm was worn by trying to repeat within three days, and in the earlier part of the game it felt like too much of a load. The muscles were so sore that it seemed as if a knife were shooting through me every time I threw a ball."

He shook his head.

"The Red Sox didn't hit me as hard today as they did the first time," he said, a trace of a smile forming. "At first I couldn't get the kinks out of my arm and I wasn't able to get the ball to where I wanted it to go. It is an admission of age. The old soup bone is not as young as it once was, when I could come back within two days and like it."

The smile disappeared.

"Even so," he said, "we should have won the game."

All around him, there was a sense of inevitability encroaching on Fenway Park. The Giants would have two days to think about their situation, since Sunday ball was still forbidden under New York City's blue laws, so Game Six wouldn't take place until Monday afternoon at the Polo Grounds. The Red Sox would gratefully spend the night in their own beds (after a full evening properly celebrating their impending coronation, of course) before leisurely training over to Manhattan, and already many of them were making arrangements to get home for the winter (after the inevitable victory rally that would be held on Boston Common or in Faneuil Hall or some such appropriate venue).

Perhaps most telling of all, Buck Herzog made a detour before heading into the Giants' clubhouse, walking straight out to center field, where Tris Speaker was limping his way in. Herzog's uniform was as filthy as his reputation as a hard-ass player, but he never minded telling a foe what he thought about him. Even a bitter one.

"You're a hell of a player, Speaker," Herzog said. "You play hard. You play hurt. You play the way I like to play."

Speaker, stunned somewhat, drawled, "Thank you."

Herzog stuck out his hand. "No hard feelings?"

Speaker stuck out his. "None."

The Boston crowd, acknowledging both an overt act of sportsmanship and a covert act of concession, cheered wildly. Someone might have said that it was all over but the shouting, but that wouldn't have been right. The shouting had already begun.

The pressmen stared at the headline.

Sox Push Giants to the Brink

"Depressing, isn't it?" one of them asked.

"Awful," another replied. "Now all we'll have to sell newspapers is that damned crooked cop. Baseball is better."

Up and down Park Row, the heartbeat of New York's newspaper community, the same conversations were taking place, between pressmen, between city editors and reporters, between publishers and managing editors. Two things moved papers better than anything in the city: baseball and blood. Blood, it seemed, never went away. But from mid-October to early March, every year, baseball did. It was always a sad time.

The Becker Trial would get the bigger headlines the next morning, in the *World* and in the *American,* in the *Herald* and the *Tribune* and the *Times* and everywhere else, and it wasn't just because thinking about the Giants made everyone a little more depressed. In what was one of the most electrifying moments anyone could ever remember in the history of New York jurisprudence, a self-confessed "collection man" named Bald Jack Rose—so named because he didn't have a single follicle of hair on his entire body, eyebrows and eyelashes included—all but tied Charles Becker into the electric chair himself with the kind of testimony normally reserved for the final five pages of a pulpy novel.

"I asked Lieutenant Becker why it had taken him so long to get downtown after I had reported to him that Rosenthal had been killed," Rose recalled of the night Beansie went bye-bye. "His answer was that he had gone by the police station. I then asked if he had viewed the body."

The courtroom on Chambers Street was practically out of oxygen by now.

"And what did Lieutenant Becker say?" asked Charles Whitman, the district attorney.

"Becker said, 'It was the most pleasing sight I have ever seen, the sight of that squealing son of a bitch,' " Rose replied. "He said that if you hadn't been standing right by him at the time, Mr. District Attorney, he would have reached down and cut out his tongue and hung it up. 'As a warning to all squealers,' he said."

The pressmen shook their heads.

"Hell of a story," one of them said, pointing at the 6,000-word article that filled half of page one and two full pages inside.

"It better be," the other one said. "It's all we'll have left soon."

Chapter Eight

Monday, October 14, 1912: Game Six

Red Sox lead, 3 games to 1, with 1 tie

NEW YORK—William Howard Taft, Woodrow Wilson, District Attorney Whitman and the Marines can cheer up. Maybe they can be quoted at length after to-day. The world's series, which has been taking the minds of the rooters off the issues at stake next month and seriously interfering with the exploitation of the fleet and the Becker trial, may end this afternoon. And then again, it may not. In which case, everyone wins.

—SID MERCER, *NEW YORK GLOBE*, OCTOBER 15, 1912

FOR THE TWO managers, Sunday's day of rest provided either a welcome respite from the fray or an unwanted spasm of inactivity, depending on which side of the field you happened to be sitting on. Jake Stahl was the toast of the Hub, always a popular mainstay as a player but thought of mostly as a figurehead who'd essentially stayed out of the way while his talented gaggle of Speed Boys ran away and hid from the rest of the American League across most of the summer of 1912. He had been hired as a favored son and he had performed his job admirably, dutifully filling out lineup cards and cajoling the boys in the clubhouse and watching with great delight as Tris Speaker and Smoky Joe Wood blossomed into the kind of once-in-a-generation superstars that can carry a team for months—even seasons—at a time, and, oh by the way, he'd had a fine season himself, hitting .301 and driving in sixty-six runs, no mean feat after spending a full year behind a bank desk and away from the batting cage.

He was no one's idea of a baseball genius. That characterization was left to the John McGraws of baseball, to the Connie Macks, to the Hughie Jenningses and Clark Griffiths and Frank Chances. But baseball has always been a funny game that way: Unlike football, where blustery blowhards tend to rule the day, and unlike basketball, where a savantlike understanding of Xs and Os can occasionally push players to perform at higher planes than those to which their talents are accustomed, the men who run baseball teams rarely have a direct impact on whether their teams win or lose. It is why they are called "managers" while every other sport goes with "coaches." Managers do what the word implies: They are handlers, they are comptrollers, they deal every day with egos and disappointments and injuries. At the end of a baseball day, a manager has little effect if the other guy's pitcher is throwing ninety-nine miles an hour on the black, or if the other guy's cleanup hitter belts three home runs, or if his own shortstop commits four errors.

"Put it this way," Stahl had said in mid-August, when his team was already nine games ahead of the rest of the American League and pulling away fast. "When the boys are hitting it well, or when Smoky Joe is slinging the sphere as he does, I look awfully good at my job. And when we run into Walter Johnson or Ed Walsh and they shut us down, I look like the biggest dope in town."

That, ironically, was one of the reasons Stahl's Red Sox loved playing for him, because he refused to believe he invented the game, or that he was ever going to revolutionize it with innovation. They knew him as a hard-nosed, strong-willed player from his first tour with the Sox, knew that he wasn't going to be a managerial lifer like Mack or McGraw because he had that cushy bank job waiting for him back in Chicago, knew that the moment Jimmy McAleer started giving him more shit than he chose to swallow he'd be back home in

Illinois on the first overnight train. But in this series, Stahl had also pushed every proper button. He'd shown faith in Hugh Bedient. He'd eschewed small ball in favor of big innings, a gamble that had paid off. Refusing to be intimidated by McGraw, he'd told his team to play the way *they* were accustomed to playing, not be sucked in by anything the Giants tried.

And for his troubles, the Sox were now one game shy of glory.

"When you look at the jobs the two managers have done," said Red Sox third baseman Larry Gardner, "I think it's plain to see which has gotten the most out of his team over the first five games, and I salute Manager Stahl for his fine work."

Back in New York, stewing over his team's fortunes, McGraw was hard-pressed to find anyone saying anything remotely as flattering about the way he'd done his job across the past week. No more stoic a source than Walter Johnson had even taken to criticizing McGraw's performance in the syndicated column the star pitcher had written for the break between Games Five and Six.

"It was McGraw's failure to have his men sacrifice that lost Saturday's game in Boston, and it was his utter disregard for the 'suicide' play that lost him Friday's game in New York," the Big Train wrote. "McGraw was expected to pull things in this series that would send the Red Sox team crazy trying to dope out what was coming next. But until now, he has not shown anything out of the ordinary."

Johnson's withering critique did exemplify one of the problems McGraw had with being McGraw: Because of his reputation, because of the high regard his peers held him in (to say nothing of the high regard with which he held himself), he was expected to do what no manager can do: win games by himself, through wizardry, through trickery, through subtle, savvy gamesmanship, as if calling for a hit-and-run can magically make a game turn on its ear. In truth, McGraw wasn't nearly the hands-on control freak many believed he was. He entrusted his players to steal, to bunt, to play the infield in or back with men on third base according to their well-trained judgment. Snodgrass insisted that one year, the only time he ever saw

McGraw use any signal at all was when Dummy Taylor, a deaf pitcher, was on the team and McGraw wanted him to steal.

"So McGraw spelled out S-T-E-A-L in sign language to him," Snodgrass recalled. "Anyone could have picked it up, but McGraw didn't care."

McGraw's graver sin in this series had been his mouth. Never a shy man, especially in regard to his team, especially when there was an opportunity to badger the American League, McGraw had opened himself up to widespread ridicule with some of his observations, the most recent of which had been his claim that the Red Sox were a one-man band incorporating Smoky Joe Wood and a cast of extras.

"It appears that those who pretended to believe that we only have one pitcher now have another guess coming," Tris Speaker gleefully said after Game Five.

"The ridiculous claim of one of the Giants that we are a one-pitcher club has been punctured so badly that we shall hear no more of it," Wood himself said.

McGraw spent some of the Sunday off day at the Polo Grounds, watching groundskeepers water the vast lawn on what would have been a picture-perfect day to play a baseball game. He could sense the city's doom. He was normally a man who couldn't walk two blocks anywhere in Manhattan without being mobbed, a face more familiar than the mayor's. But that morning, he sensed people keeping their distance. And understood why.

"It is now an uphill fight and the odds are all against us," McGraw said as he patrolled the Grounds, looking into the empty grandstand. "But we aren't beaten yet. We've had our backs up against the wall before, and I'm sure of one thing: If we can just catch the Red Sox, we will beat them in the deciding game."

He shook his head, laughed. How bad was it for his team? Even on this day, when there was no game scheduled, the Giants had managed to lose a bit of ground. The National League that morning upheld a protest by the Pirates that a week earlier, a game-winning hit that the Cubs' Dick Cotter had collected had occurred after Cotter batted out of order; the NL awarded the Pirates the win, which reduced the official margin by which the Giants had won the pennant from ten and a half games to ten.

"It really is about time," McGraw said, "that we started getting some of the breaks, don't you think?"

He had no way of knowing, as he strolled in the silence of the Polo Grounds, just how big a break he was about to enjoy. He would find out soon enough.

Jake Stahl was mocking McGraw's methods, not emulating them, when he'd said after Saturday's game, "I have a good sense that I'm going to go with Buck O'Brien on Monday afternoon in the Polo Grounds. If that doesn't work, who better to serve as an insurance policy than the great Smoky Joe Wood?"

Nobody believed that, of course, least of all Stahl himself, certainly not Joe Wood. The off day between Game Five and Game Six was almost a divine gift of Providence for the Red Sox, it seemed, because it would allow Wood the second day of rest he would need to pitch Monday, which was exactly as it should have been. No single player had done more to push the Red Sox within sight of their first championship in nine years than Wood had, so it was right that Wood would get the first shot at sealing the deal. Even the newsmen who wrote down Stahl's quote could almost see the manager winking at them.

Why would you start anyone else?

Joe Wood himself knew the answer to that as well as anyone: nobody. And while Stahl hadn't exactly told him he would get the ball Monday afternoon, he hadn't told him otherwise, either. His teammates all believed it would be Wood on Monday, and such was the unblinking belief they had in that magical right arm that almost all of them took care to make important telephone calls all day Sunday, informing all of their loved ones—brothers, best friends, bookies—that Wood was surely to be the man.

Wood definitely did. His brother, Paul, would be at the Polo

Grounds, and so he would have access to the local businessmen ply-
ing their wares in the grandstand. Paul would put down a C-note for
himself and something on behalf of his brother. Betting on Smoky
Joe, Paul Wood conceded, almost felt like stealing. Almost.

And the word soon filtered to New York: It would be Wood start-
ing Monday, no two ways about it. On the Sunday-afternoon Red
Sox train, Wood had bumped into Mark Roth, a reporter for the
New York Globe, in the dining car.

"How's the old wing?" Roth asked Wood.

"Ah, I'm hearing rumors that there's something the matter with
my arm," Wood said, smiling, rubbing his right shoulder. "They
probably mean the left one. I will be in there showing them just the
same tomorrow."

All around them, giddy Red Sox were already speaking of off-
season plans, some of them armed with pencil and paper, the better
to calculate their individual share of the $88,543.02 winner's take,
speaking of the down payments they planned to make, the investment portfolios they hoped to broaden, the farm equipment they
hoped to purchase, the vacations they hoped to take.

In their midst was Jimmy McAleer, whose own wheels were turning madly, interrupted only by a fan who recognized him on the
westbound train, shook his hand, and engaged him in a brief conversation.

"I suppose you're hoping the series will go a couple more tie
games and then three for a decision," the fan said, joking about the
very thing McAleer himself had mentioned a few days earlier, his
own wish for an endless best-of-twenty-one.

"I do not," said McAleer, sounding almost indignant at the
notion. "I want it to end tomorrow in New York."

The fan was insistent. "But look at all the money it would mean to
you."

"Ah, that's all right," McAleer said. "You see, last spring I made a
date to go deer hunting up in Wisconsin, starting from Chicago on
October 18, and I don't want to miss a day of that trip. Better to get
it over with quickly."

The fan shook McAleer's hand and went on his way, but he'd made a good point, one that McAleer had pondered already. After all, he'd been the one who'd stared with wonder at the swollen Fenway Park bleachers before Game Three. He'd been the one who'd marveled at the vast expanse of grandstand seats at the Polo Grounds before Game Four, remarking to one New York newspaper, "How grand would it be to play games in front of this many people all the time?"

Yes, McAleer's wheels were grinding.

And they carried him straight to where Jake Stahl was sitting on the train. Stahl, who even on days when he was in a good mood could barely disguise his contempt for McAleer, quietly nodded as McAleer passed, then stopped, then slipped into the seat next to his. Stahl set aside his newspaper.

"Let me ask you a question, Jake," McAleer said.

"You're the boss," Stahl said. "Ask whatever you like."

"I saw in the papers that you were thinking of pitching Buck O'Brien."

"Yup. That's what I told the papers."

"Who are you *really* pitching tomorrow?"

Stahl smiled conspiratorially. Hell, he'd already made a few calls himself, told some folks who could use such information what his plans were. Would it kill him to let the owner in on the secret, in case *he* had a few calls he wanted to make?

"Why, who else would I go with," Stahl whispered, "but Joe Wood?"

McAleer nodded. Stahl figured he'd done his loyal duty as a diligent employee. He started to snap his newspaper back open. But McAleer hadn't gotten up.

"Well," McAleer said, "let's talk that over a bit, can we?"

"Talk *what* over a bit?" Stahl asked. Suddenly, he was terribly uncomfortable.

"Well, remember, Buck O'Brien pitched really well in the third game of the series, and had his heart broken by Marquard."

"I remember. I was there."

"He won twenty games for us this year."

"I was there for every one of them. And for every one of the thirty-six that Joe Wood has won for us so far, too."

"Well, I was just thinking. If O'Brien holds the Giants to two runs again, I think we can win."

"Or he could get cuffed around. I've seen him do that, too, Jim."

"And what if he does? If he should lose it, the worst that could happen is you'll have Joe on an extra day's rest, stronger than ever . . ."

"And you'd get an extra home game."

McAleer stopped, didn't acknowledge the comment. Stahl peered at the owner, disbelief in his heart. *Is he really asking me to do what I think he's asking me to do?*

"But all the boys are expecting Wood to pitch," Stahl said. "Joe told me he's ready. And he insisted that he wants to pitch."

"He just *plays* for this team. *You* manage it," McAleer said, before adding the kicker. "And *I* run it."

There were several uncomfortable minutes of silence. Finally, McAleer rose, turned one last time to Stahl.

"Look," he said. "Think it over. I think O'Brien deserves another chance, is all. And don't forget, we'd always have Wood to go again in Boston, and what's more of a sure thing than that? We'll talk again in New York."

And with that, McAleer was gone, leaving his manager alone to stew in silence and ponder his options. Stahl could defy his boss, but that didn't seem to be a reasonable response. He could threaten to resign, but if McAleer accepted how could Stahl spend the rest of his life knowing he'd walked away from a ballclub sitting one win away from a championship? He could try to incite the players, alert them to what was happening, but they had already seen how fruitless it was to fight city hall when you were a baseball player standing at loggerheads with an owner; besides, the last thing any manager ever wanted was to reveal to his team just how little authority he truly had over them. He felt awful, he felt angry, he felt guilty: Just across the aisle sat Joe Wood, cocky and so filled with the confidence of youth.

There was zero doubt he would mow the Giants down tomorrow if handed the ball. *None.*

A few hours later, after they'd all checked into the Bretton Hall Hotel, Stahl walked up to the top floor, where McAleer and his new bride were staying. McAleer let him in his suite.

"So," McAleer said. "Are we on the same team here?"

"No, Jim," Stahl said. "We're not. We are a team that's ready to win now. Joe Wood thinks he's getting the ball tomorrow. The team thinks he's getting the ball tomorrow. They're so close to the winner's money they can taste it."

"You're telling me your club can't win one of the next three games?"

"I'm saying it's ready to win right now."

"Then win it. With Buck O'Brien."

Stahl knew there was nothing else to say. He nodded at McAleer, nodded at Mrs. McAleer, and started to leave the suite. McAleer called him back.

"One last thing, Jake."

Perfect. What now?

"Don't tell the boys tonight. There's no need for them to know anything that'll affect their night's sleep."

"What about O'Brien? He should know what his assignment's going to be tomorrow. Because it's a doozy now."

"No need to make him extra nervous, is there?"

Stahl shook his head, walked out of the suite, and started trundling downstairs, beyond furious. When he arrived on the floor he shared with his players, he thought about knocking on O'Brien's door, decided not to. Which was just as well.

Because depending on what exactly the time was, O'Brien was on either his fifth or his sixth beer of the night. And wouldn't have been much inclined to slow down.

The Royal Rooters were also squeezing as much festivity as they could out of Sunday night, with Nuf Ced McGreevy and John

Fitzgerald leading the merriment (for who better to be able to turn a dry town wet than a bartender and a mayor?). Some six hundred of them had boarded a 4 o'clock train and six hours later were descending on the Elks Club, where most of them were lodged and all of their beer was iced. So certain were the Rooters that Monday would be the day for which they'd so long sacrificed their vocal cords that their ranks had swelled by double just in the twenty-four hours since the Sox had won Game Five, and Honey Fitz had to personally call Garry Herrmann in order to ensure all six hundred could be accommodated.

"You'll have no worries here," Herrmann reported. "Last we checked, there's no lines at the Polo Grounds. I believe the Giants fans are already looking forward to 1913."

"Magnificent!" Fitzgerald exclaimed, and he officially took over the job of organizer from Johnny Keenan, charging fifteen bucks a head and guaranteeing train fare, a warm bed at the Elks Club, some cold beer once they got there, and a ticket to the coronation Monday at the Polo Grounds.

Those Giants fans who hadn't prepared concession speeches pointed hopefully to the Red Sox' own history, for in 1903 those very same Boston Americans had fallen behind three games to one to the Pittsburgh Pirates, then had rallied in splendid fashion to win four straight to capture the very first World Series ever contested. There were two asterisks that should have been attached to that loyal logic, of course. First, that Series was a best-of-nine, so the Red Sox were never as close to elimination—and the added burdens those pressures brought to bear—as the Giants now stood. More important, there had long been widespread suspicion that at least two, if not more, of those Series games had been, shall we say, "prearranged" by players on both sides who'd only been given vague suggestions as to how they would be compensated for playing the Series. Boston players and Pittsburgh players had merely been promised a "percentage of the final receipts." And it stood to reason that the more games contested in the Series, the higher that total would be.

Those were the dark old days, before the National Commission had all but eliminated the shady element from the Series by sticking fast to its policy of paying out only the first four games. Now these games were above reproach. Or so they said.

Still, history was history. "And there's no time like the present," Jeff Tesreau said Sunday, "to repeat the history of the 1903 world's series, is there?"

After spending most of his Sunday in solitude, John McGraw was happy to see his Game Six pitcher, Rube Marquard, show up late in the afternoon to loosen up his arm. He was less pleased by what he saw next: Marquard rubbing his shoulder, unable to get it loose, unable to get any life on his practice pitches. Already in a dark mood, the manager was turning downright morose.

"What else can befall the Giants?" he asked a reporter. "Why us?"

But Marquard tried to reassure his boss, calling him at home later on, saying, "Really, it'll be fine. It always hurts more when there's not a real game to be played." And later still, when a few sportswriters cornered him at his Harlem home, Marquard insisted that he would pitch through whatever ailed him: "The old arm flies right off at the shoulders if necessary to beat these alleged Boston sluggers," he said. "McGraw stuck with me when I was about as popular as the measles and I still owe him for that. This is the day that I will forever put the quietus on that '$11,000 Lemon' title." For the rest of his life, Marquard never would forgive the newspapers for dubbing him with that sour nickname.

But even those reassurances hadn't lightened McGraw's mood, as he'd had a contentious conversation with the members of the National Commission early in the day. He did score one small victory: The Commission agreed that the ball Steve Yerkes had hit into the small opening in center field in Game Five should have been ruled a ground-rule double and not a triple, and Herrmann said he would instruct the umpires that if another game were played at Fenway Park, they should honor that switch. But the other matter on the agenda had really gotten McGraw's goat. McGraw had assumed that if his team won Game Six at the Polo Grounds, and then won

Game Seven back at Fenway, they would quite reasonably receive the final game at home, keeping with the alternate games in alternate cities. "Maybe I am being too optimistic," McGraw said, "but how else am I supposed to think? Our backs are to the walls but our bodies aren't in the grave just yet."

The Commission, however, ruled that in the event of an eighth and deciding game, there would be a coin flip held to determine who should get the home-field advantage. So, somehow, in a World Series in which the Giants were originally scheduled to get four of the seven games at home, in the Polo Grounds, there stood a reasonable chance that they would get only *three* home games while the Red Sox were granted *five*. *And you want to talk about breaks . . . ?*

"By what standard do you consider that fair?" McGraw asked Herrmann.

"The tie caused a lot of problems," he was told.

"The tie caused *me* a lot of problems, and it caused my nine a lot of problems," McGraw ranted. "As far as I can tell, it was the best damned thing that ever happened to the Boston Americans. There's no way to justify granting them extra home games!"

But McGraw quickly learned the lessons his players already had: The National Commission was judge, jury, and bailiff. They ruled the whole operation.

"It's nonsense," McGraw seethed. "Pure nonsense. Nothing more."

He went to sleep angry, awoke even angrier, hoping his team would be just as furious. Dubious, in truth, that it would make a damned bit of difference if Smoky Joe Wood was on top of his game.

The word spread quickly, as bad news often does. Jake Stahl was the first man in the lobby for breakfast, and not long after that he saw Joe Wood arrive downstairs with Tris Speaker, the two of them already bearing the confident gait of champions.

"Joe," Stahl said. "I need a word. Alone."

Speaker shook his head, said he'd get a table, left the two men alone, and watched from a distance as his best friend's jaw seemed to collide with the parquet floor. He saw Stahl put his hand on Wood's shoulder, what looked like a consoling gesture. Did someone die? Is someone in his family hurt? By the time Wood reached the table, Speaker was genuinely concerned.

"Are you OK?" Speaker asked.

"Not really, no," Wood said, still sounding stunned. "I'm not pitching today."

"What do you mean you're not pitching today? Who's pitching today, Collins?"

Wood shook his head. "O'Brien."

The fury inside Speaker was immediate and it was palpable. O'Brien? The last anyone had seen O'Brien, as everyone else was heading up to bed the night before, he was on his way out, into the New York night, a few beers in him already and surely plenty more to come. O'Brien? Had Stahl lost his mind? *No, there's no way Jake made this decision. No way in hell.*

"This is McAleer," Speaker said. "This has to come from him. Has to."

Wood shook his head in agreement. "Greedy son of a bitch. Jake said it was his call, but he couldn't look me in the eye when he said it. This ain't his call."

And across the next hour, as player after player came bubbling into the cafeteria, the news would hit and their shoulders would slump and the bile in their throats would thicken. The last one downstairs was O'Brien, his eyes red and his skin clammy, a view Stahl saw clearly when he broke the news to him.

"You're going today, Buck," Stahl said.

"Going where?" the pitcher asked.

Perfect, Stahl thought. Just bloody perfect.

They were all oblivious. The happy Royal Rooters, all six hundred of them, who'd repeated the march up Broadway that had made them famous before Game One. The low-key Giants fans, who found plenty of good seats available when they walked from the elevated trains and saw small lines at the Speedway ticket entrance. The folks preparing the scoreboards in Times Square and Herald Square and Madison Square Garden in New York, where the crowds were expected to be quiet and sparse, and the ones readying the stages in Boston Common and Washington Street, where police were expecting the most raucous local gathering since the Boston Tea Party (no exaggeration).

Paul Wood was among the unaware, which was just as well, because there was nothing he could do about the money he'd already wagered on his brother and his baseball team. Certainly compared to the Red Sox themselves, who'd spent the morning stewing over winner's shares they'd already spent, to say nothing of personal wagers that suddenly seemed less than a sure thing. Joe Wood tried to send a hopeless message to his brother when he took the field at the Polo Grounds wearing a catcher's mitt, having a spirited catch with utilityman Clyde Engle. If it occurred to Paul or anyone else that this was unusual, the starting pitcher not throwing in the bullpen, it was probably muted because *nobody* was warming up in the bullpen. At one o'clock—less than ninety minutes before the scheduled starting time—there was no sign of Buck O'Brien. Same thing at 1:15. And again at 1:30. It wasn't until 1:45 that O'Brien staggered onto the field, walked slowly to the bullpen, and began his workday.

Joe Wood just glared at him, shook his head, returned to his catch, his fury building with every peg to Engle.

Marquard, meanwhile, could still feel a whisker of stiffness in his shoulder but figured he could live with it. Larry Doyle, spying him in the bullpen, yelled, "How's the wing treating you?"

"My arm is sore and kinky, but I believe it will work out all right," he said. "And if I'm wrong, I guess I'll have quite a long time to recover."

"All of us will," the captain said, winking.

The day was dark and foreboding, a heavy blanket of clouds catching Bill Klem's eye as he watched the end of pregame practice.

Klem knew how lucky everyone had been with the weather, knew that the last thing anyone on either side needed was another day away from the ball field, especially with the stakes as high as they were now. That's what his concern was, and where his mind was focused when he absently accepted the lineup cards from Jake Stahl and John McGraw and then prepared himself to call out the batteries. The startling information made him do a double take.

"Hey, Jake!" the umpire called. "You sure you got the right names on here?"

Stahl, shaking his head ruefully, nodded.

"Marquard and Meyers for the Giants!" Klem announced, to scattered applause from the pessimistic gathering of Giants fans that would total only 30,622, leaving close to 10,000 seats unsold and unoccupied.

"And for the Red Sox," Klem bellowed through the bullhorn, "O'Brien and Cady!"

The ballpark gasped. The Giants, as one, snapped their heads to the bullpen, where at last they noticed that it was Buck O'Brien, not Smoky Joe Wood, who was getting in his final few tosses out there. Up in the press box, the buzz was instant and the verdict practically unanimous.

"Son of a bitch," more than a couple of scribes surmised. "The fix is in."

Even the Red Sox, who'd been steeled to the news earlier than anyone else, seemed taken aback. Or maybe that was merely the collective look of twenty-two men convinced they'd just had their wallets stolen.

Bill Klem wasn't interested in any of that. He was interested in getting his ballgame in before the storm clouds could have their say.

"Play ball!" he yelled.

William Howard Taft was back in New York, back on the banks of the Hudson River, reviewing the whole of the U.S. Naval fleet for the amusement of an assortment of honored international guests, but he made no pretense about where he'd rather be—and with which historic engagement, other than his own, he'd prefer to be engaged—which was about a hundred blocks north and a few avenues east. He'd taken great delight in the Red Sox' victory in Game Five, the reports streaking in constantly to the *Mayflower*, and afterward he'd asked his aides to furnish him with a full accounting of runs, hits, errors, and pitching statistics. Told that the Red Sox rookie, Bedient, had outdueled the mighty Mathewson, the President had roared and said, "See? The experts don't always know who's going to win and who's going to lose." And then, after a pause, "Or who's going to finish third." Taft took consolation that the sailors in all the boats he was reviewing would be getting wireless updates from the games. He would be kept abreast of the game inning by inning.

That same afternoon, Woodrow Wilson was home in New Jersey tending to his own sporting jones, watching the Princeton Tigers practice football. Theodore Roosevelt, meanwhile, had just arrived in Milwaukee, at the Hotel Gilpatrick, where he'd enjoyed a filling lunch with aides and where he hadn't noticed that a solitary figure on four separate occasions over forty minutes had tried to gain entrance to the dining room. And on all four occasions the man, a New York City saloonkeeper named John Flammang Schrank, was told that he would have to wait until later before he could see the Colonel, who was busy and wasn't to be disturbed.

As the afternoon papers had already dutifully reported, as bad as most Giants fans thought their lot was, they surely hadn't had nearly the terrible day that another Giants fan named Charles Becker had already had, even before Marquard's first pitch was stroked to center for a single by Henry Hooper, eliciting one of the earliest groans the Polo Grounds had ever witnessed. One of Becker's former friends, Bridgy Webber, the operator of an uptown opium den, told the hushed courthouse that the day after Beansie Rosenthal was gunned down, he'd been riding in Becker's car and Becker had calmly declared, "If I had seen that squealing Rosenthal I'd have got out and backed him up against a wall and shot him." Becker himself laughed at the allegations the moment they fell out of Webber's mouth, but no one else found anything about the proceedings terribly amusing, least of all John William Goff, the judge, who announced shortly thereafter that he knew his courtroom was overrun each day with gangsters, hoods, and thugs.

"These people, whoever they are, have even obtained my private telephone number and have been calling me up almost every hour of the night since the trial started," Goff declared.

John F. McIntyre, Becker's defense attorney who'd been angling for a mistrial all week, immediately jumped up and screamed, finger pointing skyward, "And I have received death threats as well!" and to the judge: "I can show them to you!"

"I don't care to see them," Goff sniffed. "Next witness."

Marquard seemed determined to terrify himself, his manager, and the 30,000 people who still believed the Giants weren't dead yet. After Hooper's leadoff single he'd picked him off first right away, eliciting a nervous cheer from the faithful, but after then issuing a walk to Tris Speaker, Speaker showed that an extra day's rest had done wonders for his ankle, stealing second and setting the Sox up nicely. Marquard nonchalantly wiped the rubber with his spikes, reached into his back pocket for his pouch of tobacco, and stuffed his cheeks with a huge chaw, but the act was a thin one. He was visibly shaken, enough so that McGraw paid a quick visit to the mound, hoping to quell his nerves. It worked. Marquard retired Duffy Lewis on a fly ball to left and issued a long sigh of relief as he walked back to the dugout, nearly choking on his chaw. "The most terrified I've ever been on a ballfield," he would later say, describing that first inning of Game Six.

Now it was his teammates' turn to feel the butterflies. Yes, they felt like they'd been spared the electric chair when they saw Smoky Joe Wood put on his mackinaw jacket and retire to the dugout bench, but now there was even more pressure on them, somehow. They'd already lost to one rookie, Hugh Bedient. How would it look to lose to *another* rook, in the game that could shut them down for the winter? How would they possibly explain *that* away? McGraw, who wasn't usually in the business of delivering rah-rah speeches, nevertheless gathered his men around him before the bottom of the first and tried to fill them with the same spirit, the same rage now coursing through *his* veins. "Look," he told them. "*They* still have to figure out a way to beat *you*, and you're the best damned team I ever saw. Play like *you* believe that, too."

He didn't ever have to tell Larry Doyle that twice. With one out, the Giants' captain singled and stole second, pounding his hands together when he narrowly beat Hick Cady's throw, dancing off second base, trying to unnerve O'Brien, whose nerves, unbeknownst to Doyle, were plenty jangly. Still, O'Brien fanned Fred Snodgrass (suddenly unable to get out of his own way) and looked to be in good shape as he threw two quick strikes to Red Murray. But Murray fought off an inside fastball, rolled it on the slow turf toward Wagner at short, and beat the throw. Now there rose a desperate din from the grandstands and the bleachers, Giants fans offering up this final request for a miracle. Fred Merkle stepped to the plate, first and third, two outs. By now, everyone could see that O'Brien was vulnerable. Murray had thrice stepped out of the box to try to throw off the pitcher's timing, to great effect. Now Doyle darted and danced off third base, and Murray shouted illegibly at him from first, and O'Brien, almost visibly terrified that the Giants would try to pull off a double steal, kept throwing over to first to keep Murray close to the base.

Finally, O'Brien seemed to focus in on Merkle, and he brought his arms to a set position, and he swung his arms high over his head and . . . stopped. He just *stopped*: suddenly, stunningly, *inexplicably*. It took the Giants a while to realize—or even believe—what they'd just seen O'Brien do. No pitcher had ever committed a balk in the World Series before, but after a few awkward seconds it became plain to everyone that that's precisely what O'Brien had done. It was Wilbert Robinson who finally screamed "BALK! He balked! You can't do that!" before McGraw also started screaming at Klem, "Did you see that Bill? Did you see that?" Klem had seen it, and so had Billy Evans on the basepaths. Klem waved Doyle home, and Rigler signaled Murray to second. It was 1–0, Giants, and most of the fans had no idea what had happened, or why it happened, would have to read in the next day's paper the official explanation for what a balk was—according to the rulebook, "Any motion made by the pitcher while in position to deliver the ball to the bat without delivering it."

Whatever worked. It was good enough for a run. And good enough to completely destroy Buck O'Brien, whose last defenses crumbled after committing one of the greatest gaffes to that point in Series history. Fred Merkle, who surely kept a soft spot in his heart for fellow sufferers of baseball brainlock, nevertheless piled on immediately, doubling to deep right field, scoring Murray for a 2–0 lead. Buck Herzog followed with a booming double to left, plating Merkle for a 3–0 cushion.

McGraw was ecstatic. "He's gone now, boys!" he roared. "He's all done!"

Now, for the first time all Series, McGraw could taste blood, and he went for the kill. After Chief Meyers continued the assault with a single, sending Herzog around to third, the Giants' manager called for a double steal, a shocking decision with the slow-footed Meyers on base. But Cady seemed just as shaken as his pitcher, and his throw to second was late, Herzog dashing home when Yerkes couldn't get the ball out of his glove. Four-nothing. And even Art Fletcher got in the action, singling home Meyers with the fifth run before showing mercy on O'Brien and getting himself picked off first to end the deluge.

The inning had taken thirty-three minutes to play, and it had completely turned the World Series upside down. For five games, the Giants and Red Sox had circled each other like wary heavyweights, neither seemingly capable of getting more than a run or two ahead of the other. Yet here the Giants were now, up 5–0, with a twenty-six-game winner on the mound and a rejuvenated team bursting out of the home dugout. It was a sight to behold.

Which contrasted nicely to the sight of Buck O'Brien staggering off the field. Even the Royal Rooters—still bug-eyed from the shock of not seeing Joe Wood out there in a clinching game—felt no sympathy for the battered Buck. "Hey, Irish!" one of them screamed in his direction. "When did old Johnny McGraw sign you up to play for them? Back in the old country?"

None of O'Brien's teammates consoled him when he walked to the dugout, alone, slamming his mitt on the ground, completely numb to what had just happened. In the course of about six hours he'd woken with a hangover the size of the Polo Grounds outfield, then had his brains handed to him by the Giants. Not a great day so far, and it would only get worse. The Sox did scratch out two runs in the top of the second on a double by Engle, Wood's throwing partner (who'd pinch-hit for O'Brien, mercifully ending the baseball portion of his workday), briefly throwing a scare into Marquard (and forcing McGraw to tell Mathewson, "You'd better get your arm loose, just in case"). But the Speed Boys would only get one other man as far as third base the rest of the way. Their hearts simply weren't in it any longer. The final was 5–2. It felt much, much worse than that.

The Royal Rooters, to their eternal credit, tried to make the best of what had been a long, fruitless, and altogether raw afternoon, all six hundred of them making for the field in lockstep order, the band blaring as enthusiastically as it had during the first inning. Even Giants fans, pleasantly surprised by their season's remaining intact, showed their admiration by bypassing the early elevated trains heading back downtown so they could watch and listen. They saw the Rooters march for the Boston bench, saw them execute a war dance around several of the players who had not yet run for cover, and then started for the entrance gate in an emulated collegial snake dance.

Zigzagging to right and left, the Rooters passed in review. On the home plate they loitered for a moment while McGreevy addressed them:

"Tomorrow!" he began, and there he ended too, for the crowd agreed with him and carried out the slogan with a thousand voices.

"Tomorrow we'll show them!" they cried in response.

And in the middle of it all stood Honey Fitz, his voice still clear and strong, his spirit still unbowed. Before leading the procession off to the train station, he declared, "This only delays the results of the series and the reception of the Red Sox as champions by one day. Fear not!"

The Rooters' postgame loyalty oaths had briefly taken the attention away from another critical dance taking place just outside first base as soon as Heinie Wagner grounded out to third to end the game. But once the crowd behind first realized what was happening, they piled up ten deep behind the participants. A child, craning his neck, asked, "What the heck is the big deal there?"

"It's the coin toss," he was told, "to see where the decisive game will be played."

Garry Herrmann held a shiny 1912 half-dollar piece in his hands, and he made a great show of displaying it to both men, showing them the Liberty Head, or "Barber," on the front, the eagle with its wings extended and head facing left on the back. Herrmann then flipped the fifty-cent piece to McGraw, ordered him to toss it in the air.

"Mr. Stahl," Herrmann said, "call it in the air."

At its apex, Stahl yelled, "Tails."

It landed, and a few hundred people strained for a better look. All they really needed to do was look at McGraw's face, where the joy of victory had already been replaced by the anguish of another bad break.

"Tails it is!" Herrmann said, before turning to the crowd and offering with a half-smile, "Mr. Stahl will now decide where the eighth game of this series will be played, should it be necessary to play it."

Before Stahl could say a word, McGraw piped up: "Our grounds are available to you if you'd like them," eliciting a laugh from the disappointed crowd, who now understood that no matter what happened in Game Seven, New York City had seen its last baseball game of the year.

Stahl wasn't smiling.

"We shall play the game in Boston, Mr. McGraw," he said, "although I hope not to have to play it at all."

Stahl turned, the happiness of winning the coin flip hardly easing the anger he was feeling at the game he'd just managed, and all the little dramas that had led up to it, and who do you suppose Stahl saw holding court in front of a few Boston writers? Jimmy McAleer. And the dumb son of a bitch couldn't even hide his smile. He eavesdropped a little on his way back to the clubhouse.

"There is one thing to be thankful for and that is that we didn't pitch Wood, who might have been beaten," McAleer said. "That fact that we didn't make more than two runs off Marquard and probably would've been shut out if it wasn't for his error in the second will convince anyone that the saving of Wood for tomorrow was a wise move."

Jesus . . .

"There are no excuses for O'Brien," McAleer continued. "He was in good physical condition and anxious to pitch. But it turned out he had nothing at all in the box. Still, we haven't lost yet. You'll be hearing from us tomorrow."

McAleer stuck around for a good long while. Stahl didn't. He had to get to the train before he did something even dumber than not throwing Smoky Joe Wood.

Later that night, in Wisconsin's largest city, newsboys hawked evening editions of the *Milwaukee Sentinel* outside the Hotel Gilpatrick, the massive crowd waiting for Theodore Roosevelt to emerge also eagerly awaiting the results of that day's baseball game and that day's developments from the Charles Becker Trial, which had quickly seized the national curiosity.

It was just after 8 o'clock when the Colonel walked out of the hotel, waved vigorously at the delighted crowd, and stepped smartly toward his waiting automobile. As he did, a short, stocky man—later identified as John Flammang Schrank—fired a pistol toward him. The wild-eyed crowd instantly seized the gunman, and cries of

"Lynch him! Kill him!" went up before Roosevelt, relieved to be unhurt, cried out from behind an open window, "Do not hurt him! He is sick! Get him to the hospital!" before his own car sped away, toward the Milwaukee Auditorium where he was due to make a speech. It was after the car was about four blocks clear of the shocking mob that John McGrath, one of Roosevelt's secretaries sitting across from the former president in the limousine, suddenly lifted a quivering finger.

"Look, Colonel," McGrath said. "There is a hole in your overcoat."

Roosevelt found the hole, unbuttoned the big brown army coat he had over it, and thrust his hand beneath. When he withdrew, his fingers were stained with blood.

"Well, then," Roosevelt said, "it would seem that I have been shot."

"To the hospital at once!" McGrath yelled at the driver.

"Nonsense," Roosevelt said. "I have a speech to deliver. And I shall deliver it." And the car, despite howls of protest from the backseat, proceeded on to the Auditorium.

CHAPTER NINE

Tuesday, October 15, 1912: Game Seven

Boston leads, 3 games to 2, with 1 tie

> BOSTON—Dawn broke today on the restless, shattered
> slumber of two red-eyed, nerve-racked clams who were to
> rise again and face their seventh fight for the championship
> of the world. There is glory enough in a fight like this—and
> the only pity is that one must lose where another must win.
> Both have fought with too much heart and courage to miss
> the laurel which only one can wear . . .
>
> —GRANTLAND RICE, *NEW YORK EVENING MAIL*,
> OCTOBER 16, 1912

THE FORMER PRESIDENT was in no mood to be told what to do,
even now, as blood oozed from his jacket, as the shocked men
in his automobile pleaded with him to proceed on to a hospital so
doctors could tend to his wounds. Nonsense, Theodore Roosevelt
proclaimed. Though pain was just now starting to manifest itself in
his breast, Roosevelt grunted and reached into a pocket of his coat
and retrieved two items that made even this usually impossible-to-
impress man gasp.

"Well," he said. "What do you know."

In his hands he held a steel eyeglass case as well as the fifty-page
speech he was prepared to deliver. Both had small holes in them, and

Roosevelt understood that the case and the speech had blunted the bullet's path, and had saved his life, at least for the time being. By now, Roosevelt's motorcade had arrived at the Milwaukee Auditorium and the candidate had been hustled into a dressing room just off the stage, close enough that he could hear the commotion of twenty thousand excited citizens waiting to be whisked to a higher plane by the power of his words. But first he would have to audition before a pair of doctors, Scurry Terell and John Stratton, who told him in the strongest words they could summon that the place for the Colonel right now was an emergency room, not an auditorium. But Roosevelt would return their serve twice as hard.

"I will deliver this speech or die," he said. "One or the other."

He was the boss. They relented, shaking their heads at the man's pain threshold, listening as in the adjacent main room Henry F. Cochems, Milwaukee's Progressive Party chairman, introduced Roosevelt, waiting for the explosion of glee to die down before informing the multitude, "The Colonel speaks as a soldier with a bullet in his breast—where, we don't yet know."

With this, the crowd began to murmur, shock bouncing off every wall as Roosevelt appeared and walked slowly to the podium, his hands elevated.

"I'm going to ask you to be very quiet," he said, and the obedient room instantly hushed. "Please excuse me from making a long speech. I'll do the best I can but you can see there is a bullet in my body. But it's nothing. I'm not hurt badly."

The crowd was silent, but not for long.

"It takes more than that," Roosevelt boomed, "to kill a Bull Moose!"

The crowd roared its apoplectic approval. And Roosevelt delivered his entire speech. It took ninety minutes.

The details of this would crawl across the country, and most Americans who'd gone to bed either marveling over the Giants' resilience or clucking over Charles Becker's impending doom would wake up to the most unbelievable headlines imaginable.

Madman Shoots Roosevelt in Wisconsin
Colonel Shrugs Off Wounds, Delivers Speech
Doctors Fear Lockjaw, Expect Full Recovery
Roosevelt Says He Feels 'Bully' to Nurses

At the precise moment when John Flammang Schrank squeezed his trigger, three separate trains were already well on their way from New York's Grand Central Station, bound for Boston's Back Bay. All three trains contained passengers who would remain blissfully unaware of the attempted assassination until the next day, and so, for now, were fully engaged in what seemed like the most important thing in the world. It was, after all, called the "world's series" by everyone, by players and managers and newspaper columnists, and if the capital *W* and capital *S* wouldn't be formalized for some years, the sentiment was still the same.

By far the merriest train of the three was the first to pull out of the station, occupied by Honey Fitz, Nuf Ced McGreevy, and the rest of the Royal Rooters, who were just as unbowed as they'd been at the Polo Grounds. "We'll be front and center again tomorrow, and this time we'll be on our own familiar turf and it'll shake those New Yorkers all the way back to where they came from!" proclaimed McGreevy as he led the last of the Rooters onto their 5:45 train. "And we look forward to bringing the world's championship home. That's been our mission, and it will remain forever thus." By now, the Rooters were a sensation all across New England. Their train would make two stops; at New Haven, Connecticut, with little prompting, they emerged onto the platform to regale three hundred locals with a full-throated rendition of "Tessie," and at New London, forty-five minutes later, they went with "A Hot Time in the Old Town," for an even larger gathering approaching seven hundred. When they finally reached Boston, McGreevy gathered them all one last time to announce that they'd be meeting at 12:50 P.M. at the corner of Beacon and Raleigh Streets to prepare for the most important pregame march of their Rooting careers, which would commence promptly at 1:10. "You're there on time, you'll get a ticket, guaranteed," McGreevy said. " 'Nough said."

The Giants' train wasn't quite the burlesque show on rails that the Rooters' procession became, but it *did* feature twenty-three baseball players who were overjoyed to still have a season in front of them, to be embarking on another trip to Boston that, to be blunt, few of them thought they'd be eligible to take when they'd arrived for work that morning. Such is the momentum of a short baseball series, though, that they now spoke in terms that made them feel close to bulletproof, especially when it came to the prospect of again facing Smoky Joe Wood, who in their minds suddenly wasn't the invincible wonder who'd twice flummoxed them already. In the comfort of their cozy traveling clubhouse, the Giants looked, and sounded, a lot braver than the team that had seemed almost ready to accept their fate just a few hours earlier.

"Wood will be beaten," Buck Herzog boldly proclaimed, "and beaten badly."

"He is not strong after a short rest," Larry Doyle declared, "and he has already pitched two hard games. We don't get fooled thrice."

"I hope they finally start Wood," Chief Meyers pronounced. "I have no doubt that he can't come at us again the way he did the first two times. Nobody beats the Giants three times in a row if we have anything to say about it."

Three hundred similarly infused Giants fans saw the team off at Grand Central, and while they applauded each Giant as they walked up the stairs, they reserved their strongest huzzahs for the manager, for John McGraw, the one man among them who'd defiantly predicted his team's survival for two days and was now munching triumphantly from a tin box of hard candy tucked under his arm.

Just as the final few Giants were boarding, the Red Sox arrived on the other side of the vast platform, awaiting their own special coach. Spotting Buck Herzog—still a nemesis, despite the mutual truce both men entered into after Game Five—Tris Speaker yelled, "Enjoy it while you can, Giants! You fellows will have to knock Wood tomorrow!"

To which Herzog gleefully replied: "We'll do to him tomorrow what we did to O'Brien today!" Then he hopped into the train, the doors closed behind him, and the Giants were off on their jolly way. Speaker wasn't laughing. There wasn't a thing about the past ten or so hours that he—or any of the other Speed Boys—found even remotely amusing. And their mood wasn't about to brighten anytime soon.

What Herzog, the Giants' chief instigator, couldn't possibly have known was just how sore the scab he'd just picked really was. For thirty preseason games, for 152 regular-season games, for the first five games of the World Series, all the rifts and schisms that threatened at any time to break the Red Sox apart had been handled, massaged, dealt with, filed away. Sure, Heinie Wagner had been a large part of that, his knack for bringing teammates together never more appreciated, or appreciable, than during this long spring, summer, and autumn. Jake Stahl surely deserved credit, the manager making sure that whatever personal differences his players might have harbored in private, there would never be an on-field issue that would splinter them apart. Mostly, of course, it had been the players themselves who'd kept the peace in the oldest, most reliable way possible: by winning early, by winning often, by winning two-thirds of the games that didn't count, and then by winning sixty-nine percent of the games that did, and then by winning seventy-five percent of the games that *really* counted, storming to that 3–1–1 Series lead that they'd carried to the Polo Grounds that morning.

Still, from the first hour of spring training in Hot Springs, it had been a delicate, almost exhausting balance. And now, at the worst possible moment, that carefully crafted house of cards had begun to tumble. It had started on this very train twenty-four hours earlier, James McAleer inviting the wrath of the karmic gods by sidling up next to his manager. Buck O'Brien had been the next to succumb to its weight, unwittingly at first when he'd dived headfirst into the New York night, then purposefully when he'd balked home the first run and proceeded to unravel in front of the entire baseball world. The chaos quietly bled into the stands when all of those who'd put more than just their rooting interests in the hands of the Red Sox—primarily Paul Wood—saw their investments turn to ash before the first inning was even over. And everything had come to an explosive head within seconds of the final out, back in the visiting clubhouse, when the smoke coming out of Smoky Joe Wood's ears finally set off alarm bells.

"You were an embarrassment out there," Wood told O'Brien flatly.

O'Brien, in no mood for debate and already showered and dressed, answered with his right fist before being dragged out of the clubhouse, shoved into a cab, and hauled off to the train station. So it was that the alliances holding the Red Sox together—even if they were fashioned merely out of staples, paper clips, and good intentions—began bursting apart. The fact that it would occur with Wood and O'Brien as the principal combatants simply exposed every raw nerve, and every basic conflict, that had been so carefully papered over for so long.

O'Brien was Catholic, a son of Irish immigrants, very much a northerner, very much a New Englander, very much (for one unfortunate night, anyway) a drinker, the kind of player that Wood and Speaker saw as an "insider," blessed through birth or geography to always fit in perfectly in Boston. Wood was Protestant, a son of the Wild West whose soul was very much a product of the distant Confederacy, a teetotaler and, along with Speaker, the kind of player that O'Brien, Bill Carrigan, and the rest of the traditional Celts on the Sox viewed as an "outsider," bringing hard thoughts and old ideas into Boston's modern, growing, city on the hill. All year long, the papers could sense the simmering, going so far as to themselves divide the Sox by group, by the "Knights" or the "KCs" (O'Brien, Carrigan, Harry Hooper, Duffy Lewis) and the "masons" (Wood, Speaker, Cady, Yerkes). The players had long publicly denied all of it.

But they weren't in public anymore. They were in the privacy of their own train. And it would be Paul Wood—out $100 of his own money, out a whole lot more in proposition bets he'd made on behalf of a whole lot of other folks—who finally found O'Brien, drinking again, and in a dark mood.

"You bush league bastard," Wood screamed, pummeling O'Brien, blackening one of his eyes, desperately wanting more before he was hauled away, screaming that the Papist son of a bitch was lucky someone hadn't killed him.

That could have ended things, of course, but only if O'Brien had wanted them ended, only if he'd figured it was time to walk away and put a merciful close to what had already been a perfectly horrible day. The problem with that reasoning, of course, is that O'Brien didn't see where he'd done a goddamned thing wrong. He'd been handed the ball on a day he wasn't supposed to pitch. He hadn't bitched about that. He'd gone out and thrown his ass off, even with a splitting headache and a stomach that felt like the Polo Grounds' elevated train sounded. He'd given an honest effort and had nothing, and was probably the angriest player on the whole damned train, because he'd been given a chance to wrap up the World Series and he'd spit the bit but, hell, so had the rest of the team, too. And there was another thing. . . .

"If I'd have had my catcher with me," O'Brien said, referring to Carrigan, "I'd have been fine, we'd be counting our money, and none of this shit would have happened."

Hick Cady, who had caught in Carrigan's stead, was seated only a few feet away.

"What the hell does that mean, you drunken son of a bitch?" Cady raged.

"It means what it means," O'Brien seethed, not backing down.

"That's pretty fucking rich," came a louder voice still, "coming from a quitter."

It was Smoky Joe Wood, back from calming his brother down, walking back into the inferno, now hearing his favorite catcher being slandered.

"Cady caught you just fine," Wood roared. "But you're a gutless son of a bitch and you're a goddamned drunk to boot!"

And that was that. Soon, Cady was taking a swing at O'Brien, and O'Brien took another swing at Wood, and Carrigan came over to wrestle with Cady, and as one of the noncombatant players' wives, spying the whole thing, would tell a newspaper reporter the next day, "It was the most disgraceful thing you ever saw."

"Sounds like a barroom fight to me," the reporter said, shrugging.

By the time Wagner and Stahl raced back to snuff out the worst of it, they could see that all of their hard work had just been splintered to pieces. Stahl had already realized that his worst fears were brewing: At a train stop, someone had handed him an early edition of the *Boston Post*, which published a large cartoon featuring a huge satchel of money marked "extra gate receipts" surrounded by two men identified as a club owner and a member of National Commission. That was bad enough.

And now this?

As he pulled Joe Wood away, Stahl could see his star pitcher wide-eyed with fury. "Go and cool off, Joe," Stahl told his kid pitcher, normally coolheaded and even-keeled, suddenly a tinderbox of ferocity.

"Someone's gotta pay, Skip," he said, walking away, leaving his manager to fervently hope he was referring to the Giants.

By comparison, the Giants were a study in harmony, a picture of togetherness. John McGraw, for one, was feeling downright philosophical—wistful, even—as he wolfed down his candy. "If my team had stayed on the ground in the first three games, we would be going home with the championship tonight, and maybe we wouldn't even be *on* this goddamned train," he told the *New York Globe*'s Sid Mercer, the one writer among the horde of Giants beat reporters to whom McGraw felt even the slightest strain of friendship, even if Mercer was usually the one who would most gleefully poke holes in McGraw's strategy and his stodginess in his copy.

"How do you explain Larry Doyle?" Mercer asked McGraw, sipping from a glass of wine. The Giants' captain, who'd had such a masterful regular season, was trapped in a cropping October funk, his fielding spotty and his batting average barely scraping .200. Nobody was tougher on himself than Doyle, who'd worked his way out of the coal mines of southwest Illinois and saw McGraw as a role model and a father figure.

"I look for Doyle to break loose very soon," McGraw said. "He never has gone so many games with such poor results. I can pick at least eight spots where one of Larry's long wallops would have broken up a game. He is overdue. You know Doyle has the happy faculty of putting in his wallops where they're most needed. I'd still rather see him at bat in a pinch than any one else on the club."

It had been like that for McGraw from the moment he'd made Doyle his every-day second baseman five years earlier. It wasn't hard to see why McGraw and Doyle would take to each other as kindred spirits, the two of them attacking every baseball game they ever played as if someone was going to lock all the bats, balls, and bases in a closet forever. For Doyle, it was an obsession that was easy to trace. Born into a mining family, he spent five long years in those light-starved dungeons, yearning every second for something, for anything, that could liberate him from the darkness. "When you first go down into the earth there comes a sudden realization of what might happen to you," he'd written a few years before. "Nowadays the mines can be lighted by electricity, and it's comparatively simple to go through a mine. But when you get caught without a light in some deep labyrinth in the bowels of the earth, it's no picnic."

Baseball provided the life raft. At first it was just semiprofessional ball on the weekends, Doyle taking home whatever the teams were willing to pay, sometimes a dollar, sometimes two, sometimes nothing, before gaining a spot on the Springfield team of the Triple-I League. Didn't matter to Doyle, who saw what twenty hard years in the ground could do to a man's lungs, and to his spirit, who saw six of his former coworkers for the Breese & Trenton Coal Company perish in a horrific Christmas Eve accident in 1906 when the cage that lowered the miners toward their grim tasks unspooled and crushed them. Whenever Doyle fretted about his batting average—as he certainly was now—or grew angry at McGraw's heavy-handed guid-

THE FIRST FALL CLASSIC

ance, it didn't take much to snap him from even the shallowest throes of self-pity. It was seven months after the mining disaster that McGraw forked over $4,500 for his services to Dick Kinsella, president of the Springfield club, at the time the highest amount ever paid for a prospect.

For a day or two, McGraw had to wonder what he'd done. Doyle's train from Springfield arrived in Jersey City on July 21, 1907, and he was directed toward a ferry that dumped him on Manhattan's West Side. Still as green as weathered copper, Doyle approached a policeman and asked for directions to the Polo Grounds.

"See that elevated train?" the cop said. "Take it to the last stop. You can't possibly miss it."

Doyle missed it. He took the train to the end of the line, walked out, looked around for a magnificent baseball stadium, but all he saw was ocean.

"I was at South Ferry," Doyle would explain years later. "It was the wrong end of the line. I tried explaining that one to McGraw later in the day, and all he said was, 'I hope you know your way around the basepaths better than you do around the train tracks.' And from there, we got along like two peas in a pod."

Now McGraw worried about his captain.

"I hung on to Doyle when the New York fans and critics were calling for his scalp, and that includes you," McGraw told Mercer. "And today I wouldn't trade him for any man playing baseball."

He *would* trade the impostor who'd been wearing Larry Doyle's uniform the past six games, however.

By the next morning, Boston was a scalding porridge of rumors, whispers, half-truths, and speculation. "I'm disgusted," one Red Sox fan declared inside a coffee shop not far from Fenway Park. "If the fix was in, that's the worst thing there is. But if the fix *wasn't* in and they just played lousy baseball? I think that's twice as bad."

James McAleer, he heard the rumors clearly and concisely,

because wherever he walked in Boston this Tuesday morning, October the fifteenth, there were people pointing at him, sneering at him, cupping their hands over their mouths as they slandered him. Six months ago, McAleer had been toasted as the people's choice, a commoner who'd risen to the owner's suite, a man who before spring training could be found in the city's barrooms and bowling alleys mingling with the people, hawking his team, selling his product, inviting them to the shining new palace by the Back Bay Fens. But that was a long time ago. Now the people wondered if the very man who'd tried selling them on a championship vision had sold that very dream out from under them. McAleer began instantly spinning his own version of the calamitous fate that had befallen his team the day before in New York.

"I was in the dressing room immediately after the game at the Polo Grounds and can truthfully say there was no trouble among the players," McAleer insisted. "The boys had counted on winning the game and were intensely sorry that they lost but there was not the slightest trace of friction."

Some believed him, the hardest core of Boston fandom that couldn't allow themselves to believe that any games would ever be compromised, *especially* World Series games. Many others, however, smiled knowing grins. They understood that baseball wasn't exactly populated by altar boys or choirboys, whether you were looking in the dugout or inside the executive offices. There had been all those ugly rumors swirling around the 1903 World Series, after all. If you went to a ballgame, any ballgame, everyone knew what section of the ballpark you could visit if you had a few extra dollars burning a hole in your pocket.

Few of them were inclined to allow their outrage to manifest in anything resembling a boycott. Besides, once the morning newspapers started arriving on doorsteps and at newsstands throughout the town, there were more important things about which to aim their outrage. Theodore Roosevelt had concluded his speech at Milwaukee Auditorium the night before, the stubborn act of a physical marvel who held one last captive audience in the palm of his steady hand even as the bullet in his breast precluded him from breathing regularly. By 10:30 he was lying on an operating table at the city's Emergency Hospital, talking politics with doctors who took X-rays, declared the wound superficial, and approved Roosevelt's request that he be transferred to a surgical hospital in Chicago.

It was well past two in the morning when Roosevelt was helped off the train at Union Station, but he was immediately approached by an army of newspaper photographers and cried, "Oh, no! Shot again!" before emitting a hoarse laugh. It wasn't until 3:30 that he was finally at rest in his private room, visited by Dr. George F. Butler, who first offered an excellent prognosis for a full recovery and then exclaimed, "Mr. President, you were elected last night. It was the turning of the tide in your favor."

To which Roosevelt declared, "Bully!"

That was a popular sentiment. Both Woodrow Wilson and William Taft pledged to suspend campaigning for as long as Roosevelt was recuperating, a stunned Wilson confiding in one of his aides, "I believe Colonel Roosevelt has found the most direct line possible to the people."

It was such talk that replaced the Red Sox and the Giants for much of Tuesday, which allowed James McAleer to slip away to Fenway Park and to make his way down, one more time, to a private audience with Jake Stahl. Stahl hadn't slept much once the Red Sox' boisterous train finally reached Back Bay Station just past midnight, and he'd come to the ballpark early. Just not early enough.

"People are saying a lot of nasty things today," McAleer told his manager.

Stahl shrugged. What did the man expect him to say?

"I have a favor to ask," the owner said.

"What could you possibly want now?" Stahl asked.

"I'd like to speak to the team before the game," McAleer said.

"I don't think that's such a great idea," Stahl said, shaking his head, amazed at how tone deaf one man could be.

"That's your opinion."

"You pay me for my opinions."

"I pay you to manage this team. But I *own* this team."

Stahl knew what was coming next, verbatim.

"And that means I own *you*, too, don't forget."

Stahl just smiled. He'd expected to be boarding a train back to Illinois that afternoon, back to his family, back to the bank. Now he was listening to lunacy, watching his season leak away drop by drop by drop.

"I can make them hear you," he finally said, "but I can't make them listen."

And so ninety minutes later, with the players having arrived quietly, after they'd dressed in silence, Stahl gathered them around to listen to an old-fashioned pep talk.

"I know you fellows don't believe the stuff in the papers," McAleer said. "I know you're professionals. And I know you're gonna win today's game. How much confidence do I have in you? I've arranged a postgame celebration already, with the finest fish, the finest champagne, the finest of everything. It will be an appropriate celebration to toast you, the finest baseball team in the land."

"Great!" a voice called out. "What time should we be there?"

McAleer's silence confirmed what everyone in the room already knew: None of *them*, the lumpen proletariat, was invited. Most of the Speed Boys were already too exhausted, and too disgusted, to be angry. Smoky Joe Wood? He was plenty of both. And he'd already left the room, hadn't listened to a word McAleer had to say. He'd heard it all before, anyway.

New York City, which had fallen very much out of love with the Giants just twenty-four hours before, was suddenly crashing hard, fast, leading with its collective heart. Once it was clear that Roosevelt, the city's favored son, would be all right, there was nothing blocking Giants fans' affections from spilling into the streets and filling the city with an odd, addictive miasma of hope and good cheer. Even the Becker Trial had lost its momentum for one day, seemingly conceding to the Giants every eye, every ear, and every second of spare time. Men arrived to work early, knowing they'd be trying to leave early, too. Children were encouraged to go to school because a fleet of truant officers would be patrolling every corner, especially where the baseball scoreboards were located. And even the women of many households made an important decision. In those years, each day of the week was assigned a chore: Monday was Wash Day, Thursday was Market Day, Saturday was Baking Day. Well, Tuesday was supposed to be Ironing Day, but as many men discovered when they got home that night, *this* Tuesday was not.

This Tuesday would be Baseball Day.

Two hours before first pitch, there were 40,000 people already crammed into Herald Square. At Madison Square Garden, every seat was sold and occupied long before the pregame entertainment began. And at Times Square, extra policemen were called in to protect the crowds from themselves: People were so close together, so close to the outer through streets, that they were in danger of getting crushed.

"Oh," a frenzied observer named Kenneth Jackson, caught up in the moment, yelled at a reporter from the New York *American*. "To be in Boston right now . . . to be watching this glorious game in person . . . how lucky those fans are. *So* lucky . . ."

Those fans knew it, too. Red Sox fans had weeded through the paper talk and the discourse and decided: The hell with it. How many times in a lifetime do you get to see your team win a championship? They flooded the streets around Fenway Park, flooded the ballpark itself, all but knocking down the ticket kiosks in an effort to be first through the doors.

In the middle of this glorious merriment, of course, were the Royal Rooters, out in force and in full voice, close to a thousand of them, meeting as planned at the corner of Beacon and Raleigh, taking their march on time, singing and chanting at the top of their vocal cords, their arrival at the Jersey Street entrance to Fenway greeted by the fans and the street vendors with the same appreciation as if they'd just spotted Tris Speaker or Harry Hooper. Players came and went, after all, but the Rooters were forever, the Rooters never got too old to play, never got traded away, never held out for more money.

"The Rooters," John Keenan, one of their organizers, had said back in New York, "will be here perpetually, rooting on the sons and the grandsons of the Speed Boys long after they've passed this mortal coil."

The Rooters, knowing how important the day was to them, to the Red Sox, to all of Boston, decided it would behoove everyone to move their routine up fifteen minutes in order to ensure a peaceful start to the day's true festivities. So around 1:40, they started filing onto the grounds, taking their pregame lap, encouraging fans to get on their feet and root for the Red Sox, and for Smoky Joe Wood, who'd finished a listless session in the bullpen and was now preparing to take the mound for the top of the first inning. The band blared "Tessie," and the Rooters were joined in the familiar lyrics by the other 32,000 or so jammed into the park. The Red Sox took the field, and that was the Rooters' cue to make the last segment of their journey, out to left field where they'd spent the first three Boston games of this Series crowding the temporary stands set up in front of the huge Fatima Cigars advertisement in left field. Joe Wood began his warm-up throws. Game Seven of the 1912 World Series was seconds away. Josh Devore walked from the on-deck circle to the batter's box.

Billy Evans, working home plate this day, shouted, "Play ball!"

But no ball was played, not at that instant and not for some time. Because suddenly everyone was well aware of a commotion exploding in left field, near where the Royal Rooters were supposed to be sitting and were, instead, standing. And still on the field. With John Keenan yelling at a large segment of fans, "Remove yourselves and make way for the Royal Rooters! These are *our* seats!"

To which he was told, "The hell they are. We bought them with our own hard-earned money. Look at our tickets!"

But neither Keenan nor Nuf Ced McGreevy nor any of the restless thousand people cooling their heels behind Duffy Lewis in left field cared even a little bit about their tickets. What were these people *doing* here? Had they never heard of the *Royal Rooters?* It was Captain Thomas Goode of Station 16, in charge of the police detail, who approached Keenan and alerted him that it was true, the Rooters seats had been sold out from under them.

"Secretary McRoy ordered me at one o'clock to throw the section open," Goode explained over the growing tide of acrimony. "He said he couldn't be sure that the Rooters were going to honor their tickets."

Keenan listened in astonishment.

"McRoy? *He* told you to sell our tickets, a carpetbagger from Chicago? And you *listened* to him?"

Goode wasn't inclined to have a debate. The game was already supposed to start. Joe Wood was already warmed up. The other 30,000 people, dispersed elsewhere in the ballpark, started murmuring testily. And the people in the Rooters' usual seats, who really *had* bought their tickets honestly, were hardly inclined to budge.

"Well," Keenan said, "we aren't going anywhere either."

And then it got strange: From far down the field, a shout went up and in an instant a half a dozen mounted horsemen appeared, their steeds speeding toward left field, charging full tilt, intending to scatter the Rooters, the horses kicking up the dirt and grass of the carefully manicured infield, pounding divots into the outfield, all the ballplayers watching this unfold with bemused smiles on their faces. One especially interested observer, sitting in a VIP box behind the home-team dugout, immediately stormed the field himself, waddling out toward left field.

"This is an outrage!" John Fitzgerald boomed. "An outrage!"

A good ten minutes had passed. Heinie Wagner, red-faced, breathless, sprinted to where Keenan was standing. "This game will be forfeited if we don't get going the right way," the Red Sox shortstop said. "And if the crowd comes on the field again the umpires will declare the Giants the winner. They just told me so."

Keenan looked at Wagner in disbelief, unable to fathom that this player to whom the Rooters had given such unconditional devotion would turn on them. "We are *not* responsible for this state of affairs.

We came here expecting to find our seats and they are taken. We don't blame the people in them—they have a right to them as well as we have. But where are we going to go? What can we do? It is not the fault of the Rooters and it is not the Rooters who are causing the troubles. We will do everything within our power to let the game go on and you can rest assured every member of the Rooters party will assist you in every way they can."

It wasn't until Honey Fitz made it to the scene that order was finally restored. The Rooters reluctantly agreed to a compromise: They would stand wherever room allowed. That would mean no chants, no songs, nothing resembling the atmosphere they'd contributed their hearts, souls, and voices to. "I will deal with Mr. McRoy and Mr. McAleer later," Fitzgerald promised his most ardent constituents. "And they will rue the day they picked a fight with the Royal Rooters."

Finally it was time to play ball, and Billy Evans said so (again), and Smoky Joe Wood shook his head (again). You couldn't make this stuff up if you tried.

No video exists of what followed next, and only a handful of grainy photographs have made it through the better part of a century, and all of the participants are, to quote Casey Stengel, dead at the present time. There is no way to judge with certitude what precisely was lurking in the hearts of the Boston Red Sox as Smoky Joe Wood threw his first pitch of the afternoon toward Josh Devore, a straight, soft meatball of a misnamed fastball that bisected the heart of the plate for a strike and left Devore stunned and John McGraw wide-eyed with fanatical glee.

"He has *nothing*!" McGraw yelped from the third-base dugout. "Get your hitting shoes on, boys, because he has *nothing*! Get after that fastball!" It was all McGraw could do to not run from the coaching box and grab a bat himself. Devore obliged, swung at the next pitch, pounded the ball into the ground toward shortstop, and beat the throw to first. Devore had been so anxious, his hands so attuned to Wood's fastballs, which normally dripped gasoline, that he'd almost overswung. He joined McGraw's chorus, yelling toward Larry Doyle, "Cappy, he has *nothing*! He has *nothing*!" Doyle would discover that soon enough on his own, lining a clean single toward center that seemed to lift a thousand-ton building from his shoulders and put the Giants very much in business.

Fred Snodgrass stepped to the plate, only half believing what his manager and his teammates were saying about the great Smoky Joe Wood, who'd already struck him out twice in this series, who'd limited him to only one hit in eight at-bats so far, the base-knock coming his first time up in the first game when he'd spun a ball into the dirt at home plate and beaten the throw, a ball that traveled, tops, eleven feet. But Snodgrass's eyes wouldn't lie to him, and he described later on what Wood's first offering to him looked like.

"A lob," Snodgrass said. "Like something you'd get in batting practice, only slower, and softer."

Snodgrass laid off, the ball drifted outside, and then he stepped out of the box, noticing Doyle at first and Devore at second exchange knowing glances, and Snodgrass knew what that meant: a double steal. No matter how slow the next pitch was, he would keep his bat on his shoulder, give the runners a chance to advance. What he didn't expect—what no one in their right mind could expect—was what happened next: Inexplicably, Wood started into his full windup. Understand that since the beginning of baseball time, pitchers have always thrown from the "stretch" position with men on base; it prevents runners from having their way on the base paths. It is something pitchers do from sandlots to semipro all the way to the big leagues. It is as basic a fundamental as running. And yet, somehow, Joe Wood wound up, either forgetting there were two runners on base or—worse—not caring.

Devore slid into third and Doyle into second before Wood's big, sweeping curve could even reach Hick Cady's mitt. It was inconceivable. It practically disgusted Larry Doyle, grateful for the gift but easily pushed to anger whenever a player lost his head on the field.

"Wood couldn't have gotten by in the bush leagues on a dark day with what he had," Doyle would assert. "And that goes for his brain as well as his arm."

Snodgrass badly wanted in on the action and he all but licked his lips as Wood delivered his next pitch, another straight fastball. Snodgrass stayed back on the ball as long as he could and then pounced, smacking a hard line drive down the right-field line that scored Devore and Doyle, nudging the Giants out to another early first-inning lead, and quieting most of Fenway Park—all but that segment of irate Royal Rooters who suddenly couldn't be more delighted by any misfortune that visited the home team. *They* cheered lustily.

Wood wasn't himself, wasn't even remotely resembling a major league pitcher, and the malaise was spreading. Red Murray laid down a bunt, an odd decision by a cleanup hitter, and it rolled right for Jake Stahl at first but the Sox' player-manager, already stunned by what he was watching, nearly forgot to field it, recovered, then barely beat the hard-charging Murray by half a foot. Up stepped Fred Merkle, who lofted what looked to be a routine fly ball toward the normally sure-handed Duffy Lewis in left field, but the wind started blowing it back toward the infield and Lewis nearly twisted himself into a pretzel trying to track it down, and couldn't. When it landed with a thud in short left field, Snodgrass raced home with the third run and Merkle was standing on second base. Wood had thrown exactly eight pitches and the Giants already led 3–0. It looked like Wood would finally stanch the bleeding on his *ninth* pitch, another fat fastball that Buck Herzog drilled up the middle. The ball bounded hard off the sod, smacked into Wood's glove almost by accident, and the overeager Merkle (who else?) wandered too far off third base and was eventually thrown out in a rundown. But Herzog took second base on the play, and he immediately scored the fourth run of the game when Chief Meyers stroked a single—again on a first-pitch fastball.

"Look at him," Jeff Tesreau, the Giants starting pitcher who was delighted with such early run support, exclaimed on the Giants' bench, pointing at Wood, who seemed oddly serene considering the beating he was absorbing, "there must be something wrong with his arm."

Wilbert Robinson, the old coach who'd seen about 2,000 more professional baseball games in his time than young Tesreau, spit out a stream of tobacco, and crossed his legs, and replied, "Or his head."

The Red Sox were ruined. Art Fletcher lined another first-pitch fastball for a single to right field, and the slow-footed Meyers should have been dead at third base when Harry Hooper's throw beat him by about ten steps. But Larry Gardner couldn't handle the throw, then couldn't pick the ball up in time to tag Meyers before he finally poured himself into third base. The Giants' catcher picked himself up, dusted himself off and trotted home when Tesreau scalded still another first-pitch fastball up the middle, "the hardest-hit ball I've ever hit in my life," he would report, "and the hardest-hit ball I ever *expect* to hit in my life." Five-nothing. One pitch later it was six, when Tesreau took off from first base trying to steal, got himself caught in a rundown, and stayed in it long enough for Fletcher to dash home from third a second or two before Tesreau was finally tagged out to end an inning that never seemed like it was ever *going* to end.

It was a surreal moment for everyone. Even the revenge-minded Rooters couldn't bring themselves to cheer any longer, because this wasn't just a beating, it was a *battering*, a smearing of the great Smoky Joe Wood, who incredibly, almost unbelievably, had thrown all of *thirteen* pitches in the inning. Thirteen! It was an appalling display on many different levels, the most sinister of which helped empty almost half of the Fenway Park grandstand before the Red Sox were even finished with their first turn at bat. On one hand, few wanted to believe the Speed Boys would be so audacious as to throw a World Series game in front of 32,694 witnesses, even those who knew what a highly motivated band of vigilantes the Sox might have been, seeking both visceral revenge for their owner's sabotage and financial gain if they'd all decided to bet the Giants at the long local odds still being offered that morning. On the other hand, few could believe that a team that had won 105 regular-season games and had been so clearly the dominant of the two teams for the Series' first five games would be *this* bad, *could* be this bad.

Wood was the most obvious culprit, of course, since he plainly had enough motivation to take part in a conspiracy if he'd wanted to, thanks to his brother's fiscal loss and his own anger at being replaced as the Game Six starter to benefit McAleer's fiscal greed. And later in his career, Wood would be implicated alongside Ty Cobb and Tris Speaker with betting a game they all knew was fixed in 1919, less than two weeks before the Black Sox scandal that nearly drove the sport out of business. But there were others, too. There was Duffy Lewis's shaky pursuit of the fly ball. There was Larry Gardner's suspect error. Most important, there was the fact that the Red Sox never did mount a serious threat after falling behind so early, falling meekly 11–4 and setting up an eighth and decisive game.

"We finally looked like a real club today, and the Red Sox didn't look very much like one," Larry Doyle said when it was over, after he'd justified his manager's faith in him by collecting three hits, including the Giants' first home run of the Series in the sixth. "We are a whole lot nearer to that winner's money today than we were Saturday, and we have also given Smoky Joe Wood a terrible trimming. Now for the big battle: one game, winner take all. Just like it ought to be."

The Red Sox, for their part, didn't sound the part of a team that had just been taken to the woodshed. Even Joe Wood, whom you would have expected to seem shell-shocked beyond recognition (assuming he was, in fact, "shocked" by what had happened to him), was downright sanguine.

"I had all my usual stuff," he insisted, "but perhaps I was too confident. Those Giants batters just stood up there and banged away at a fast one, the curve, and my slow one. I will be back in there this afternoon if the manager says the word. There is nothing the matter with my arm."

James McAleer, meanwhile, fresh from canceling his victory celebration and locking his best champagne in the cellar, was spinning wildly when reporters caught up to him, many of them more suspicious than ever that he was more marionette than martinet now, that he'd pulled these strings all along.

"Nonsense," McAleer said. "I believe that Wood was bothered considerably by the heavy gale which blew directly in his face. He couldn't get his curve ball working and for some reason his speed was lacking. Something evidently was wrong with him, and when he found he had nothing he became bullheaded and just sailed the ball over the plate trusting in his fielders to pull him out of the mire. If Wood had been at his best we couldn't have lost today."

Then, in either a Freudian slip or a who-gives-a-shit glimpse of arrogance that too many Red Sox had seen too often lately, he said, "I haven't decided whether to start Bedient or Wood tomorrow but you can bank on one thing: the Red Sox will be there fighting for the victory until the last man has been retired."

Jake Stahl, who was the man ostensibly charged with making that decision, figured that his owner had done enough talking for the both of them.

"I'll worry about tomorrow, tomorrow," he said. "I have enough things to worry about right now."

He wasn't the only one.

Giants fans had all but taken to the streets when word swirled around the city of their team's first-inning explosion. At Madison Square Garden, an engineer had to be called in because the six-run first inning had made people wonder if the floor wasn't really shaking (it wasn't). The engineer was called again when the gathering exploded once more; when fan favorite Doyle's home run was announced, many were convinced the foundation had cracked (it hadn't). Uptown, at the Imperial Hotel overlooking the Hudson River, the biggest Giants fan of all, John T. Brush, was nearly overcome with emotion as scoring updates were relayed to him minute by minute. Brush had been feeling well enough during Games One and Four to actually spend the games in a parking area beyond the outfield fence, but he'd grown too weak to do the same for Game

Six, and much as he'd have given anything to make the trip to Boston for the deciding game, he knew that would not be possible. Still, he was reported to be "ecstatic" by his club's resilience.

Everywhere else that ecstasy was evident and it was deafening, and it nearly caused a riot in Herald Square, where close to 55,000 people had kept a steady vigil for the sixth time in the past seven days. The choking crowds had finally become too much for a shopkeeper who shared Broadway with the *Herald* and the *Telegram*, and he'd filed a complaint with the Tenderloin Police Station accusing Frank B. Flaherty, circulation manager of the *Herald*, of maintaining a "public nuisance." Captain Harold Thor had personally come to arrest Flaherty that morning as the crowd in the streets—and the crowd above the streets, lining the neighboring windows and rooftops—booed. Later that day, before Magistrate Lawrence Barlow in Jefferson Market Court, the anonymous shopkeeper pled his case and Flaherty argued his.

Barlow, who declared he "had no interest in who wins this world's series," nevertheless issued a verdict that was music to the ears of baseball fans across the city. "If you will produce the necessary evidence against the owners or operators of all the bulletin boards and display advertising signs in the city in a form which will require that I consider the issuance of warrants for all I shall take this matter under advisement. I certainly shall not take any action in this case alone. The case is dismissed and the prisoner discharged."

Yes, it was a good day all around for the Giants.

The Red Sox? Their problems seemed to mount by the hour. Somehow, someway, someone had found a way to alienate the most passionately loyal fans in the country, fans who put not only their hearts but their wallets behind the Red Sox and earlier in the day had been thanked for their fealty with the back of Fenway Park's hand. When Game Seven was over, the Royal Rooters made their displeasure known by playing Tessie, as always, but then they marched over to the extreme left end of the grandstand and one of the rooters, William Shea, produced a megaphone.

"Three cheers for Secretary McRoy of Chicago!" he cried.

Booooooooooo! Booooooooooooo! Booooooooooooo!

"Well then! Three cheers for the Giants, and for their management!"

The grounds shook from the cheering.

No less a studied eye than the one belonging to the *Globe's* Tim Murnane instantly declared this the lowest point in the history of Boston baseball, the moment when the Red Sox had not only humiliated themselves on the field but distanced themselves from the very people who'd helped make them such a civic phenomenon. Murnane followed the Rooters as they retraced their steps back to Raleigh and Beacon, then disbanded—forever, if you believed some of the angrier rooters, especially those who chose to cool their heels (and moisten their parched voice boxes) at McGreevy's Third Base Saloon.

Theirs was a noble complaint, instantly picked up by empathetic voices.

"Secretary McRoy—who is from Chicago—should be retired from all connection with the Boston Baseball Club and a Boston man who understands conditions here given the place," roared Mayor Fitzgerald, who vowed he would sooner step foot in a Republican clubhouse than Fenway Park for Game Eight after what the Red Sox had done. "Boston money supports the club and there is certainly enough baseball brains in Boston to furnish a secretary. It seems a pity, when New York has been willing to set aside 300 seats for the Rooters that the home club could not be equally courteous. If the owners of the Boston club know their business, a Boston man will be found in the secretary's office by the time next season begins."

McRoy himself tried to backtrack, swearing to reporters, "I hadn't heard from the Royal Rooters representative up until 12:45 at which hour I saw the bundle of tickets allotted to them on my desk. I didn't want to get stuck with the tickets so at one o'clock I sent one of the clerks to tell the policemen to throw the section reserved for the rooters to the public." There was one problem with that: He was lying. McRoy, and McAleer, knew full well the Rooters were coming. They'd sold the seats because they figured the Rooters wouldn't mind standing, because they figured they could treat their most loyal supporters any way they wanted to. It was Timothy Mooney, chief of the Bureau of Information in the mayor's office, who exposed the ruse. "I called up the office of the secretary at noon and received the usual block of tickets for the Rooters," he said. "I signed for them. McRoy doesn't know what he is talking about."

Amid the tumult, the Red Sox announced that tickets for Game Eight would go on sale promptly at 8 o'clock the next morning (after McAleer had unsuccessfully lobbied the National Commission to move it back a day so there would be more time to sell more tickets). Yet as McAleer finally left Fenway Park late that night, he looked around, turned to his wife and said, "Isn't that queer?"

It was. The long lines that had snaked around Fenway Park before each of the first four games played in Boston were gone. Nobody was in line. Not one soul. "Maybe they didn't get the message," McAleer wondered, but it was worse than that.

The fans had gotten the message, all right. Now they were sending one of their own.

CHAPTER TEN

Wednesday, October 16, 1912: Game Eight

Series even, 3 games apiece, with 1 tie

> BOSTON—There's a set of foolish people in Boston this
> morning. They had an option on seats for yesterday's game
> between the Red Sox and the Giants and didn't go. They
> missed seeing the one baseball game of ten years. The Red
> Sox and the Giants had fought out a whole season of
> heartbreaking travel and play up to the heads of their
> respective leagues. Then they came together in a world
> series that won't soon be forgotten by anyone who saw it . . .
>
> —FRANK P. SIBLEY, *BOSTON GLOBE*, OCTOBER 17, 1912

Dawn broke over Boston, and still the streets and avenues
around Fenway Park were barren, the only people on the
premises a gaggle of speculators with fistfuls of tickets and no one to
unload them on. One bemoaned, "I'm going to take a loss that I'll
feel the rest of the year," to which another retorted, "A loss? I'm taking a bath! These ducats ain't worth the paper they're printed on if
no one will buy them!"

The locals were bitter, and there were so many candidates for
their ire, so many culprits, you needed a program to get all the
names right. There was Smoky Joe Wood, of course, right at the top
of the list. Wood had only known glory since he'd arrived in Boston,

and even if the Irish-Catholic KCs who ruled Fenway Park made Wood queasy, made him feel the forever Mason outsider, they'd adored him as they'd adored few other baseball players in their time. And how had Wood repaid them? By throwing thirteen pitches that would make a bush leaguer blush and then calling it a day. With the *World Series* on the line, no less!

There was James McAleer, formerly the favorite of working-class fans across New England, recast now as a greedy buffoon who'd tampered with a sure thing, who'd ruffled the magic carpet ride that Jake Stahl had going, who'd tempted karmic calamity by trying to steer the championship back to Fenway Park (despite all his denials), who'd then gone the extra miserable step of alienating the Royal Rooters, of all asinine things.

"If he can treat the Rooters that way," a Red Sox fan named Paul Halloran was quoted in the morning newspapers, "then what kind of chance do the rest of us have? The Rooters spend their own money to go to Baltimore and Pittsburgh and New York, and *they* get spit on? This McAleer is a fool and I won't support any fool with my hard-earned money, no sir."

Mostly, there was the Red Sox roster, the whole lineup, a group who'd gotten behind in Game Seven and didn't seem the least bit interested in mounting a comeback. Was this the result of that heartbreaking first inning? Was it the result of something else?

Either way, Boston countered with a response impossible to misinterpret.

It had had enough. It was staying away.

Elsewhere, however, there was no more important festivity than the one scheduled for the Fens at 2 o'clock Eastern Time. When word spread that there were likely to be plenty of good seats available for what was already being hyped as the baseball game of the (admittedly still young) century, a fair number of New Yorkers booked train tickets. Some of them were even baseball fans. Most, however, saw this opportunity as the ultimate business trip, so notable among the pilgrims were the most famed gamblers and bookmakers in New York City and, thus, the world: Max Blumenthal, Honest John Kelly, Leo Mayer, Jakey Josephs, Edward G. Downey. They were offering odds of 10–7 on the Giants. Theirs were the most popular seats on every eastbound train.

In Chicago, Theodore Roosevelt arose to a dull pain in his chest and a team of surgeons eager to tell him he could expect a full recovery.

"When the time comes for you to give your inauguration speech," Dr. Alexander Lambert, the Colonel's personal physician, told him, "you'll be strong as an ox."

"You mean strong as a bull moose," Roosevelt said.

Later, to the newspapermen, Lambert said, "I shudder when I realize how narrow an escape from instant death Colonel Roosevelt had. The bullet struck him from below at an angle such that unless deflected it would have surely passed through the little lobe of his right lung upward and inward through the auricles of the heart or the arch of the aorta. The folded manuscript and heavy steel spectacle case checked and deflected the bullet so that it passed up at such an angle that it went outside the ribs and in the muscles. If this hadn't happened Colonel Roosevelt would not have lived sixty seconds."

Roosevelt, a lifelong New Yorker, was eager to get back to his house in Oyster Bay, on Long Island, and just as eager to read a box score from Game Seven. A newspaper was provided him and there it was: His local nine had prevailed to live another day. Just as he had.

"Outstanding," Roosevelt said.

Throughout the country, one last time, crowds began to flock to the local newspapers late in the morning to secure ideal positions to follow the game on the remote scoreboards. In downtown Newark, where the *Evening News* had its board set up, a dockworker named Daniel Connon unwrapped a brown paper bag filled with his lunch and prepared himself for a long day of anxious baseball-watching. Three thousand miles away, outside the *Los Angeles Times* building, the mostly male group of early-morning arrivals noticed a rare sight in their midst, a slight, gray-haired woman whose smile seemed permanently affixed.

"Do you have a rooting interest?" she was asked.

"I most certainly do," she said. "I'm for the Giants!"

The men laughed. "Why, you must have picked them for their uniforms," they said, slapping their knees. But the woman shook her head.

"No, sir," she said. "I root for them because my son plays for them. He's the center fielder. His name is Fred Snodgrass."

In Manhattan, extra police had already been called to work because authorities were expecting the entire city to play hooky. The opening bell on Wall Street was greeted quietly, the floor of the stock exchange barely populated. Schoolrooms were scarce. Trial judges—at least those not presiding over Charles Becker's Trial of the Century—granted adjournments and continuances without thinking twice.

The biggest crowds gathered in Times Square, watching the *Times'* electric scoreboard on the north façade of the *Times* building. Before noon, the crowd already extended ten yards out from the building to the Astor Hotel in Seventh Avenue and the Criterion Theater on Broadway, while the plaza from Forty-third to Forty-fourth Streets was thronged with eager fans. People were also able to see from the air, since the big electric sign on the roof of the Hotel Rector was being wired during the contest. The main board was sixteen feet in length and seven feet high, continued the batting order of the two clubs, and showed what player was at bat and the result of every ball pitched, showing whether the ball was hit safely or fouled, ball or strike, putout or error. The Herald Square Playograph, a few blocks away, drew secondary crowds that were already being measured in the tens of thousands. A half-mile east were the more modest presentations along Newspaper Row, and a half-mile south the elaborate showplace at Madison Square Garden, both ensnared by humanity.

"There is no reason," Damon Runyon would write, "for any New Yorker at any time in their day today to be unaware of exactly what is transpiring in their sister city to the east. Listen closely enough and you may be able to hear the pop of a glove in Boston all the way in Greenwich Village. Although I can't promise you that."

There was but one place in all of New York where the singular conversation didn't revolve around baseball, and that was on Chambers Street, early in the afternoon. It was then that Mrs. Herman Rosenthal walked into the courtroom, locked eyes briefly with Mrs. Charles Becker—her former best friend, the wife of the man now accused of making her a widow—and raised her right arm to be sworn in. She was asked about a night the previous April, just before her husband's murder, when Becker led a raid on the family business.

"When they came to the house that night, there was so much hammering that I went down to see what was the matter," Mrs. Rosenthal told a rapt gallery. "I said to Becker, 'For God's sake, stop hammering and I'll open the door!'

"I couldn't find the key. So they broke the door in. Then I ran upstairs. Becker followed me there. I said to him, 'What does this mean?' He said, 'Sssh! It had to be Herman or me.'

"I said, 'Please don't let them break the furniture. Then Lieutenant Becker said, 'Tell Herman to call that debt off. Tell him to go and see that man and tell him to call off that mortgage for $1,500. Tell Herman it's all square. He knows what man to see."

There was a pause. Maybe it lasted only a few seconds. It felt like a few months.

"Two days later," Mrs. Rosenthal said, "my Herman was dead."

Finally there was a recess. The newspapermen in the gallery raced for the banks of telephones located in the hallway, and one of them, the man from the *Journal*, was livid; he couldn't get anyone on the phone back in his newsroom. What the hell!

It was the man from the *World*, who looked at his watch.

"Two-thirty," the man sighed. "The ballgame's started."

The man from the *Journal* shook his shoulders and hung up the receiver.

In the morning, slumped in a chair in the corridor of the Copley Square Hotel, there sat a gaunt figure with hollow cheeks and deep furrows in his brow, a man who looked to be fifty years old, whose hair was graying at the temples, who looked badly in need of a hot meal and a warm bed, who might have been mistaken for a vagrant but for the fact that he was bedecked in a soft hat, brown three-button sack suit, two buttons of the waistband showing, knitted tie, high turndown collar, and tan shoes.

In reality, the man had only recently celebrated his thirty-second birthday, and while he might never have had it in him to challenge Jim Thorpe for the title ceded him by the King of Scotland, there wasn't a soul striding in this hotel lobby—or anywhere else in America, for that matter—who wouldn't have acknowledged that this was one of the greatest athletes on earth if they'd known his true identity.

"I'm tired," Christy Mathewson had admitted that morning in his syndicated newspaper column.

"I think all of the fellows on both teams are tired. The baseball season is a long grind, and if you're lucky enough to play in the World Series, the way we are and the way Boston is, it can be exhausting. But we also know there's nothing to save ourselves for now. After today, we can relax. But we have a ballgame to play first."

Mathewson had been the first one to hit the coffee shop, just past 8 o'clock, and he'd ordered the fifty-five-cent club breakfast of cereal, bacon and eggs, and a pot of coffee. Tired as he was, as much as fatigue may have been eating at his bones and muscles, he wasn't nervous, and he wolfed down his food. Nervous? It was far too late in the game for Matty to get nervous for one pitching assignment, no matter how high the stakes might be. His legacy was already secure, as was his future: Most simply assumed that when his right arm finally ran out of gas, he'd succeed his very good friend, John J. McGraw, as manager of the Giants—unless he was more inclined to pursue business interests, or law school, or politics. He would have no lack of secular suitors if he ever opted for life outside the white lines.

"Mathewson," McGraw once said, "is the greatest man in America. Not simply the greatest pitcher, or baseball player, or athlete. The greatest *man*."

Theirs had long been a most improbable (if not utterly implausible) friendship, the hard-charging, hard-living, single-minded manager and the urbane, sophisticated Renaissance Man of a pitcher. McGraw's own wife, Blanche, had once said, "Life without baseball had little meaning for John. It was his meat, drink, dream, his blood and breath, his very reason for existence." No one would ever think to associate such a sentence to the Christian Gentleman.

Yet starting with a 2–0 shutout thrown by a twenty-one-year-old Mathewson on July 24, 1902, just after McGraw had moved north from Baltimore to assume the reins, McGraw and Mathewson, star pitcher and ultra-ambitious manager, were virtually inseparable. In 1903, John and Blanche McGraw moved with Christy and Jane Mathewson into a furnished seven-room apartment at Eighty-fifth Street and Columbus Avenue, a block from Central Park. The couples split the fifty-dollar monthly rent and other living expenses, and would share those accommodations for three seasons, or until young John Christopher Mathewson (named for McGraw) was born early in 1906.

By then, the Giants had won two National League pennants and dominated the Philadelphia Athletics to win the 1905 World Series, and Mathewson had emerged as the greatest pitcher of his generation by throwing three shutouts at the A's. Both men believed that there would be many more seasons just like it, believed they were on the ground floor of the greatest baseball dynasty ever assembled. But then the Cubs had usurped the Giants for a few years in the National League, and they'd lost that rematch with the A's in the 1911 Series, and now here they were, seven years later, the two of them hoping to drink championship champagne one more time (if not one last time).

Mathewson wanted to win the Series.

But he believed his friend *needed* to win the Series.

"It is right that McGraw be seen as the greatest manager in the game, because it's what he wants and it's what he deserves," Mathewson had written. "If we win this series, I'm sure that's how he will be seen."

In the home clubhouse at Fenway Park, nobody was much concerned with niceties. This was a simmering, blistering cauldron of a room this Wednesday morning, a place where hard feelings were no longer camouflaged, a place where the tension was so thick as to be almost unbearable. It didn't help any that as soon as the Speed Boys reported for work they were greeted by yet another stuffed suit wanting to tell them what was expected of them and what they had to do. This time it was Ban Johnson, the founder of the American League, better known to the angry souls in the room as one of the three cheap sons of bitches who'd denied them an extra gate after the Game Two tie.

"Boys," Johnson said, "you have *got* to win this game. You have the ability, both mentally and physically, to beat the Giants. Go in and play for all you are worth and don't stop fighting until the last man has been retired. Upon you depends the future popularity of the American League. The Giants are going to make a desperate stand and will be hard to overcome, but if you play your best game you will be triumphant. Now buckle down to work and show the Boston baseball people how game you are!"

As quickly as he'd materialized, Johnson disappeared, and if the Red Sox were moved by his speech they did their best to hide those emotions. They continued to dress in quiet, looking like a beaten team, when Smoky Joe Wood finished buttoning his jersey and went across the room, knocked on the manager's office door, and stepped inside.

Jake Stahl glanced up from his newspaper, nodded his head.

"Come on in, Joe," Stahl said. "Take a load off."

Wood's message was a simple one.

"I'm ready to pitch today, Skip," Wood said. "You can count on me."

Stahl nodded his head. It wasn't in him to interrogate Wood, to ask what had happened the day before. As far as he was concerned, for the record, Wood simply hadn't had it against the Giants. All pitchers get raked every now and again, even the great ones. Stahl couldn't crawl inside Wood's brain. He could only go by what his pitcher told him.

You can count on me.

"Stay ready," Stahl said. "But I'm going with Bedient to start."

Stahl gave Wood a stern look that said a couple of things, primarily this: This time, it's *me* keeping you out of the game, no one above me, and that's the manager's prerogative. But there was also this subtle message, too:

Whatever you did yesterday, it was what you needed to do.

This is what *I* need to do.

"I'll stay ready," Wood said, rising from the chair, walking toward the door and back into the chilling quiet of the clubhouse. It was almost too much to bear, and there was only one man who would be able to pierce it.

"Listen up," Heinie Wagner said, and instinctively his teammates gathered around the Red Sox shortstop. All season long, it had been Wagner who'd called team meetings, who'd soothed hard feelings, who'd massaged egos, who'd made certain everyone kept their eyes firmly fastened on the prize. One last time, he'd have to do it again, he'd have to recalibrate this fractious, delicate baseball apparatus.

"Look, whatever's happened, we still have a shot to win the world's championship and to get our hands on that winner's share," Wagner said. "We don't have to like each other. Hell, I'm past believing most of you guys can even *tolerate* each other and I have to tell you: I want to punch a couple of you in the jaw myself right now. But we got nine innings left in the season. No reason why we shouldn't get after it with everything we got. Is anyone with me?"

There was a quiet pause, as if they were all pondering their options.

And then, louder: *"Is anyone with me?"*

With that, Wagner got his answer. First, a voice from a distant corner of the room: *"I am."* And then a few more: *"Yeah." "Count me in." "Let's beat their asses!" "Let's go for the big money!"* If it wasn't the kind of classic locker-room speech that would come to define American sports over the coming decades, it was enough to roust the Speed Boys from their wicked slumber.

Hell, they'd put up with each other for close to seven and a half months.

What was three more hours? What was nine more innings?

The Giants walked onto the field laughing, whistling, singing, practically floating in the grass. This was the way they'd spent most of their summer, after all, showing up for work in a ballpark in Boston, or Chicago, or Pittsburgh, or Cincinnati, and knowing they were going to steamroll some helpless opponent and have a hell of a time doing it. It was that swagger that pissed off so many National League teams, that made so many opposing fans want to pelt the Giants with rotten tomatoes and rocks and other assorted projectiles.

"When they lose, they feel like they've been set crooked," Frank Chance, the recently dismissed manager of the Cubs, had said earlier in the year. "And when they win, they all act like some paragons of virtue. They take their cue from the manager. When they're playing well, they can infuriate an archbishop."

Soon enough, Chance would learn even more about Giants arrogance, because he would soon be appointed the manager of the Yankees, meaning not only would he have to keep a daily tally of how much farther ahead the Giants were in the National League than the woeful Yanks were in the American, he would actually have to pay McGraw money every month in order to play their home games at the Polo Grounds. McGraw would fully delight in this landlord-tenant relationship for the next decade, minding the Yankees' existence far less than he used to now that he could count on their rent checks. Sharing the town—coupled with his team's dreadful .411 winning percentage—would soon drive Chance to distraction, and then out of baseball entirely for a time.

"McGraw," he would say, "is despicable when he wins."

Now, with his baseball team suddenly nine innings away from restoring him to the roof of baseball's Pantheon, McGraw was hoping the rest of his sport would soon find him similarly contemptible. As the New York press corps gathered around him in the hours leading up to the first pitch, the Giants' manager sounded every bit as loose and carefree as his players looked on the field.

"The Red Sox had us on the ropes," said McGraw, the big boxing fan using his favorite boxing metaphor. "But we survived, and now we're ready to take what is rightfully ours. We still haven't even played *one* game worth a damn, but that's OK. I think today will make up for the rest, and once we win today nobody's going to care how we played in the other games."

Fenway Park had the look and the feel of an exhausted, burned-out vaudeville house. There were dry brown patches all over the outfield grass, and the infield was a lumpy mess, as if the grounds crew had taken their cue from the Sox themselves and mailed in the past few days of work, too. Not that there were many to complain: Good as their word, the Royal Rooters all stayed away from the yard—with one glaring exception. For once, the two masters that John Fitzgerald served—his baseball team and his city—had irreversibly collided. He felt a loyalty to his Rooters. But he felt an even stronger duty to his constituents. *Boston* still had a chance to be crowned king of the baseball world (and at New York's expense, no less), and so even if Fitzgerald the fan would be absent in spirit, Honey Fitz the mayor would be there in body. And in voice.

It wasn't only the Rooters who were drenched in disillusionment, either. Before the game, down at the Park Street subway entrance, speculators were vainly trying to sell their tickets, and a full hour before the game they'd already started scrambling, agreeing to settle for face value. Even then, there were only a few takers, and soon the scalpers threw up their hands and started giving them away for whatever people were willing to pay . . . and *still* business was as slow as one of Joe Wood's Game Seven fastballs. The ballpark reflected this: By 1:40, twenty minutes before the scheduled first pitch, the stands were only half full, a shocking sight to anyone, but especially to Red Sox players accustomed to playing in front of a full house. The first-base extension stands were practically empty, the third-base grandstand was barely half full, the bleachers a vast sea of unoccupied slabs of wood. The Red Sox, hoping to make up for numbers with decibels, distributed thousands of wood rattlers to those customers who professed to be Sox fans (Giants invaders were given nothing but quiet thanks for filling the Sox' coffers another three dollars).

Despite their bravado, there were a handful of Giants who copped to feeling an unusual case of nerves. After all, none of them had ever played a decisive World Series game before, since only twenty-one men had *ever* played a decisive World Series game before. That was the dirty little secret of this annual baseball event that some newspapers had already dubbed "The Fall Classic": In many cases, there was nothing "classic" about any of it. In the eight previous Series, there had been one sweep, three one-sided five-game walkovers, two equally unbalanced six-game affairs, and the very first one, in 1903, when Boston and Pittsburgh had played eight games in an unruly best-of-nine competition.

Only once had the World Series come down to the "ultimate" game, a Game Seven, when in 1909 the Pittsburgh Pirates and Detroit Tigers split the first six games, setting up what should have been a timeless showdown between the Tigers of Ty Cobb and the Pirates of Honus Wagner but was instead a grisly 8–0 whitewash for the visiting Pirates in the seventh and deciding game. Across the next century of baseball, there were few terms that would conjure more magic or more romance in the whole sport than the words "Game Seven," but every single example of why was still very much in the future as the Giants and Red Sox went through their final pregame paces.

During batting practice, Larry Doyle, the Giants' captain, broke his favorite bat completely in half. Sensing that his favorite team-mate was all but grinding his teeth to dust from the pregame ten-sion, Buck Herzog walked over, took the handle out of Doyle's hands, drove it into the ground, and announced, "you have to punish them properly."

Doyle wasn't amused.

"That's a jinx," he yelped, his voice shaky. "Now I *know* I won't get a hit!"

Herzog roared with laughter; there was little doubt in his or any-one else's mind that it was long past time to get this thing started and settled. The two managers continued to play their little games, Jake Stahl sending both Hugh Bedient and Joe Wood out to the bullpen to warm up, McGraw, naturally, countering with *four* pitchers: Christy Mathewson, Rube Marquard, Jeff Tesreau, and Red Ames. By the time they met at home plate for the conference with the umpires, both McGraw and Stahl had to smile as they shook hands one last time.

"I've enjoyed this series very much," McGraw said.

"I have also," Stahl said. "May the better team win."

"I think," McGraw said, unable to resist, "that you can count on that."

With that, they were back in their dugouts, and the Sox (with Bedient ambling toward the mound) were jogging out to their posi-tions, and one last time Silk O'Loughlin, taking one more turn behind home plate, announced the batteries—"For the Red Sox! Bedient and Cady! For the Giants! Mathewson and Meyers!"—and then, for what was sure to be the final time in calendar year 1912, he cleared his throat.

"Play ball!" O'Loughlin roared.

In a time of reform in America, few things were more sacrosanct than the antitrust legislation that filled every courthouse docket in every jurisdiction in the land. It was Theodore Roosevelt who'd seized the subject during his presidency, who'd gleefully embraced the reputation of a no-nonsense trust-buster who would brook no obstacle in the fight to make sure the United States remained an economy free of monopolists and robber barons. It was both an irony and an indication of how fast the nation was moving that, in the weeks before the attempt on Roosevelt's life in Milwaukee, both Woodrow Wilson and William Howard Taft had tried to paint a picture of Roosevelt being too *soft* on trusts, too lenient on big business, too willing to get cozy with the Rockefellers and Carnegies and Morgans who were alleged to be anathema to antitrust legislation.

So it was little surprise that early in the afternoon of October 16, 1912, the U.S. Supreme Court was engaged in a bench hearing on the famed "Bathroom Trust" case, officially titled *Standard Sanitary Manufacturing Company v. United States.* The justices were preparing to listen to the government's case when the lunch recess hit, just before two o'clock. Associate Justice William Rufus Day, before repairing to his chambers, summoned one of his clerks and sent him on a sacred mission.

"Take these," Day said, stuffing several dozen thin slips of paper into his clerk's hands. "I want regular updates."

The justices all knew what was taking place in Boston that very afternoon—that very moment, in fact. Not all of them were baseball fans. But enough were. And so for the duration of the lunch hour— "And," Day asserted to his clerk, "for as long as is necessary thereafter"—they would be kept apprised of whatever was happening at Fenway Park within minutes.

So nine men in black robes would join thousands of truant schoolchildren and thousands of recalcitrant workers in having their attentions greatly and grandly divided by the final baseball game of 1912, and like their fellow citizens they would remain riveted for the next three hours, rendered practically breathless by a baseball game that, even as it was unfolding, was slowly taking its place alongside— and, ultimately, far beyond—the greatest baseball games ever played to that point.

And everyone knew it. There may only have been 17,034 people inside the yard, but from the beginning they made the noise of twice that number. They were loud, they were enthusiastic, and they celebrated both teams. There was a fair segment of Giants fans, but this went beyond pure partisanship.

"Rarely," Runyon would write, "have paying customers ever gotten their money's worth the way these partisans did."

For much of the afternoon, it would be Christy Mathewson who would command the most attention, the loudest cheers, and the deepest devotions. There wasn't a man anywhere near Fenway Park who would testify that Mathewson bore even a shadow of a resemblance to the pitcher he'd once been. And yet, as the innings mounted on this day, as his pitch count grew, so too did his aura. Even as a youngster he didn't have Joe Wood's fastball, and even though he would collect two hundred or more strikeouts five times in his career Mathewson truly earned his legend as a *pitcher*, not a *thrower*, as a craftsman rather than a marvel of nature. And never was he more at one with his craft than on this day. Across the first six innings, he would strike out only four hitters and he would be anything but overpowering.

"You would watch from the bench, and you could barely contain yourself, you'd want to grab a bat and get up there and take your swings," Tris Speaker would recall many years later. "And then you'd actually have a bat in your hands, and it was almost like he could read your mind. He knew *exactly* what he had to throw to make you look incredibly foolish. That's what great pitchers can do, even to very good hitters."

Speaker reached Mathewson for a first-inning single and reached second base when Doyle (proving he really was a bundle of jangling nerves) committed an error, but Mathewson calmly stranded him there by striking out Duffy Lewis. In the second, the Red Sox had two on and one out, but a pop-up and a ground ball quickly ended that threat. And in the sixth, when the Sox finally got a man as far as third base (after Steve Yerkes singled, moved to second on a walk, and to third on a fielder's choice), what did Mathewson do? He picked Yerkes off third base. End of inning. End of trouble. And what looked like the start of a very, very, *very* long winter for the Speed Boys.

There was only one problem.

The Giants were having just as much trouble getting to young Hugh Bedient, the pride of Falconer, New York. They stranded one man in the first and another two in the second before finally scratching a run off Bedient in the third, Red Murray continuing his Series-long redemption tour by stroking a two-out double that scored Josh Devore.

Of course, they should have had at least two more runs.

And, of course, there was a story behind both of those failures.

In the fourth, with Fenway finally starting to buzz nervously, Buck Herzog smoked a line drive that soared over Speaker's head in center field. McGraw, coaching third, started jumping wildly: A ball could ricochet forever out there, and the question, in McGraw's mind, was a simple one: Should he play it safe and hold Herzog at third with a triple? Or should he really press the issue, send him home for a chance at an inside-the-park home run that would surely crush the Red Sox' spirit? So many choices, so many . . .

Hey! McGraw heard himself yelling, *What the hell is Klem doing . . . ?*

What Bill Klem was doing was enjoying the rare pleasure of using McGraw's own words, his own affinity for capturing every conceivable edge, and dropping them right back in McGraw's lap. What Klem, umpiring at second base, had seen was the same thing Tris Speaker had seen: The baseball, instead of rattling around the cavernous outfield, had somehow settled into a tiny hole in the extreme corner of the bleachers—the *same* tiny hole, in the *same* extreme corner of the bleachers, that Harry Hooper had found four days earlier, in Game Five.

Suddenly, chillingly, McGraw remembered his own words.

"How is that not a ground-rule double, Silk?" McGraw had yelled at Silk O'Loughlin that day. *"It's common sense, Silk!"*

"Take it up with the Commission," O'Loughlin had urged, and that's

exactly what McGraw had done, and for once they had actually *listened* to him, they'd changed the grounds rule, and McGraw had taken such satisfaction when they'd done it. It was *his* rule, changed at *his* insistence. And now it was going to bite him in his trousers.

"Bill," McGraw asked sheepishly, "are you *sure* the ball went in the hole?"

"Saw it with my own eyes, John," Klem said. "It's a double."

On another day, in another situation, McGraw might have offered up a few choice observations about the quality and the reliability of Klem's eyesight, but not now, not in the fourth inning of the decisive World Series game, not with McGraw knowing who'd caused the rule change in the first place. So instead of an inside-the-parker, or instead of having a man on third and nobody out, it was a man on second and none out. Big difference. Made even bigger when Chief Meyers, Art Fletcher, and Mathewson could not drive Herzog home.

That was one galling, missed opportunity.

The next one came an inning later, when with one out Larry Doyle stepped into a Bedient fastball and absolutely pulverized it, sending it on a majestic path toward the bleachers in right field. Doyle knew he'd gotten all of it.

"So much for the jinx!" he crowed to himself as he slowed into his home-run trot.

There was only one problem: In right field, Harry Hooper hadn't conceded the play yet. He was still tracking the ball, even as he ran out of outfield, even as his back collided with the short fence, even as the ball kept soaring behind him. Hooper figured he had little to lose, so he jumped, lunged his glove hand toward the ball, then disappeared into a tangle of humanity.

Doyle was still trotting, unmoved.

"There's no way he caught that ball," he muttered to no one in particular.

Klem and Cy Rigler, the first-base ump, raced out to right field just in time to see Hooper's head emerge from the crowd, and then to see him lift his glove—with a baseball safely nestled inside—in triumph.

Rigler, satisfied, raised his arm.

"Batter is out!" he yelled.

Doyle was apoplectic, screeched, "I *was* jinxed!" but he was stoic compared to his manager, who came roaring out of the dugout and dashed to greet the umpires.

"There's *no way* you can tell for sure that he caught that ball!" McGraw raged. "For all you know, he picked it up off the ground after he fell in the stands! For all you know, a fan gave him the ball!"

Rigler listened to McGraw, let him have his say.

Then repeated, "Batter is out!"

Unbelievable, McGraw thought. By rights, his team should be up 3–0, and there was no way Matty was capable of giving up a three-run lead. Hell, as good as he was pitching, 1–0 might well be enough. But 3–0 sure would have been better.

McGraw was reminded of that as the Speed Boys mounted one more desperate push in the home half of the seventh inning. With one out, Jake Stahl blooped a single into the unoccupied gap between left and center, and then Mathewson issued a full-count walk to Heinie Wagner. Suddenly, there was one more set of raindrops for Matty to dance through, the tying run was in scoring position, and the Sox fans inside Fenway Park began loudly waving their wooden rattlers, trying to shake Mathewson in any way that they could.

But Mathewson was equal to that challenge, jamming Hick Cady on his fists with a fastball, coaxing an easy pop-up to Art Fletcher at short for the second out. Now Stahl had a decision to make. Bedient had pitched well, but he knew the Sox might never get a better chance than this to score the equalizer. From second base, he ordered Joe Wood to remove his mackinaw jacket and hustle to the bullpen to start throwing. And then he pointed to the dugout and ordered into the batter's box a twenty-four-year-old reserve outfielder born in Kirkerup, Denmark, named Olaf Henriksen.

Or, as a ten-year-old boy loudly and boldly asked in Times Square, amid the nervous, quiet throng surrounding the *Times* scoreboard:

"Olaf *Who*-riksen?"

It was a fair question.

There have been close to 17,000 men who have played at least one inning of major league baseball since 1869. Olaf Henriksen is the only one ever born in Denmark. His family emigrated to the United States just before the turn of the century and Henriksen's schoolmates dubbed him "Swede," of course, since geographic accuracy was never of any concern in the half-second it took to come up with a nickname (hence the dozens of ballplayers of German descent through the years who would be called "Dutch"). Henriksen grew into a fine baseball player, a slender athlete who could run and throw and whose hitting caught the eye of the Red Sox scouts after a single season playing for the Brockton club in the New England League.

Henriksen had shown a proficiency with the bat from the moment he arrived in Boston in 1911, hitting .366 in ninety-three at-bats as a rookie in 1911 and .321 in fifty-six at-bats in 1912 (to go along with fourteen walks in both years, exhibiting a fine eye that would serve him well throughout his career). But the Red Sox outfield was virtually impossible to crack; Tris Speaker and Harry Hooper would both wind up in Cooperstown, and Duffy Lewis was the best left fielder in the league. And, more important, all three men were built out of iron. The Red Sox played 154 games (including two ties) in 1912; Lewis played all 154, Speaker played in 153, and Hooper played in 147. All three had played every inning of the World Series, too, meaning that Henriksen's opportunities to stir from the bench were practically nil. His only Series appearance had nearly been a memorable one, however: He was racing around the bases at the end of Game Three with the potential tying run when

Josh Devore made his spectacular, game-clinching grab of Hick Cady's drive in the darkness.

Still, Henriksen had a sense he would be called upon to do something special here, with the season growing short on the Red Sox. "Somehow, in that seventh inning, I got a hunch that I would be sent up as a pinch hitter," he would say after the game. "After Gardner had flied out to Devore [for the first out], I pulled for Jake to get on for I felt if Stahl reached first the chance I had been waiting for would come."

And now it had. Now, Olaf Henriksen, with exactly 149 at-bats under his belt in the major leagues, would face Christy Mathewson, Big Six, the Christian Gentleman, the most decorated pitcher in history, the most beloved sportsman in America. You would think those might be some overpowering odds for the kid from Kirkerup. You would be wrong.

"I was certain—cocksure—that I could beat Matty," Henriksen asserted later.

Mathewson was never one to be especially gracious to younger generations of players who happened to play on opposing teams. As helpful as he was to his younger teammates, he always saw foes of any age as logical successors to his throne, be they hitters who would try to beat him (and take food off his table) or pitchers who might threaten his pitching records (and take money out of his pocket). Joe Wood, for one, would remember bitterly for decades after that as often as he tried to engage Mathewson in conversation during the 1912 World Series, Mathewson was cold, distant, aloof, and completely uninterested in forging a friendship with the younger man.

Now Mathewson peered in at Henriksen and the Swede instantly understood the great pitcher's hesitation: *He's never heard of me! He has no idea what kind of pitches I like, which ones I avoid. He has no idea how to get me out!* It was here that Henriksen decided he'd let Matty's first offering pass by, no matter how inviting it looked. So he just stared at a sweeping curve, which dropped in for strike one.

"Atta boy, Matty!" Meyers, the catcher, screamed. "Two more just like it!"

Henriksen figured Matty would stay with the curve, the pitch that had made hundreds of major-league hitters squirm, and he was right: As a left-handed hitter, Henriksen could pick the ball up from the moment it left Mathewson's right hand, the ball seemingly starting somewhere near third base then spinning slowly and magnificently back to the plate. It came in slow and inviting, and Henriksen whipped his bat around, and just like those hundreds of vanquished hitters before him the ball seemed to have a mind of its own, seemed to dance clear around the bat before falling softly into Meyers's glove. Strike two.

"He's yours, Matty!" Meyers roared. "He's yours!"

Mathewson came back with a couple of fastballs, a couple inches wide of the plate, figuring Henriksen might chase them. He didn't. Now, at 2-and-2, with the tying run still sitting there on second base, with his team now seven outs from a championship and $4,000 a man, Mathewson and Henriksen both knew what was up next. When it left Matty's hand, it was waist high, and right before home plate it dipped straight down, like a diver jumping off a cliff. Mathewson had thrown this pitch so many times before, and he knew when he'd thrown it well. He'd thrown this one *perfectly*.

Henriksen was beaten, but he wasn't fooled. Knowing the curve was coming, he'd kept all his weight back. Somehow, as the ball acceded to gravity, he readjusted his swing, looking as if he were lunging at it with both hands. And the most curious thing happened: The ball met the bat squarely. It wasn't hit hard, but it was hit hard enough: It hugged the third-base line and found the patch of dirt between the bag and Buck Herzog's glove, squirting through. Stahl, not a fast runner, could have crawled home with the tying run. Henriksen, a very fast runner, didn't stop until he reached second.

"Then it occurred to me for the first time that I had done something," Henriksen would recount. "So I stood on second base, and I was almost hypnotized by the racket of the crowd. I wondered: *Is some of that meant for me?*"

All of it was. Mathewson stood blankly on the mound, wondering if there really was some mystical force greater than he who was hell-bent on making him pay, retroactively, for those three shutouts from the '05 series. He stared at Henriksen, who had no business beating him in such a critical spot. He quickly retired Hooper on a lazy fly to center, keeping the game tied. Smoky Joe Wood entered the game and (surprise, surprise!) looked nothing like the pitcher he'd been twenty-four hours earlier, blazing through the Giants' lineup in the eighth and ninth, allowing only a scratch single and a walk. Mathewson received a small scare in the bottom of the ninth, allowing a one-out double to Jake Stahl, but he induced easy fly balls from Heinie Wagner and Hick Cady to escape the jam.

So it wouldn't be enough for the Red Sox and the Giants to wrestle with each other for three wins apiece, for one hard-fought tie, and for nine more innings of an eighth game. No, they would have to go to a tenth inning (and who knew how much longer beyond?) to settle this most remarkable World Series.

Silk O'Loughlin looked at the sky; there would still be time for a good hour more of baseball. He could only hope that would be enough time.

"We may have to play this in moonlight," he joked to Hick Cady when he came out to catch Wood's warm-ups for the top of the tenth.

"Might as well," Cady replied, stone serious. "I have nowhere else I have to be."

Or anyplace he—or the others—would rather be. On to the tenth inning it was.

CHAPTER ELEVEN

Wednesday, October 16, 1912

Tenth inning, Game Eight, Giants 1, Red Sox 1

BOSTON—It was a series which combined the wildest
mixture of brilliant and wretched playing, of impossible
catches and easy chances marred, of wonderful and bush
league pitching, of desperate chances and dumb, bush league
work—a veritable swirl of all that goes to make up baseball
from every angle of the game. Games were saved by
miraculous work and lost by schoolboy muffs and the only
regret both teams might have is that such a drama should
close and swing upon a fly ball popping from an outfielder's
hands or an easy foul fly fluttering safely when it should have
been snagged with both eyes shut . . .

—DAMON RUNYON, *NEW YORK AMERICAN*, OCTOBER 17, 1912

H E LOVED THE action, John McGraw did, and it didn't always
have to be contained to the neat geography of a baseball diamond to get his blood racing, even if it was there where all of his
diverse passions coagulated neatly. In his youth, in Baltimore, he'd
opened up the first duckpin bowling alley alongside his friend
Wilbert Robinson, and it had been a huge hit. Later, after he hit the
Big Town, he opened up a string of billiard halls, and because he was
the famous manager of the New York Giants, nobody ever seemed

terribly bothered by the fact that his silent partner was a man named Arnold Rothstein, who a few years down the road would nearly destroy the very game that had made John McGraw famous. He was a well-paid thespian, of all things, spending many of his off-season hours in vaudeville houses in the employ of B. F. Keith, the most renowned theater impresario of the day. In 1912, he would do fifteen weeks on the road, performing a monologue titled "Inside Baseball" that was a mishmash of his own stories and embellishments penned by Bozeman Bulger of the *New York World*. It was, admittedly, a fairly routine (or "dull," or "sleep-inducing" if you listened to some of the critics) bit that was usually tolerated by the sold-out crowds because McGraw invariably followed Keith's featured performer, Odiva, "The Goldfish Lady," who would immerse herself (and her considerable talents) in a glass tank filled with water for two and a half minutes. For his efforts, McGraw would clear close to $60,000 on the stage (and in those pre-income-tax years, he kept every penny of that windfall, worth $1.3 million in 2008 dollars). He even did a silent film, *The Detective*, in which he played an Irish gumshoe.

But it was the ponies that truly captured McGraw's attention and most of his non-baseball devotion. As a player in Baltimore, he'd often frequent the famed Pimlico Raceway, and after the original Orioles were dissolved and McGraw had been shipped out to St. Louis, he took solace in the fact that the city's most popular track was located right next to Robison Park, where the Perfectos played home games. Every off day in New York would find McGraw leaning against the rail at Belmont Park, or Aqueduct Raceway, or at nearby Empire City Raceway in upstate Yonkers. Once, in fact, there was a widely circulated (and widely accepted) tale that McGraw had dispatched two players to Yonkers to lay down money on a horse named Confessor that was going off at 10-to-1. Five hundred dollars richer, it was easier for McGraw to swallow the 20–5 shellacking the Pirates had laid on his team that day.

It was this equine affinity that had led McGraw to Los Angeles in the spring of 1907. McGraw had sold John T. Brush on the idea of the Giants training in Southern California by emphasizing the public-relations coup of a big league team visiting virgin baseball territory. In reality, McGraw had heard about the many wildcat racetracks that dotted the L.A. area, and figured that was as good a place as any to hold his annual baseball boot camp. And so it was, that early in that spring of 1907, a catcher for St. Vincent's College, against whom the Giants were scrimmaging, caught McGraw's eye.

A year later, McGraw was back in California (on his own dime now, as Brush had caught on to his game) and was working out on his own in between visits to the track, when he was trying to fill out two teams to put together a pickup game, and he badly needed a catcher.

"What was the name of that kid from St. Vincent's?" he asked one of the locals.

"Fred Snodgrass," he was told. "He's the best semipro catcher in California."

Snodgrass was summoned, played, and played as well as McGraw remembered. Afterward, he approached the twenty-year-old backstop and shook his hand.

"Are you thinking of playing pro baseball?" McGraw asked.

"A little," said Snodgrass, "but not too seriously, to tell the truth."

McGraw reached into his pocket, removed a contract, told Snodgrass to bring the contract home, talk it over with his parents, and if he still wanted to stay home and play ball only on weekends, no hard feelings. But if he wanted to go to spring training with the New York Giants, the train for Marlin, Texas, was leaving in four days and he could expect to earn the princely sum of $150 a month.

"And really," Snodgrass would say years later, "what choice was there to make?"

Two months later, Snodgrass broke camp with the Giants as a third-string catcher, and over the next two years McGraw kept moving him around the diamond, looking for a place for him to play. Snodgrass was quick to anger and he had a fresh mouth, and some managers would have sent him home the moment he popped off about playing time. Not McGraw. He liked young players who believed in themselves. Hell, he would say, I'd be more inclined to send him home if he *wasn't* mad about not playing more. Guys like that, guys who were in it just for the paycheck, they were stealing money, and you couldn't win with guys like that. But you could win with guys like Snodgrass. So on the Giants' first road trip of the 1910 season, McGraw knocked on Snodgrass's door in the Cincinnati hotel.

"Hey, Snow," McGraw said. "How would you like to play center field?"

Snodgrass was furious. This son of a bitch was sending him to the minor leagues! "For which club?" he asked, his face reddening.

"Why, for *this* club, of course."

Snodgrass was stunned, but he was also ready. He hit .321 for those 1910 Giants, who won ninety-one games and finished second behind the Cubs. He hit ten triples in 1911 and stole fifty-one bases (while getting on base nearly 40 percent of the time), and he'd learned his defensive position so well that he'd become among the most reliable outfielders in the National League. McGraw loved him, because he was proof positive that not only could McGraw spot talent in even the most far-flung places on the map, he could mold that talent into something approaching stardom.

But there was a cost to that fealty, a blind spot that sometimes prevented McGraw from being as hard on Snodgrass as he was on other players. Snodgrass had some spasms of selfishness and incivility that angered his teammates, especially when there were no visible ramifications. During the 1911 Series, he'd caused an unnecessary furor when, in the bottom of the tenth inning of Game Three, in a 1–1 struggle, he'd tried to intentionally get hit by a ball thrown by Jack Coombs. When the umpire didn't buy it, Snodgrass eventually worked out a walk but kept chattering about how he'd been screwed, then made the ill-fated decision to take second on a short passed ball. The throw beat him by ten steps, but Snodgrass kept coming, kicking his spikes deep into Frank Baker's shins.

The move not only fired up the Athletics (who won that day and two of the next three, too, to sew up the Series), it nearly cost Snodgrass something greater: Death threats poured into the Giants' offices, and into their hotel, and a rumor quickly spread that Snodgrass had been shot dead by a furious Philly fanatic. His teammates never forgot that, and neither did the press, and so when Snodgrass picked that silly fight with the members of the bleachers prior to Game Five, it lit a lot of smoldering embers.

"Fred Snodgrass is, off the ballfield, apparently as level-headed a fellow as one could meet, but when he dons his uniform and goes into an important series before a big crowd when everything is at stake he seems fated to make some bull-headed move that queers not only the situation but himself and his fellow players," Sam Crane had written in the *Journal* after his Fenway Park antics. "He not only makes himself obnoxious to the people he is evidently striving to anger but he aggravates the Giants themselves and their friends and rooters to a degree that is dangerously effective as a boomerang."

Perhaps that sounds sensationalistic. But there was another correspondent in another newspaper that day who seemed to concur fully:

"It is not my policy to criticize, since I have my own soul to take care of," opined temporary sports columnist Christy Mathewson, in close to three hundred newspapers nationwide, "but Snodgrass simply has to be better than that."

McGraw heard, saw, and read all the criticisms and flicked them away. The Giants had gotten this far with Snodgrass and all the regular dramas and furies that sometimes traveled in his wake. He was McGraw's boy. Surely, when the chips were down, he would be equal to the task.

For now, though, the moment got to Fred Snodgrass, leading off the top of the tenth inning. Snodgrass looked at one Joe Wood fastball whistle right down the heart of the plate and then swung at the next one, drizzling a ground ball right back to Wood, who lobbed to Jake Stahl for the first out. It wasn't until Snodgrass returned to the dugout that he realized how much it hurt to try to straighten out his fingers; that was how tightly he'd been gripping his bat.

Which was perfectly understandable. The Giants and the Red Sox were in uncharted waters, engaged in a battle that was beyond exciting now and had reached a point of utter excruciation. And everyone could feel it. The moment the Red Sox had tied the game in the seventh, Ban Johnson had left his seat and started wandering around Fenway Park, trying to burn off nervous energy that had him practically muttering to himself. In the dugouts, where reserves could only watch and bite their fingernails and whittle away the minutes, there was an almost unbearable tension. Jeff Tesreau and Rube Marquard, who'd both done their jobs to simply allow this decisive game to occur, talked gibberish to each other, neither able to keep their brains focused on anything but the pitch at hand. In the stands, John Fitzgerald had long allowed his anger to abate—especially since he'd already visited John McAleer and extracted the promise of an apology, win or lose—and was now absently thumbing the rosary beads in his pants pocket.

Everywhere else, the pressure was pure and it was palpable. In New York, the police had simply given up the ghost when it came to crowd control; there were a hundred thousand people in midtown alone, between the *Times* scoreboard and the Herald Square Playograph, and the word was the only time a crowd had even approached this one was for the presidential election returns of 1900, 1904, and 1908. Most of the masses near the *Times* building had virtually adopted a ten-year-old boy from the East Side of Manhattan named James, who'd climbed the subway kiosk and had been cheering— pleading, almost—ever since the Giants took the lead and who had to be consoled in the bottom of the seventh when news of the Red Sox' tying run had reduced him to a whisper: "That can't be! Matty wouldn't let that happen!"

In Boston, the Royal Rooters boycott may have kept Fenway freed up with breathing room, but as word of the epic struggle crisscrossed the town, 50,000 citizens gathered along Newspaper Row, living and dying and breathing with every pitch. If they'd so desired, they could have walked a few more blocks to Fenway itself, where a disconsolate bunch of ticket brokers was getting ready to throw the ducats into a bonfire, but why would you want to go there, anyway? There were three times as many people right *here*. In New Jersey, as the "zero" was slotted under both teams in the ninth inning on the scoreboard sponsored by the *Newark Evening News*, Daniel Connon tried to ignore the tightness in his chest and the shortness of his breath. And in California, Adie Snodgrass peered intently at the *Los Angeles Times*'s scoreboard during her son's tenth-inning at-bat, exhaled when the announcer said, "Ground ball to the pitcher, one away," and hoped Fred would have other chances to distinguish himself, and deliver the Giants, before the afternoon was through.

Back at Fenway Park, the relief that greeted Snodgrass's ground-out was soon replaced by a groan that bounced all over the grand-stand: Red Murray, one more time, had found a pitch he liked and crushed it, putting a little more space and a little more distance between himself and that calamitous 1911 World Series, the 0-for-21 millstone he'd carried around his neck for fifty-two weeks. This was his tenth hit in thirty-one at-bats in this Series, and as he cruised into second base standing up, he pounded his hands together, and in the quiet still of a panicky ballpark you could hear his satisfied applause from every seat.

Up to the plate stepped Fred Merkle.

For four years, Merkle had been searching for just such a moment, for an opportunity to reclaim his good name and restore a reputation that had already taken more of a beating than any twenty-three-year-old should ever have to absorb. He was another unpolished gem that McGraw had uncovered, born in Watertown, Wisconsin, and raised in Toledo, toiling with Tecumseh in the South Michigan League when, late in the summer of 1907, McGraw's bird-dog scouts noticed him and urged McGraw to sign him. Merkle played parts of fifteen games that year, and he saw sporadic duty in 1908, as well, and at nineteen he had the distinction of being the youngest player in the National League. It was hardly enough to make him famous, however. Few outside the Giants' most ardent supporters had ever heard of him.

That would all change, forever, on September 23 of that year.

In the morning, the Giants' iron-man first baseman, Fred Tenney, who hadn't missed a game all year, awoke with a terrible case of lumbago, and when he reported to the ballpark it was clear he couldn't play. This was a terrible break for the Giants, who were to host the Cubs, the teams each sporting identical 87–50 records atop the league standings. McGraw could have gone a number of different directions, but he decided to go with the kid, and Merkle certainly did his part to justify that faith: In the bottom of the ninth, with two outs and Moose McCormick standing on first base in a tight, tense 1–1 game, Merkle singled sharply to right field, pushing McCormick to third, extending the most critical rally of that 1908 season. And when the next Giants hitter, Al Birdwell, delivered another single, bedlam instantly ruled at the Polo Grounds: McCormick trotted home with the winning run, the Giants had nudged themselves into first place all by themselves with sixteen games to play, and a mob of fans descended on the field to celebrate with their heroes, who were all hustling toward their clubhouse, Merkle included.

There was one problem:

Merkle had never reached second base, and once pandemonium invaded the Grounds, he never bothered to—which meant the run technically wouldn't count if someone had noticed, retrieved the ball, and stepped on second for a force-out. And Cubs second baseman Johnny Evers had noticed. Across the decades, various accounts of how Evers actually got his hands on the ball amid the madness have muddled the details, but this much was certain: Evers yelled at umpire Hank O'Day, pointed at Merkle, then made an elaborate show of stepping on the bag. O'Day had no choice. He called Merkle out, nullifying the run, necessitating a suspended game since there was no way to resume the game with 30,000 people trampling the grounds. As fate would have it, the Giants and Cubs would each go 11–5 over their next sixteen games, so they were forced to play one game for the pennant on October 8. The Cubs won, 4–2 (beating Mathewson). And Fred Merkle, at age nineteen, instantly acquired the worst kind of nickname.

Bonehead.

It was a testament to McGraw's stubbornness—and to Merkle's own talent—that despite cries for Merkle to be traded, released, tarred and feathered, McGraw didn't only keep him around, he made him the starting first baseman beginning in 1910, and by 1912 he'd emerged as the Giants' most reliable, productive hitter with a .309 average, eleven home runs (third in the league), and eighty-four runs batted in. People in New York and everywhere else still referred to "Merkle's Boner" relentlessly, still razzed him unmercifully, but Merkle had survived.

And now he was about to put all of that behind him: He connected with a Smoky Joe Wood fastball, looping a sinking line drive toward center. Tris Speaker, as proficient at the position as anyone in the game, knew the smart play was to play it on a hop, hold Murray (who'd had to wait to see if the ball fell safely) at third, and hope that Wood could weasel his way out of a first-and-third, one-out jam. But even the great Speaker wasn't above losing himself in a nervous moment, especially now that his ankle was pain-free: He ran hard after the ball and made a dive for it, hoping to pluck the ball before it hit grass. Instead, it rolled underneath him. Murray came roaring home, his cleats audibly hitting home plate in the now church-still ballpark, and Merkle raced to second as Speaker retrieved the ball.

The Giants led, 2–1, news that was greeted, about nine seconds later, with uninhibited delirium in Times Square, in Herald Square, in Madison Square Garden, along New York's Newspaper Row, and everywhere else in the five boroughs, where the news spread citizen-to-citizen, mouth-to-mouth, fan-to-fan. Newspapers were shredded and tossed in the air like confetti. Young James, the new Times Square baseball mascot, was hoisted into the air, carried on grown men's shoulders. The Giants' dugout was a noisy cauldron of sweaty glee, the joy and relief so overwhelming that few of them noticed when Smoky Joe Wood recovered to strike out Buck Herzog on what he would insist were "my hardest three pitches of the season" ("I never saw 'em," Herzog would later confess, "I just heard 'em."). With two out, Chief Meyers connected squarely on another Wood fastball and sent a line drive right back through the box; if it got through, Merkle would have scored a critical insurance run and the Giants would be even farther along to the greatest comeback in baseball history.

But it never got through.

Wood, acting on instinct, stuck his pitching hand out and the ball collided with his thumb; he gathered the ball up off the ground, lobbed it over to first, and trudged angrily and wearily off the mound. He was scheduled to lead off the bottom of the tenth, and if Jake Stahl had any question about whether to pinch-hit for him or not, it was quickly resolved when Wood showed the manager his priceless pitching hand, specifically a swatch of flesh that, until two minutes ago, had served as his right thumb.

"That son of a bitch," Stahl said, "is broken."

As, so it seemed, was the Speed Boys' destiny.

The truth is, it was astonishing that Tris Speaker acclimated himself as well as he did to his adopted hometown of Boston. The world of the late nineteenth century and the early twentieth century was a far more immense place, the chasm between Up Here and Down There so vast that it really did seem like separate countries sometimes, regardless of how the Civil War had turned out. And if you happened to be from Texas, then New England had to feel like it belonged on another planet to you. Not only did most of the people talk in that odd local brogue, but there were accents of every sort speaking at every street café and restaurant in town: Irish, Italian, German, Hungarian, Yiddish. Maybe the culture shock would have been worse in, say, New York City, which actually *prided* itself on being a place where all these people mixed their blood, their histories, and their futures, but Boston, Massachusetts was about as far removed from Hubbard, Texas, as a man could wander in 1912.

In Hubbard, in many ways, the Civil War, only forty-seven years in the distance, had yet to be settled, and the issue of why had little to do with the battles that had been fought and the causes that were espoused. It was a condition far more prevalent in Texas than any-where else in the former Confederacy, even battleground states like Virginia, Louisiana, and Mississippi where people still harbored bullet-riddled flags and hard-to-shake beliefs, because Texas had been in the war business far longer than any of its brethren. Old-timers still recalled Texas's short but bloody War of Independence against Mexico in 1836, where thousands of innocents on both sides were senselessly slaughtered and where the Alamo was, indeed, still remembered. Many who survived that had eagerly joined the U.S. Army to fight the Mexican War ten years later, so the Texans who took part in the Confederate cause were no virgins to the bloody authenticity of war, they'd been raised and reared on its realities for generations.

It was with this history coursing through their veins that a pair of brothers newly recruited to the Texas militia, Byron and James Speaker, rode north of the Red River in 1861 to fight Union-sympathizing Indians. Across the next four years they would visit three separate theaters of the war, they would fight Yanks all across Arkansas and Mississippi, and they would fight Ulysses Grant's men in Tennessee and William Tecumseh Sherman's invaders in northern Georgia. James would manage to survive even after being captured by Sherman's men in October 1864 and shipped to a Union prison camp in Illinois in which a quarter of the 26,000 inmates would die of hunger and be buried in unmarked pauper's graves; Byron would merely survive, against the long odds of regular conflict. When the brothers reunited after Appomattox, they returned to Texas and filled the ears of their youngest brother, Archery, with tales of their exploits and of Northern atrocity. And Archery, in turn, relayed these stories to his youngest child, Tristram, named for one of the knights of King Arthur's Round Table.

So Speaker, very much an outsider in his new city, was just as much an outsider in his own clubhouse when he was called up to the Red Sox in 1907, and his whole life he felt compelled to fight, if not with his fists then with his antics and his actions; he learned early on that no one was going to sponsor you in this world. What you wanted, you had to take. As a child he'd broken his right arm falling off a horse, forcing him to rely on his left hand, and even after the injured arm healed he kept throwing, hitting, and eating left-handed. Later, while playing college football at Fort Worth Polytechnic Institute, he hurt the left arm so badly that his doctors wanted to amputate. Speaker told them to forget it, he healed, and two years later he'd shown up in Boston, gotten three hits in his first nineteen at-bats, and so impressed the Red Sox that they traded him to the Little Rock Travelers of the Southern League in exchange for the use of the Travs' spring training facilities in 1908.

Outraged and humiliated at, quite literally, being swapped for a bag of balls, Speaker decided to make the forty-five-mile pilgrimage from Hubbard to Marlin in the spring of 1908 to present himself to John J. McGraw and offer his services as a center fielder. It is worth noting that if this meeting had gone smoothly, then it could well have been Tris Speaker roaming center for the Giants this October 16 instead of Fred Snodgrass, but the meeting went anything *but* well. "McGraw said he had no place for me," Speaker would recount decades after the fact. "I did everything I could, but I couldn't get him to change his mind."

It wouldn't take long for McGraw to second-guess himself; during their 1909 postseason exhibition, Speaker had dominated the series so completely that McGraw was moved to marvel, "I had read a lot about that young fellow but I didn't think he was that good. He is without doubt one of the greatest players of all time."

For now, though, Speaker's misplay in center had helped nudge McGraw's Giants to within three outs of the world championship, and as McGraw's friend and meal ticket, Christy Mathewson, eased out of the dugout McGraw approached, put his hand on Matty's shoulder, and exchanged wordless glances.

Finally, *finally* their moment was at hand.

Larry Doyle, the Giants captain who'd worshipped Mathewson from the moment the great pitcher had shaken the nervous infielder's hand upon his arrival in New York five years before, jogged out in front of Matty and excitedly shook his fist. Mathewson smiled and told his captain, "I'll float my old arm out there right after the ball if I have to in this inning. I'll win the game."

Mathewson warmed up quickly and efficiently, and was somewhat surprised when he didn't see Joe Wood (who'd hit a perfectly respectable-for-a-pitcher .290 in 1912) greeting him in the batter's box but instead a pinch hitter named Clyde (Hack) Engle, who'd been the Sox' incumbent first baseman until Jake Stahl had been lured out of retirement. Engle had accepted his demotion reluctantly but quietly, and he'd hit only a soft .234 in 171 at-bats during the season (though he'd doubled off Rube Marquard and driven in the Sox' only two runs pinch-hitting for Buck O'Brien during their Game Six meltdown at the Polo Grounds two days earlier). Chief Meyers jogged out to the mound, went over the signals with Mathewson, then pointed to the Sox' dugout where team trainers were looking grimly at Wood's thumb.

"I got him right square on the hand," Meyers said. "No way he can pitch again, much less hit here."

Mathewson, with uncommon boldness, said, "Let's make that a moot point."

Engle took Mathewson's first pitch right down the middle for strike one, and Fenway Park was so quiet that the ball popped in Meyers's mitt and echoed all across the ballpark. And when Engle made contact with Mathewson's second pitch, another rising fastball, such was the hush that you couldn't only hear the unmistakable thud when Engle threw his bat down in disappointment after lifting a lazy fly ball toward left center field, you could hear two voices rise above the melancholy. One was a joyful Larry Doyle, who tracked the flight of the ball from his spot at second base and gleefully squealed, "That's one of 'em!" The other belonged to Fred Snodgrass, who clearly and loudly proclaimed:

"I GOT IT! I GOT IT! I GOT IT!"

In the dusty miasma of memory, there would be some through the years who would insist that by rights Red Murray, in left field, should have called for the ball, that because Hack Engle was a soft-hitting right-hander Snodgrass was shaded toward right field to start the at-bat, that he'd had to cover some ground to get to where the ball was landing in left center. There are others who would swear that Murray, after being called off the ball, had taken a knee, an overenthusiastic way of getting a good, up-close look at the first of the three outs the Giants would need to make them champions, and still others who would testify that even as the ball was descending toward earth, acceding to gravity's wishes, Murray was yelling at Snodgrass to flip him the ball after catching it, so he could say he was a part of an historic final inning. All of these theories tend to dissolve when you remember one of John J. McGraw's most fundamental rules:

If the center fielder believed he could catch the ball, he caught the ball.

It was the statute by which Snodgrass and Josh Devore had abided in Game One, you may remember, when Speaker's ball fell between them for the fly-ball triple that broke up Jeff Tesreau's no-hitter and awakened the Sox' slumbering offense, and it was surely in play now, with Snodgrass easing over to plant himself under the fly—a "can o' corn" in the parlance of the day, since it resembled the ease with which a general store owner could drop canned vegetables from high shelves into his waiting hands—and calling for it loudly. What all the excuses and all the conspiracy theories speak to, in all probability, is the basic hidden terror that lurks within every ballplayer, from T-ball to Little League to the majors, from Wiffle ball games to stickball games to softball games, the innate fear that when a ball is right over your head, the easiest play in the game, that somehow, someway, you will do the improbable, the impossible, and drop it.

Fred Snodgrass dropped it.

In Herald Square, the name "Engle" suddenly appeared next to second base and a puzzled voice cried out, "A fellow named *Engle* hit a double off Matty? That can't be!" Then the board showed what had happened: error, center field. "Surely, it had to be a hard play," another patron yelled. "They are notoriously difficult scorers in Boston, you know." In Newark, people started to notice that Daniel Connon was sweating a little more than seemed natural on such a cool autumn day, and asked if he was all right. And in Los Angeles, there was no immediate explanation for why a runner suddenly appeared on second base with nobody out, and Adie Snodgrass listened to the lunchtime crowd talk about how overrated the Great Mathewson must be if he let a man named Engle get a hit off him with the World Series on the line.

Out There, there was so much mystery attached to what had just happened.

In Here, inside a Fenway Park that now sounded as if someone had just pushed a plug back into the wall, there was nothing but the simplest truth abounding.

As Snodgrass himself would say later: "I just dropped the thing."

And now Engle, who'd been running all the way in what felt at the time like fruitless hustle, was standing on second base, already in scoring position, amazed at the whims of fortune. Mathewson was dazed. He waved his glove hand in disgust, and it was hard to know if he was directing his emotions at Snod or at God; probably both, since both had forsaken him at that moment. But whatever self-pity he might have felt evaporated in a few seconds; now he had to face the top of the Red Sox batting order, and he had to rein in all the swirling emotions and feelings raging inside him.

Harry Hooper was due up, naturally, as if Matty needed *another* reminder that this game, by rights, should already be over, and they should all be on a Gotham-bound train sipping champagne if not for Hooper's defensive magnificence. Now Jake Stahl had a decision to make: Should he have Hooper bunt, sacrificing Engle to third? McGraw, who *absolutely* would have played it that way, had his corner infielders, Herzog and Merkle, pinch in so close to home plate it looked like they could grab Hooper's bat. But Stahl, one last time, proved he wasn't McGraw. Hooper, grateful for the freedom, took a vicious hack at Mathewson's first pitch and the moment it struck his bat the faithful inside Fenway began to roar: It was a blast, heading deep into the gap, deep over Snodgrass' head, and not only was Engle going to be able to walk home with the tying run, Hooper was surely going to make it all the way to third with the potential *winning* run, and . . .

And just as abruptly as Snodgrass had stuck the plug in the wall, he kicked it back out again. Because somehow, someway, running as fast as he could, reacting as quickly as he could, and diving as far as he could, he made one of the most extraordinary catches in baseball history. Now, no video exists of it—the way it does of Al Gionfriddo in 1947 or Willie Mays in 1954 or Ron Swoboda in 1969, and some of the other spine-tingling catches in World Series history—so all we can do is go by the accounts of those who watched it. And even decades after the catch, they were *still* shaking their head.

"I saw thousands of games," Tris Speaker said in 1949, "and I never, ever saw a catch like that before or after. It was like a magic trick."

"It was so impossible, it was hard to describe," McGraw would say in 1931.

Engle, as awestruck as anyone, was already around third and had to scramble back to second to avoid being doubled up. One more time, Mathewson waved his glove, although this time it was to acknowledge the shared munificence of the almighty and the outfielder. But even the Great Matty could get rattled and now, after one brutal break and one extraordinary one, he sabotaged himself by walking Steve Yerkes, the least-potent, least-threatening bat in the entire Boston lineup. It was an unfortunate piece of timing. Now the Speed Boys had the tying and winning runs on base, and up to the plate walked Speaker, who was—McGraw's words, remember?—"without doubt one of the greatest players of all time." Of course, Speaker would be facing—everyone's words—one of the greatest pitchers of all time, and even without the blessing of historical context, everyone was on their feet now—in Fenway, in Boston Common, in New York City, Newark, Los Angeles, Des Moines, Little Rock, everywhere. Speaker—who would hit .345 across twenty-two years (sixth all-time in major league baseball's 139-year history through 2008), and collect 3,514 hits (fifth all-time)—had gone 2-for-5 in Game Two against Mathewson. Mathewson—363 career victories (third all-time) in seventeen seasons, a 2.13 lifetime ERA (eighth all-time)—had limited Speaker to just one single in three at-bats in Game Five, and a single and a walk in four plate appearances so far in Game Eight. So as Speaker walked to the plate, with the ballpark in an uproar and what seemed like the whole world peeking in from as many as 3,000 miles away, he dug his spikes in knowing he'd done quite well against his fellow immortal, going 4-for-11 with a walk, a nifty .363 average.

Now they eyed each other warily. Mathewson took a long stride into the stretch, gathered the ball back into his glove at the waist, looked over his shoulder at Engle leading off second, spied quickly at Yerkes at first. And reached back across seven or eight years and uncorked the kind of fastball that used to regularly fly from his fingertips in his youth, one that only occasionally graced him with its presence now, at age thirty-two, one that started out around the hitter's thighs and kept rising as it made its sixty-foot, six-inch way toward the hitter, upward to the belt, upward near the stomach, upward near the lettering, upward near the armpits.

Speaker swung. Almost immediately, his heart sank. A hitter swings his bat thousands of times during a season, in games, in exhibitions, in batting practice. Instantly, the moment he hears the crack of ball against bat—the moment he *feels* it—he knows what he's done. If he feels nothing at all, it means he's connected with the sweet spot and that ball will be traveling a long, long way. If it collides with the lower half of the bat, start running, because it's on the ground somewhere. If it hits the upper half, forget it: It's going to be a lazy fly ball or a pop-up. And if you hit it on the wrong *end* of the bat, you can *really* forget it since it won't even stay in fair territory.

That's where Tris Speaker's bat hit Christy Mathewson's fastball, and immediately there was a sad groan stretching over Fenway Park, because everyone could see that he'd popped the ball straight up over the right side of the infield, and with the wind swirling softly it easily drifted the ball into foul territory near first base.

Where Fred Merkle, of all people, was waiting to catch it.

Now, it is impossible to know exactly what was going through Christy Mathewson's thoughts at this moment. He should have been greatly relieved; he'd done the heaviest lifting already. He'd induced a pop-up from the great Speaker. And he could see, because *everyone* could see, that Merkle had a bead on the ball. Still . . .

Mathewson had been at the Polo Grounds that surreal day four years earlier when Merkle failed to touch second base. He'd seen how the criticisms and the heckling had affected the young player. More than anyone, he should have appreciated how hard Merkle had worked to overcome that gaffe. Still . . . it was *Merkle* out there, under the pop-up. Merkle of "Merkle's Boner" . . .

"CHIEF!" Mathewson suddenly blurted. "YOU TAKE IT, CHIEF!"

Chief was Chief Meyers, the catcher, and in truth it was Meyers's responsibility to select the man who should field, or catch, any ball in front of him. That's what catchers did. And this catcher could see that it was Merkle's ball all the way. But Meyers, like the rest of the Giants, was a Matty acolyte. What he said was law, on all matters. And so when Meyers heard his name, he made a quick stab for the ball. When *Merkle* heard Meyers's name, *he* backed away.

And the baseball fell, untouched, in the grass beyond the first-base line.

As it lay there, the three Giants surrounding it could hardly believe it, could hardly bring themselves to touch it. John McGraw, in the dugout, said nothing; what could he say? His head hung limply on his shoulders and listened to his stomach growl. Fenway remained silent for half a heartbeat, then erupted in laughter and another wave of bombastic cheering, many of them no doubt thinking: Wasn't it *our* team that was supposed to be on the take?

And Tris Speaker, halfway down the first-base line, could contain himself no longer.

"Well, Matty, you just called for the wrong man," Speaker said, not bothering to hide either his relief or his resolve. "Now it's gonna cost you the ballgame."

And on the very next pitch, this one a hanging Mathewson curveball that looked every bit like it was thrown by a man of thirty-two and not a kid of twenty-two, Speaker laced a single to right field, sending Engle home with the tying run, sending Yerkes to third with the would-be winning run, sending himself to second when Devore foolishly overthrew the cutoff man trying to nail Engle at the plate, and sending Fenway Park into a frenetic spasm of elation. It was all so impossible to believe. One more time, these teams were dead even, tied at three games apiece, tied at two runs apiece, with Steve Yerkes standing but ninety feet away with the run that would topple all of New England, send it upside down.

McGraw was shaken, and never bothered to send anyone to the bullpen, just in case. He did wave four fingers in the air, ordering Mathewson to intentionally walk Duffy Lewis, loading the bases, setting up a force at any base or a double play that could help Matty weasel out of this most unpleasant pickle he was in.

Now all eyes turned to Larry Gardner, the third baseman whose shattered little finger had nearly caused him to miss the series. Gardner understood that, with only one out, he was a man with many options: He could win the game with a clean base hit, of course. He could win it with a slow roller, assuming he beat a double-throw relay to first. He could win it with a long fly ball to the outfield. He could win it if Matty uncorked a wild pitch, or if an unnerved Chief Meyers let one get past him for a passed ball. He could win it by getting hit by a pitch, or by letting four balls go by him. A hitter with options was a hell of a dangerous man.

He watched ball one sail by him.

He watched ball two cruise past him.

Fenway was an asylum now, and it was obvious that even Mathewson had been affected by it. He had no choice: He had to throw a strike. He did, right at the knees: Gardner swung and missed. The din died down for a few heartbeats. The next pitch was another fastball, shaving the inside corner thigh-high.

My God, Gardner thought. *Right where I like it.*

The left-handed Gardner turned on the pitch, pulled it, lofted it high and deep toward right field, and as soon as he hit it Mathewson started walking off the mound. Matty knew it was staying in the ballpark, but he also knew that Devore, in right, could place the ball in a cannon after catching it and it wouldn't make a difference. Devore tried, circling under it, getting a running start once the ball fell in his glove.

But it didn't matter. At third base, Yerkes had his left foot on the base, his head was focused on home plate, and he waited for Clyde Engle—now coaching third—to tell him when to go.

Engle listened for the thud of ball hitting glove.

"GO!" he screamed.

And off Yerkes went, and here came Gardner's throw, and it never had a chance. Jake Stahl, the triumphant manager who was waiting on deck and standing behind the plate, shot both hands in the air, alerting Yerkes that he wouldn't have to slide and so he didn't, sprinting right past Chief Meyers, whose eyes were glued to the plate, making sure Yerkes's spikes touched it. They did.

It was over. It was official. It took roughly six seconds for the news to reach Boston Common and Boston's Newspaper Row, and when it did, when everybody learned about Boston 3, New York 2, there was an immediate celebration the likes of which the city had never seen before. As it was, most of the city's workers had knocked off early in order to join in these communal gatherings, so when the word finally arrived that Yerkes had crossed the plate, there rose a yell from tens of thousands of people gathered near the public scoreboards, from the people in the street, in the windows, in stores and doorways along the row. The yell told the story. Men danced and waved and shook hands and slapped one another on the back. Women cried.

The Royal Rooters, scattered to the wind, all knew instinctively to gather anew at McGreevy's saloon, where they spent the rest of the night and a few hours of the next morning enjoying some let-bygones-be-bygones revelry, making plans to attend the next day's celebration at Faneuil Hall in force, using Nuf Ced's spittoon whenever the name McAleer entered the conversation, and buying round after round in honor of Snodgrass.

Snodgrass. What could you say about him? What could you say *to* him? The center fielder knew that he might be in for a long day—and a long life, for that matter—when Sox fans gratefully, gleefully chanted his name as he walked off the field, lost in his own suffocating misery. His teammates weren't sure what to do. Most of them would admit later, in the angry haze of aftermath, they wanted to walk up to him and say, "How could you drop that ball? A first-grader could catch that ball!" But to a man, all of them showed restraint, overcome with compassion when they saw tears flowing down his cheeks, his body racked with agony.

"After the game," Jeff Tesreau would recall, "Snodgrass came to the bench and picked up his blazer. He did not speak to anyone but acted as if he were a criminal, and then he walked off the field alone."

Later, Tesreau and Josh Devore were climbing into a taxi on their way to the train station when they noticed a forlorn, solitary figure: Snodgrass.

"Snow!" Tesreau yelled. "Ride with us!"

He hesitated, and then Devore grabbed him by the lapel of his coat and dragged him into the backseat. There they sat, in silence, none of the three men knowing exactly what should be said. Then, with the hotel in sight, in a voice barely audible over the hum of the cab's engine, Snodgrass finally broke the icy silence:

"Boys," he said, "I lost the championship for you."

Neither Devore nor Tesreau knew how to respond to that.

"Because he really had," Tesreau later explained. "And there was no use in trying to deny it. Ten chances to one he will read some similar comments in the papers in the morning if he cares to read them. So we just naturally kept quiet and if silence means assent Snodgrass knew that we admitted he had lost it. Two or three times Josh started to break out and tell him so, because he was terribly sore over it, but he took one look at Snodgrass and quit. He was the most dejected looking person I ever saw."

Tesreau was correct, of course. At that very moment, the knights of the nation's typewriter keyboards had already begun a vicious assault on Snodgrass, conveniently overlooking Mathewson's equally costly blunder two hitters later—or, more conveniently, blaming old piñata Merkle for the drop. Within five minutes of the

end of the game, the sportswriters already had a nickname for it—
"Snodgrass' $30,000 Muff"—commemorating the total difference
between winner's share and loser's share that was, to be precise,
$29,514.34. (A further irony: It cost each individual Giant
$1,458.22—which, in 2008 dollars, would amount to exactly
$30,958.11.)

The lead paragraph in the next day's *New York Times*, written
without a byline by Harry Cross, would reflect much of the coverage:

> Write in the pages of world's series baseball history the name
> of Snodgrass. Write it large and black. Not as a hero; truly
> not. Put him rather with Merkle, who was in such a hurry that
> he gave away a National League championship. Snodgrass
> was in such a hurry that he gave away a world championship.
> It was because of Snodgrass' generous muff of an easy fly in
> the tenth inning that the decisive game of the world's series
> went to the Boston Red Sox this afternoon by a score of 3 to
> 2, instead of to the New York Giants by a score of 2 to 1 . . .

Anger was not the foremost emotion for every scribe, though. As
he typed out close to two hundred inches of copy for the *New York
Globe*, Sid Mercer occasionally had to pause because he was weeping
uncontrollably. On the bench, Wilbert Robinson slumped, virtually
paralyzed, unable to move for half an hour. In a field box, fat Harry
Sparrow, McGraw's friend and bodyguard, reacted the same way,
and so did many of McGraw's Broadway friends, just staring blankly
into space, hurting for their friend, knowing how much a second
World Series would mean to him.

McGraw himself, as was his wont, was remarkably upbeat, his disappointment subservient to his belief that—much as a fictional manager named Jimmy Dugan would say on a movie screen eight
decades later—there was no crying in baseball, that there was no
shame in losing to a great baseball team in the tenth inning of the
eighth game of the World Series. His first priority was to seek out

Mathewson, who had been magnificent all afternoon, and all Series long, pitching to an ERA of 0.94 across twenty-eight and two-thirds innings even though he would take an 0–2 record away from his week's work. Mathewson's eyes were red and moist, but they were tears of exhaustion rather than sadness. McGraw, his own heart breaking, wrapped Mathewson with both arms, then shook his hand firmly.

"I never seen a gamer pitcher than you, son," McGraw rasped. "You're the greatest boxman that the world's ever seen, I wish I had ten more just like you. It's a bad day for the Giants, but it's a wondrous one for you." And in a classy showing of sportsmanship, the Boston fans took two minutes from their celebration to agree with McGraw: As Matty slowly pulled his sweater on, they roared their approval and offered up three cheers for the great pitcher. Later, after getting showered and dressed (and playing a few hands of therapeutic bridge in the clubhouse), Matty emerged to find Sox fans lined up to pump his hand and wish him well as he walked to the taxi stand outside Fenway.

By then, McGraw had already found more trouble than he bargained for. Sprinting across the field to shake hands with Stahl, a Boston fan ran into McGraw and almost tipped him into the bench pit. McGraw turned and delivered a straight left, knocking the *fan* into the pit instead. By the time he reached the Sox' manager his hand was bleeding, and Stahl had to chuckle at the sight even as he was touched by McGraw's words: "I want to congratulate you and the Boston team on this victory," he said. "It was a tough battle and all the credit that goes to the victor belongs to you and your team."

"Thank you, Mr. McGraw," Stahl said. Somewhere in the past eight days, he'd lost the stomach to call the man Muggsy.

The Sox were euphoric; all the old quarrels were forgotten, all the lingering bitterness. Wood sought out O'Brien, shook his hand, asked for forgiveness for being quick-tempered; O'Brien told him to forget it, and invited him and Speaker to come see him sing an Irish tenor solo at the National Theater in six days. Wood said they'd be honored to attend, and they did. Carrigan and Cady shook hands, burying their bitterness. Speaker, Yerkes, and Engle, three of the primary figures in the tenth-inning rally, were detained on the field and kept from the celebrating by a bevy of women fans who left the stands to plant kisses on their cheeks; none seemed to mind.

And while other Royal Rooters offered their own salutes and tributes off-campus, the biggest Rooter of all entered the clubhouse, his cheeks crimson with triumph, announced officially a civic party the next day at Faneuil Hall while all but falling over himself to gush loudly and proudly in the midst of his most-favored constituents: "I want to congratulate each and every member of this team for the grand victory scored today," John Fitzgerald roared. "It is a remarkable achievement when one considers that Boston, one-sixth the population of New York, has had the unflinching backing of its citizens. Tomorrow I hope to be able to show what the city thinks of you."

There would be plenty of time for that. Everyone loves a winner.

It's hard to be on the other side. Daniel Connon finally conceded as much, after Yerkes's run was posted on the *Newark Evening News* scoreboard, when he walked two blocks to a nearby hospital and had doctors examine him. They decided his heart was sound, but his nerves seemed frayed.

Three thousand miles away, just after the final score was posted, someone in the crowd yelled at the man with the megaphone working the *Los Angeles Times* scoreboard.

"Hey!" the voice yelled. "Who committed the error on Engle?"

The announcer scanned his papers, tried to decipher the strange-sounding name, then lifted his megaphone to the sky.

"The center fielder," he intoned. "Snodgrass."

Upon hearing that, one of the spectators fainted immediately, and it wasn't until she was on her way to a downtown hospital that Adie Snodgrass came to, and whispered, "My poor boy."

Epilogue

We hold no beef with what he's done
Nor classic "bone" he may have spun
No booster for a man who's down
Who helped to lose the great game's crown
But from the throng with glaring glim
Who curse what happened there, let him
Who's yet to make his first mistake
Step up and pan him for the break . . .

—GRANTLAND RICE, *NEW YORK EVENING MAIL,*
OCTOBER 18, 1912

ALL WAS FORGIVEN the next day in Boston. Everyone was friends again. At Faneuil Hall, the City of Boston put on the wildest celebration that anyone could remember, beginning with a parade, ending with Fitzgerald presenting keys to the city after making an impassioned valedictory praising the world champion Speed Boys.

"I want you to be as quiet as possible," he told the assembled masses, several hundred thousand of whom would take part in some segment of the downtown celebration that day. "Faneuil Hall is crowded as I never saw it before. We meet here to honor the team, which has worn the Boston uniform in the big cities of the country.

It has won after the hardest of seasons and in the World Series then only in the tenth inning of the last game."

The crowd halted him here, cheering ever louder, drowning out even the loudest notes of one of the loudest orators of the day. Honey Fitz had to plead with them to simmer down so he could talk and get out of the way.

"I am proud to have the honor to preside at this meeting to congratulate Manager Stahl. I am not here as Mayor of Boston but to thank the team in the name of the national game. I also want to say that the players are entitled to their share of the fifth game which is morally theirs."

With this, the crowd truly went ballistic, and the players did, too, and there was little doubt that when the next mayoral election rolled around in two years, there were at least twenty-three men who would vote a straight Democratic ticket.

Jake Stahl took the stage.

"This has been a stiff year for us," he said. "I want to thank the Rooters for helping us, as they did. You all know what good they did for us."

The roar from the crowd said that they knew well, especially since the loudest cheers of all came from the temporarily lapsed Rooters themselves, now fully restored to the faith. That had been assured earlier in the morning when McAleer, chastened at the embarrassment that the greatest game in baseball's history to that point had been witnessed by 17,000 empty seats, had issued a statement expressing abject contrition:

"On behalf of the Boston American League Baseball Club, I desire to make an apology to the mayor of Boston and the Boston Rooters for the failure to secure the seats at the fourth game of the world's series in Boston. We regret very much that this unfortunate affair should have occurred to mar what was on every respect the most sensational series of games ever played and we appreciate the splendid support and encouragement given the Red Sox in their efforts to bring Boston the championship of the world. A mistake was made in not holding the usual seats until game time but I can assure Mayor Fitzgerald and all the Royal Rooters it was unintentional."

Honey Fitz, on behalf of the Rooters and Red Sox fans across New England, accepted the owner's apology, but with a caveat: "Mr. McAleer," he said, "I urge you to re-consider raising ticket prices for next year's Boston games at Fenway Park. I further urge you to make available a certain number of twenty-five-cent tickets at every home game so every citizen in Massachusetts and beyond who wants to see the Red Sox can see the Red Sox."

You had to give the mayor this: He was damn good at his job.

The Giants' disappointment was neutralized somewhat within minutes of the team train pulling out of Back Bay Station for the final time, for that is when National Commission secretary John E. Bruce walked over to McGraw's seat and ripped a bank check out of his leather folder, payable to the manager in the amount of $59,028.68. The next day, Stahl would receive his own check in the amount of $88,543.02 and deposit it in his account in the State Street Trust Company. It would have probably upset Giants fans to know just how soothing that payment was to the ballplayers' nerves, since so many of the people who watched these games, fretted over them, lived over them, died over them, had yet to get a good night's sleep during the whole Series, while most of the Giants were asleep within thirty minutes of stepping on the train.

The more things change, the more they stay the same.

"We are professionals," Christy Mathewson said during the Series. "The name of the game is to get paid, and paid a fair wage. Winning and losing is important. But money feeds our family."

Maybe the Christian Gentleman would have fit in during the next century far better than he—or anyone else—could ever have imagined.

Mathewson would remain one of baseball's most dominant talents for two more seasons, winning twenty-five more games in 1913 and twenty-four in 1914, but in that last year his ERA ballooned to 3.00, the worst since his six-game cameo as a rookie in 1900. By 1916, his arm all but ruined, McGraw agreed to trade his old friend to the Cincinnati Reds for a package of players that would include, ironically, Buck Herzog, who in 1914 had been named Cincinnati's player-manager. But the Reds were sitting in seventh place in late July, and so Herzog received a double dose of bad news: Not only was he losing his job as the Reds' skipper, he was going back to New York to play for McGraw, whom he loathed. But Mathewson, understanding McGraw was only going to leave the Polo Grounds' manager's office at gunpoint, eagerly accepted the trade, knowing he'd finally get a chance at running a club. And he did very well, too, elevating the Reds from seventh to fourth to third, to the point where they would make a successful run at the 1919 National League pennant.

By then, however, Mathewson would be out of office and in uniform, having volunteered for the Army's Chemical Warfare Service in August 1918, at the height of the Great War, and earning the rank of captain. It was yet another chapter in the fabled legend of Matty, who was just about to turn thirty-eight and could easily have avoided service without much criticism. It was a fateful decision. After arriving in France, Mathewson was assigned to examine ammunition dumps left behind by the Germans and while doing so was exposed to residual deposits of mustard gas. Already suffering from the flu, the encounter with the deadly poison weakened him greatly, and after he was discharged he would spend much of the rest of his life suffering from tuberculosis. Though he returned briefly to the Giants as a pitching coach, he would split his declining days at his home in Saranac Lake, New York, and at the Trudeau Sanitarium on the other side of the city before dying on October 7, 1925, at the age of forty-five.

By then, his good friend McGraw had finally risen from a decade and a half of frustration to regain his reign as baseball's preeminent manager. After losing a third straight World Series—the capital letters permanent now—in 1913 to the Athletics, McGraw oversaw a steep decline to last place in 1915 that nearly cost him his Polo Grounds fiefdom, yet by 1917 the Giants were back in the World Series (and losing a fourth straight Classic, this time to the White Sox) before finally, in 1921 and 1922, winning McGraw his second and third Series, both of them extra delicious as they came at the expense of the Yankees (still paying rent to the Giants at the Polo Grounds) and their newly acquired slugger, Babe Ruth.

That was the final high point, however, in a career awash with them. By 1923, the Yankees built their own gleaming baseball palace on the other side of the Harlem River and defeated the Giants in six games, and it was the start of both a literal and a lyrical takeover by the American League club, which would go on to win nineteen more championships in the next forty years, establishing the kind of dominant dynasty that McGraw tried, and failed, to build. McGraw grew embittered at this turn of events and also by Ruth's emergence, which rendered his brand of "inside baseball" quaint and outdated. Within a few years he spitefully built a grandstand extension that was hardly needed to meet public demand, but did serve to blunt out the sight of Yankee Stadium sitting in the horizon beyond the Polo Grounds' grandstand. He retired abruptly from the Giants on June 3, 1932, and took one final spasm of satisfaction in the fact that his announcement wound up dwarfing the news that Lou Gehrig of the hated Yankees had swatted four home runs the same day. Much as his wife had feared, though, without baseball McGraw found he had little to live for; he died less than twenty months later, on February 25, 1934, six weeks before his sixty-first birthday.

By then, Tris Speaker had not only completed an extraordinary playing career, he'd finished what could well have been one of the greatest managerial careers, too, if not short-circuited by one terrible lapse of judgment.

In 1914, Speaker had resisted the advances of the Federal League, the start-up that not only hoped to earn a place as the "third" major league but also allowed players to dream that they could finally earn a salary commensurate with their worth and their talent. Dozens of players jumped to the new league, which would barely last two seasons, but Speaker stayed in Boston thanks to a two-year contract awarded by new owner Joseph Lannin that paid him the lordly sum of $18,000 a year. Speaker rewarded Lannin's faith by anchoring another Red Sox championship team in 1915, a five-game stomping of the Philadelphia Phillies.

Lannin rewarded Speaker's loyalty by cutting his salary in half for 1916.

The Federal League was dead. Refugee players by the dozen were taking whatever they could get from their old teams (if they were welcome back at all), and there was no place for Speaker to play if he wasn't willing to play for $9,000. That was also roughly what Lannin offered Speaker's best friend, Joe Wood, but that was an entirely different circumstance.

While Speaker had continued to blossom after 1912, Wood's spectacular starship of a career began a rapid descent almost immediately. He'd feasted on his triumphs that year and also spent the winter allowing the thumb he'd hurt in the last inning of the last game to heal completely. By the time the Sox reconvened in Hot Springs, the smoke was back in Smoky Joe's arm and he was ready for an encore.

"Then," he would recall some fifty years later, "it happened."

It was a routine play during pitchers' fielding practice, the most basic and most mundane part of any spring training morning. He went to field a ground ball, slipped on wet grass, and fell square on the thumb. The same thumb. His pitching thumb. Attached to that meal-ticket arm. It was immediately encased in a cast, kept there for three weeks. Of course, it needed more time to heal; of course, the Sox couldn't afford Wood such a luxury, and besides: Wood was barely twenty-three years old. He was young. Indestructible. Bulletproof.

Finished.

"I don't know whether I tried to pitch too soon after that, or whether maybe something happened in my shoulder at the same time, but whatever it was, I never pitched again without a terrific amount of pain in my right shoulder," he said years later. "Never again."

After winning those thirty-four games in 1912, Wood would win only thirty-six more the rest of his career. When he could lift his arm to throw he could still twirl magic, but sometimes he would have to take two weeks off in between starts. For the champion Sox of 1915 he somehow managed to grit his way to a 15–5 record and a career-best 1.49 ERA but he struck out only sixty-three in 157⅓ innings and he was in agony; he didn't make one appearance in the World Series. And when Lannin decided to play hardball with him the next spring, Wood decided to go to Pennsylvania and leave baseball behind.

Speaker, however, was going nowhere except to Cleveland, which is where Lannin traded him just before the start of the season. In Boston, the outrage was palpable, almost mutinous. In truth, in real time it far surpassed the level of indignation that another owner's trade of another star would generate four and a half years later, when Harry Frazee famously sold Babe Ruth to the Yankees. And while the Red Sox would survive without Speaker, winning two more titles in 1916 and 1918, Speaker would also gain a measure of revenge, surpassing a .380 average four different times, single-handedly elevating the Indians to a championship in 1920 when he had his most explosive season, a .388 average with 107 RBIs, 137 runs scored, and 214 hits. By then, he had also been named manager of the team and as such had lured back to the game his oldest and dearest friend, Joe Wood . . . as an outfielder. It was a triumphant reunion, and even if Wood never approached his past level of pitching greatness he would hit .283 in close to 2,000 major league at-bats. Wood would become a longtime baseball coach at Yale following his 1922 retirement, and would spend the rest of his life—and he lived to age ninety-five—hearing fathers and grandfathers and great-grandfathers tell their children, grandchildren, and great-grandchildren: "You see that old man over there? That was Smoky Joe Wood. He used to be the greatest pitcher who ever lived."

Speaker himself could easily have become one of the greatest managers who ever lived, such was his brain for the game and the respect he commanded from players who weren't a fraction as accomplished as he. From 1919 to 1926 he managed 1,139 games and won 617 of them, a winning percentage of .543 that's far higher than Connie Mack (.486), Casey Stengel (.508), Leo Durocher (.540), Tony La Russa (.534), and Tommy Lasorda (.526), to name just five managers who are either in the Hall of Fame or sure to wind up there. But in 1926 an old, embittered pitcher named Dutch Leonard all but drove a stake through that career by charging Speaker, Wood, and Ty Cobb with fixing a game late in the 1919 season.

It was the wrong thing to stand accused of in that rigid law-and-order baseball time. Baseball had a commissioner named Kenesaw Mountain Landis, an old federal judge brought into office by terrified owners in the wake of the 1919 World Series, won by Christy Mathewson's old Reds team, thrown by the Chicago White Sox, and masterminded by John McGraw's (and Beansie Rosenthal's) old business partner, Arnold Rothstein. Eight of the Sox players who'd been accused (and acquitted) of fixing the Series were unceremoniously banned from the game for life by Landis, whose zero-tolerance policy led directly to the creation of Rule Twenty-one, which clearly spelled out the consequences of gambling on the sport and would, beginning in 1927, hang inside every clubhouse in every stadium forever. Leonard, angry with Cobb (by then managing the Tigers) for allegedly running him out of baseball, and with Speaker (an old teammate on the Red Sox for three seasons) for not picking him up after Cobb had released him, said he had possession of letters from Wood and Cobb that implicated themselves (and Speaker, by proxy) of fixing a game on the last day of that same, fateful 1919 season.

It seems that on the afternoon of September 24, 1919, Leonard and Cobb of the Tigers met under the stands at Detroit's Navin

Field to "talk baseball" with Wood and Speaker of the Indians. There, Cobb talked about how much he wanted his team to finish "in the money," which meant climbing into third place. And a win the next day over Cleveland (which had already clinched second-place money) would all but ensure that. Speaker, according to Leonard, told Cobb he "needn't worry about tomorrow's game. You'll win tomorrow." And the Tigers did win the game, 9–5, and did finish in third place. And, according to Leonard, the other three at the meeting had all benefited from this arrangement by placing calls to bookies—though not as many as they'd hoped.

When the charges were leaked to the public, Cobb and Speaker were both immediately dismissed from their jobs. They were spared any kind of Black Sox–level punishment mainly because Leonard refused to appear at hearings in January of 1927, forcing Landis to clear them (and Wood). But while Speaker would manage in the minor leagues for two years with Newark, and while he'd become a part owner of the American Association, a top Triple-A-level minor league for a while, he was done with the major leagues for good.

However, because Landis has spared him from baseball's blacklist, Speaker was able to secure an important measure of immortality that four other participants in the 1912 World Series enjoyed. In 1936, Christy Mathewson had been selected as one of six original inductees into the newly chartered National Baseball Hall of Fame in Cooperstown, New York. A year later, he would be joined by John McGraw and by Tris Speaker; it would take another thirty-four years, but in 1971 both Harry Hooper and Rube Marquard joined them in Cooperstown and, happily, both men were still alive. Marquard, at eighty-four, spent much of his post-baseball life working the pari-mutuel windows at racetracks in New York and Baltimore (which would no doubt have made his beloved manager, McGraw the horse lover, beam with as much pride as if he'd tossed a two-hitter), while Hooper, at eighty-three, was appointed the Postmaster of Capitola, California, by President Franklin Roosevelt in 1933 and served in that capacity for twenty-four years.

On the eve of his induction, Marquard sat with a reporter and said, "Those eight games in 1912 were as good as it gets, as good as baseball gets. They wanted to beat us so bad, you could see it in their eyes. We wanted to beat them so bad that it still hurts me to think of us coming up short. But those were . . ."

He paused, emotion catching his voice.

"Those were glorious times, glorious times. I wish we could gather everyone together and play a game number nine tomorrow. . . ."

Unlike his manager, Giants owner John T. Brush would never see his beloved Giants win another world championship. Immediately after the series, Brush caused something of a firestorm when he refused to hand over to the National League the one-quarter of the $147,028.85 in profits that was part of the standard league agreement. "I cannot understand what Brush's contention is," Pirates owner Barney Dreyfuss said, "but perhaps he'll explain at the December meeting." He never got the chance. Weakened terribly, his doctors urged him to take a train to Pasadena, where the warm weather might restore his strength, but in the early-morning hours of November 26 he died near Seeburger, Missouri. He was sixty-seven years old.

Despite his attempts to regain favor with the citizens of Boston, James McAleer was as good as dead as the Red Sox' principal owner. His relationship with Jake Stahl, never a good one, exploded in 1913 when the Red Sox got off to a slow start and McAleer couldn't help himself from meddling. Then, in July, McAleer caught wind that Stahl was angling to replace him as the club president—not entirely stunning, since it was, after all, Stahl's own father-in-law who'd helped to quietly put the Sox' ownership group together. Feeling threatened, McAleer fired Stahl, who was more than happy to return to life as a banker. Ban Johnson, furious at McAleer's impetuousness, decided then and there that he would find a new group to own the Sox, and soon he would steer the club toward Joseph Lannin. McAleer's last years were lonely and unhappy, and on April 28, 1931, suffering from cancer, he was listening to a baseball game on the radio when a spasm of pain pushed him to the bathroom, where he loaded a pistol and shot himself dead at age sixty-nine. Stahl, his sparring partner, would live a prosperous, if sadly brief, life as a bank executive, dying of tuberculosis at age forty-three in 1922.

Both team captains aspired to be big-league managers, but only Heinie Wagner would get that chance, and it was an unfortunate one: By 1930 the Red Sox were barely surviving as a franchise, years of mismanagement and bad baseball reducing the club to a shell of its former glories, and while Wagner still had great passion and energy for the game, the best he could do in one year at the helm was a 52–102 record and last place in the American League, some fifty games behind pennant-winning Philadelphia. And while Doyle remained a loyal Giant for more than twenty years after retiring as a player in 1920, managing farm clubs in Nashville and Toronto, he was passed over in favor of Bill Terry when McGraw finally retired in 1932, and by the time Terry retired Doyle was fifty-five years old and starting to suffer the effects of all those long-ago days and nights spent in the coal mines of rural Illinois. Within a year he had full-blown tuberculosis, and it was Jane Mathewson, Big Six's widow, who suggested that Doyle move to Saranac Lake, Matty's final home, to be treated at Trudeau, the same sanitarium where Mathewson had spent so many of his final days. Unlike his idol, however, Doyle was destined to live a long life, staying in Saranac Lake until his death at age eighty-eight in 1974.

Fred Merkle never could outrun his slew of nicknames—"Bonehead," "Leather Skull," "Ivory Pate"—and, however unfairly, his failure to ignore Mathewson and catch Speaker's ninth-inning pop-up in Game Eight only added to his sad legacy. Luck was just never much on Merkle's side; in 1926, after finishing his playing career as a Yankee and spending a year as a coach, he was replaced by Art Fletcher—his old teammate, the shortstop who nearly blew Game Two of the '12 Series all by himself with his malfunctioning glove—and so it was Fletcher, and not Merkle, who took part in ten World Series between 1926 and 1943 (and cashed the checks that went along with them), and it was Merkle who wound up suffering during the darkest days of the Depression, grinding jobs at the Works Progress Administration and, later, with a fishing manufacturer. Whenever newspapermen would approach to do where-are-they-now features, he would slam the door in their face, and it wasn't until 1949 when he finally accepted an invitation to attend a Dodgers game at Ebbets Field that he started to loosen his grip on bitterness. Dodgers announcer Red Barber saw him crying during the game, and Merkle told him, "Past sins should be forgotten. I've been paying forty years." He died seven years later, at age sixty-seven.

Boston's three unsung World Series heroes each enjoyed the spoils of their success completely and unabashedly. Olaf Henriksen joined a vaudeville troupe and never again had to worry about buying a meal inside the Boston city limits. Larry Gardner, who drove in the winning run with his sacrifice fly, admitted, "I was disappointed at first because I thought the ball was going out. But then when I saw Yerkes tag up, then score to end it, I realized it meant $4,024.68, just about double my earnings for the year. And that was just fine by me." After his playing career he returned to his alma mater, the University of Vermont, and coached baseball for twenty years before becoming the school's athletic director. When he died at eighty-nine in 1976, he left his body to the university's Department of Anatomy, a proud Vermonter, quite literally, from cradle to grave. And while Hugh Bedient spent much of the 1912–1913 off-season feted from one part of western New York to the other, he always knew baseball wouldn't sink its hooks into him forever. After his sparkling 20–9 rookie season, he turned in records of 15–14 and 8–12 with the Sox the next two years, then essentially played in his backyard when he jumped to the Buffalo Blues of the Federal League in 1915, going 16–18 for a sixth-place club and calling it quits at age twenty-five. He left with no regrets, with a scrapbook overflowing with clippings from that splendid 1912 season, and with regular appearances in *Ripley's Believe It or Not!* for his forty-two-strikeout performance against Corry all those years ago.

"I was going good and felt fine," Bedient would explain to his local newspaper many years later. "I really can't explain why I quit but I felt the strain of trying to produce every fourth day would be a little too much so I came home."

That was one end of the spectrum. On the other resided Duffy Lewis, proprieter of "Duffy's Cliff," one-third of the "Million-Dollar Outfield," and likely the only man who saw Babe Ruth's first major-league home run (on May 6, 1915, when Ruth was pitching and Lewis was playing for the Red Sox against the Yankees at the Polo Grounds) and his 714th and final home run (on May 25, 1935, with Ruth playing and Lewis coaching for the Boston Braves against the Pirates at Forbes Field). A year later, he became the team's traveling secretary and stayed with the team for twenty-six years, following the franchise to Milwaukee. But he never severed ties with the Red Sox. In 1962, he attended a celebration of Fenway Park's fiftieth birthday alongside most of the surviving members of the Speed Boys, and in 1975, the Red Sox asked Lewis, by then eighty-seven, to throw out the first ball on Opening Day to honor the team's seventy-fifth season. Six months later, Lewis repeated that honor before Game Six of the World Series against the Cincinnati Reds. Some have tried to call that twelve-inning, 7–6 Red Sox victory the greatest game ever played.

But Duffy Lewis and forty-four other members of the 1912 Red Sox and 1912 Giants would probably all beg to differ.

Theodore Roosevelt would recover from his wounds, but his campaign never did get off the ground fully. Always at odds with the Bull Moosers, the Republicans in 1912—knowing they had zero hope of getting their own man, William Howard Taft, reelected—made it their mission to make sure Roosevelt wouldn't be able to secure a third term, and at that they succeeded. Although taken together, Roosevelt and Taft would win 50.6 percent of the vote—far outpolling Woodrow Wilson's popular tally by 1.3 million votes—it was an electoral landslide for the bespectacled governor of New Jersey and former president of Princeton University, Wilson garnering 435 electoral votes to only eighty-eight for Roosevelt and a paltry eight for Taft, who would now be free to watch as many baseball games as his oversized heart desired. John Flammang Schrank, the man who shot Roosevelt, was quickly declared insane by doctors and would spend the remaining thirty-one years of his life at Central State Mental Hospital in Waupon, Wisconsin, forever proclaiming the justness of his cause trying to prevent a man from running for a third term in office. Ironically, he would live long enough to see Franklin Roosevelt, Theodore's cousin, become the only man ever to secure a third term—and he would die less than fourteen months before he would win a fourth.

In Boston, anyway, it is unlikely that any of the candidates could have beaten John Fitzgerald, who was at the peak of his powers that October of 1912, with his eye on ever-higher offices. But for all the friends Honey Fitz made along the way—notably Nuf Ced McGreevy, whose own business would thrive until the advent of Prohibition eight years later—he also accrued a substantial list of enemies, among them James Michael Curley, the upstart boss of the city's South Side. Fitzgerald badly wanted to serve another term as mayor starting in 1914, but Curley wanted the job, too, and wasn't above going on the lecture circuit of Boston, weighing in on such matters as "Great Lovers: from Cleopatra to Tootles," alluding to widespread (though unsubstantiated) rumors of a romance between Honey Fitz and a blond cigarette girl named Tootles Ryan. Before Curley could go through with that one, Honey Fitz withdrew.

Four years later, Fitzgerald won back his old seat in the U.S. House of Representatives by 238 votes, but a challenge and subsequent investigation uncovered that numerous Fitzgerald votes came from falsely registered voters who didn't live in the district, or were in the military, or were, in some cases, not living at all. There were charges of voter intimidation and other fun methods of electioneering, and his term would last exactly 231 days before he was unseated by the House and replaced by his opponent, Peter F. Tague. Far from disgraced, Fitzgerald would regularly mount ill-fated runs for governor or senator over the coming decades, including a final one, in 1942, at age seventy-nine, in which he ran merely to make life difficult for one of his oldest political nemeses, Henry Cabot Lodge, Sr. In 1946, it was an indefatigable Honey Fitz who plotted out much of the main strategy (and shook most of the important hands) that helped secure a congressional seat for his twenty-nine-year-old grandson, John Fitzgerald Kennedy. At the victory celebration, Honey Fitz danced an Irish jig, sang "Sweet Adelaide"—always a favorite of the Royal Rooters—and predicted that his grandson would one day be president of the United States. He would not live to see that, dying at age eighty-seven on October 2, 1950, but you have to believe he was smiling somewhere in November of 1952 when Kennedy defeated Henry Cabot Lodge, Jr., for a U.S. Senate seat. And he must have *really* wanted to sing a few verses of "Tessie" eight years later when Kennedy fulfilled his grandfather's vision by winning the White House and defeating a Republican ticket headed by Richard Nixon and balanced out by . . . yes, Henry Cabot Lodge, Jr.

Nuf Ced.

Despite the mounting evidence against him, Charles Becker believed in the power of the badge, and thus believed no self-respecting jury of honest New Yorkers would ever dare convict him of killing Beansie Rosenthal. Oh, they might well believe he *did* it— but they were more likely to congratulate him for ridding the earth of one more scummy gambler than convict him for it. Before the jury went out, he told the reporter from the *World*: "I have no fear of what will happen." And he told the reporter from the *Journal*: "What happened was supposed to happen. There was no crime in it. None whatsoever. I will walk out of here when the jury comes back. You'll see."

But when the jury did come back three minutes before midnight on the evening of Thursday, October 24, they had a surprise for the fallen policeman. After a deliberation of just nine hours and thirty-seven minutes, jury foreman Harold B. Skinner pronounced the verdict to the charge of murder in the first degree:

"We find the defendant guilty as charged in the indictment."

With a mandatory sentence of death by electrocution.

All during the trial Becker had exhibited an air of confidence bordering on contempt for the whole process, as if disbelieving that this rogues' gallery of nicknames and yellow sheets could possibly sway twelve reasonable men away from his title, his authority, and his badge. Now, as all twelve men were polled and all came back with votes of guilty, Becker was transformed before the gallery and the eyes of fifty journalists to just another skell who couldn't buy off a jury: His legs weakened, his face paled, he could control neither his muscles nor his bowels. He would recover only slightly as he was dragged from the courtroom, blowing kisses at his wife, who was overcome with grief. "At last," said Charles Whitman, the ambitious district attorney, "the monster can sleep where he deserves to be for the rest of his short life."

The story didn't end here, of course. Though Judge Goff sentenced Becker five days later to die in Sing Sing's electric chair on December 12, just six weeks after the verdict, Becker's appeals process took well over a year to play out, and when it did, the verdict was overturned on February 24, 1914, the Court of Appeals criticizing both Goff's perceived pro-prosecution conduct and his handling of basic criminal procedure; in essence, Goff had become America's first celebrity judge, and the appellate was none too pleased. In the meantime, all of Becker's colorfully monikered accomplices—Dago Frank, Whitey Lewis, Lefty Louie, and Gyp the Blood—were found guilty and condemned to death, and as they were led to the gallows early in the morning of April 13, 1914, Dago Frank threw something of a red herring at the public, issuing his final statement as a breathing human being: "So far as I know, Becker had nothing to do with the case. It was a gambler's fight. I told some lies on the stand to prove an alibi for the rest of the boys."

Undeterred, Whitman forged forward with his case even more

forcefully than before. His earlier victory had greased him an all-but-certain path to a much higher office, but if he wanted to complete that journey he would need to make the conviction stick this time, and the odds were against him: Never before in the history of New York City had a man whose guilty murder verdict was overturned been reconvicted of the same crime. Bald Jack Rose was again the star witness. Judge Goff was replaced by Judge Samuel Seabury, thought by prosecutors to be a "defendant's judge," though he was also a crusader against corruption by such public trusts as the police department. This time, the trial took sixteen days and the result was the same: Guilty. Becker's date with Sparky the electric chair was scheduled for July 16. But, again, Becker's attorneys clogged the system with more appeals, more pleas, more attempts to spare the lieutenant the fate of dozens of common crooks he'd put away himself through the years. But by July 30, 1915, all those appeals were exhausted, and Becker's last hope was that the governor of New York would take mercy on his soul and commute his death sentence to life instead.

But Governor Charles Whitman was not inclined to uncap his pen.

So at 5:30 A.M., with Becker dressed all in black, his trousers slit up the sides, he took the grim walk down death row. While dozens of reporters jotted down his every breath and every motion, he was quickly strapped into the chair before issuing his final words: "Into thy hands, O Lord, I commend my spirit." A signal was given. A switch was thrown. Two thousand volts of electricity crackled into Becker's body. When that failed to kill him, a second jolt of two thousand volts was applied, and then a third. It took eight minutes for the grim task to be completed, and for decades advocates who wished to abolish the death penalty would cite Charles Becker's awful demise as one of their chief pieces of testimony.

His bitter widow ordered a headstone on which were listed Becker's vital statistics (July 26, 1870–July 30, 1915) and another message, etched in stone:

MURDERED BY GOVERNOR WHITMAN.

The police department ordered her to take it off. She did.

Unlike his old teammate, Fred Merkle, Fred Snodgrass never allowed his defining baseball moment to consume him in anger or bitterness. Though the fans of the day could be just as cruel as fans of today, though media of the day could be just as vicious, and opponents (to say nothing of teammates) just as biting, Snodgrass was confident enough in his own talents and comfortable enough in his own skin that even the prospect of seeing his name attached to something like "The $30,000 Muff" for the next sixty-two years only made him smile, never made his blood boil, always simply amazed him at the power of the American public to remember missteps and misdeeds.

As crushed as he was in the hours after the dropped fly, it simply wasn't in Snodgrass's nature to wallow in self-pity. By the next day, as he gathered with his teammates to pick up their checks, the players decided to sign a baseball for Eddie Brannick, the Giants' courtly assistant secretary. Snodgrass's full autograph read: "Fred '$1,400' Snodgrass," referring to the approximate amount he cost himself and each of his teammates. A few days later, after arriving in Los Angeles and consoling his poor mother, Snodgrass opened his door to local newsmen and offered no excuse: "I was frozen to the marrow when I muffed the fly. I didn't seem to be able to hold the ball. It just dropped out of the glove and that was all there was to it."

Part of Snodgrass's recovery, no doubt, can be credited to John McGraw, whose reputation as a win-at-all-costs megalomaniac belied the compassionate, forgiving soul that better represented who Muggsy really was. To the press in the weeks after the muff, he said of Snodgrass: "I have no complaint to make. I do not censure a player for muffing a fly ball. The loss meant more to me than anybody except myself knows. But I am not complaining. It's the luck of the national game." Then he repeated to the scribes a vow he'd already made to Snodgrass: Not only would he not hold the muff against him, he intended to raise Snodgrass's salary by $1,000; a few months later, when a contract arrived at Snodgrass's home, he saw that his manager had made good on that promise.

Snodgrass enjoyed as prosperous a post-baseball life as any ballplayer of the time could have asked for. He played four more full years with the Giants and the Boston Braves before retiring at age twenty-eight with a lifetime .275 average. The fact that he ended his career in Boston was one of the wonderfully quirky accidents baseball sometimes provides, especially given what happened one September day in 1914, two years after the muff, a year before he was traded. The Braves were in the middle of a miracle push from last place to first place, but the Giants had their number that day, especially Snodgrass. Late in the game, a Brave started lobbing a baseball to himself and then dropping it, mocking Snodgrass, and the frustrated crowd lapped it up. Snodgrass responded by thumbing his nose at the crowd as he walked out to center field; by the time he arrived, he realized he wasn't alone out there. A man had walked out of the stands, followed him all the way, then identified himself as James M. Curley—the newly elected mayor of Boston. Curley demanded Snodgrass's ejection. Bill Klem, who by now was laughing uncontrollably, told the mayor to forget it and get back to the stands before *he* got Klem's thumb. Snodgrass loved telling that story.

He went home to California, became a successful businessman and banker in Oxnard, and then served three terms in the City Council before being appointed acting mayor, a job he held for about a year before making a final move to Ventura, where he grew lemons and walnuts and regaled anyone who asked him with tales of his playing days. He was especially grateful one evening, many years after the Series, when he ran into Harry Hooper at a function in downtown Los Angeles. All those years later, Hooper *still* couldn't believe the catch Snodgrass had made on his line drive immediately after the muff, and he told Snodgrass, as he'd told anyone who would listen for fifty years, that it was the greatest defensive play he'd ever seen.

"Well, thank you," Snodgrass said, smiling. "Nobody ever mentions that catch to me. All they talk about is the muff."

"Well, people can say what they want," Hooper said. "I still see the catch like it happened yesterday."

A few years earlier, speaking to a reporter on the thirtieth anniversary of the Series, Snodgrass had said: "Hardly a day in my life, hardly an hour, that in some manner or other the dropping of that fly doesn't come up, even after thirty years. On the street, in my store, at my home, in Oxnard or Ventura, it's all the same. They might choke up before they ask me and they hesitate—but they always ask.

"Now, if I honestly felt that I, Fred C. Snodgrass, was really alone to blame for losing that series to the Red Sox I don't think I could go on. I could not have played baseball later and I could not now be in business. Many things happened to lose that series, and I'm sure you'll understand."

Funny thing, though? It's doubtful anyone understood. When Snodgrass died on April 5, 1974, this was the headline that appeared above his obituary in the *New York Times*, of all places:

FRED SNODGRASS, 86, DEAD;
BALL PLAYER MUFFED 1912 FLY.

In response to this, the next week's edition of *The New Yorker* featured an editorial that Snodgrass himself would no doubt have enjoyed and endorsed.

"It often happens with the *Times* that when a man dies certain unpleasant aspects of his life are given charitable short shrift in its obituary. For example, if a once-honored member of Congress has been convicted of a crime and put in prison, the *Times* obit writer nearly always makes as little as possible of this ugly, necessary fact: in the writing of his life, the dead man receives a sort of posthumous pardon in ellipsis and abbreviation.

"There is an exception to the rule. When it comes to sports, and especially to baseball, the *Times* rarely follows the principle of *de mortuis nil nisi bonum*: it would seem our National Pastime is too important a subject to be tampered with in the name of kindness."

Here, the magazine reprinted the headline.

"With a brisk matter-of-factness, the *Times* might have hesitated to employ the obituary of an unregenerate mass murderer, the account began, 'Fred Carlisle Snodgrass, who muffed an easy fly that helped cost the New York Giants the 1912 World Series, died Friday at the age of eighty-six.'

"Note that the deed took place sixty-two years ago. The passage of six long and presumably penitent decades has done nothing to soften the heart of the implacable obituary writer. Mr. Snodgrass isn't to be let off with a simple, unmodified fly. Oh, no, it was an 'easy' fly that Mr. Snodgrass had the misfortune to muff.

"How lucky we are, those of us who go to the grave without having played a professional sport! Our errors, whatever they may be, are not in the record books. The *Times* will be gentle with us, and a miscalculation that occupied less than a second on a sunny fall day when we were twenty-four will not be made the means by which we win a place in history."

Still, for all the tumult, it was a hell of a life, being a baseball player and a hell of a time to *be* a baseball player, and for the rest of their lives, they understood what a privilege it had been. And they almost certainly would have echoed the words of Fred Snodgrass, as told to author Lawrence S. Ritter half a century after the 1912 Series was played, contested, and decided:

"My years in baseball," Snodgrass said, "had their ups and downs, their strife and their torment. But the years I look back at most fondly, and those I'd like most to live over, are the years when I was playing center field for the New York Giants."

Acknowledgments

All of us who delve into the wonderful, practically limitless world of baseball history will eternally owe a debt of gratitude to Lawrence S. Ritter, who for several years in the 1960s traversed the country with a tape recorder in his hand and a special inquisitiveness in his brain and made it his mission to get into the public record the recollections and the remembrances of old-time baseball players before these wonderful athletes—and their memories—were lost to us forever. The resulting masterpiece—*The Glory of Their Times*—not only established an entire genre that those of us of future generations hungrily read for pleasure, it established a limitless supply of subject possibilities. Baseball is a magnificent game in 2009; it was magnificent in 1912, and in 1893, and for as long as it has been played and people have cared about it.

I am an avowed junkie of both history and of baseball, so this project was a joy in too many ways to count. Ninety percent of the research for this book took place in libraries and archives, in darkened microfilm rooms and in basements and attics where hidden scrapbooks almost always yield priceless results to patient eyes. I am indebted to the research staffs at both the New York and Boston Public Libraries, as well as to the men who filled the newspapers and magazines of 1912 with so much copy that if you closed your eyes every now and again during this project, it was impossible not to feel like you were wearing an old fedora, clacking away at a manual type-writer, and listening to paperboys screaming "Extra! Extra!" on every street corner. Primary source material was found everywhere you wanted to look, but specifically from these newspapers:

In New York City: The *Journal*. The *American*. The *Herald*. The *Tribune*. The *New York Times*. The *New York Post*. The *Daily Press*. The *Daily Mail*. The *Telegraph*. The *Telegram*. The *Sun*. The *World*. In Boston: The *Globe*. The *Evening Globe*. The *Boston Post*. The Boston *Record*. The *Herald*. The *Traveler*. Elsewhere: The *Los Angeles Times*. The *Washington Post*. The *Chicago Tribune*. The *Sporting News*.

Several books were very helpful, serving as road maps for some of the key figures of this book, among them: *The Glory of Their Times*, by Lawrence S. Ritter; *Sportswriter: The Life and Times of Grantland Rice*, by Charles Fountain; *Baseball As I Have Known It*, by Fred Lieb; *Tris Speaker: The Rough-and-Tumble Life of a Baseball Legend*, by Timothy Gay; *Red Sox Century*, by Glenn Stout and Richard A. Johnson; *John McGraw*, by Charles C. Alexander; *John McGraw: My Thirty Years in Baseball*, by John McGraw; *The Giants of the Polo Grounds*, by Noel Hynd; *Matty: An American Hero*, by Ray Robinson; *1912: Wilson, Roosevelt, Taft & Debs—The Election That Changed the Country*, by James Chace; and *Boston's Royal Rooters*, by Peter J. Nash.

On the Internet, there were two sites that were absolutely invaluable on an almost daily basis, and they are resources I urge all baseball fans—not just authors—to visit every day they sit in front of a computer. The first is www.baseball-reference.com, which is the greatest invention for baseball fans since the scorecard. The other is the Baseball Biography Project, put together by the amazing people who comprise the Society for American Baseball Research. Access that site here: www.bioproj.sabr.org, and if you have even a little interest in baseball's history, its legacies, and its amazing assortment of characters past and present, I urge you to join SABR.

I have been blessed to write three books now, and for all three I have had the great good fortune to work alongside Jason Kaufman, my editor at Doubleday, who not only shepherds the words but also manages to make the craft of writing seem, and feel, as joyful and as fulfilling as all writers want it to be. My career, and my life, are immeasurably richer for having collaborated with him. My thanks also to his assistant, Rob Bloom, who never fails to provide an encouraging voice and a helpful hand when it is needed most, and to Peter Grennen, a fellow Flyer who took such care and skill in copy-editing the manuscript; whatever errors remain are mine alone to answer for. Frank Scatoni and Greg Dinkin, my agents at Venture Literary, are the reason I have been able to live out this wonderful dream of writing books; they were the ones who showed initial faith and have provided endless support, and I can never express properly the depths of my gratitude for that.

As marvelous a life as it is to write books, it almost seems like an excess of riches that I also have a day job that I treasure. Greg Gallo is the man who hired me to write a sports column at the *New York Post*, which means all he's done for me is open the door to the rest of my life, a debt I'll never be able to come close to repaying. Every day I appear in that newspaper is a joy to me, and honors the memory of my father, Mickey, who encouraged my dreams from the start and helped foster them by bringing the *Post* home with him every day. It was my humble honor to work under Dick Klayman for five years, and my lone regret that I didn't get twenty more under his guidance and friendship. The daily encouragements of Tim Sullivan, Pat Hannigan, Dave Blezow, Mike Battaglinio, and Kevin Kenney all bring me to a better place with my words and my work. And every day Col Allan, the big boss, inspires me to want to kick a little more ass than I did the day before.

Baseball has become such a deep part of my professional life, it's been a privilege to work alongside the best baseball columnist in the country, Joel Sherman, who has helped broaden my depth of knowledge with his wisdom and his generosity. He is just one of an amazing corps of professional confidantes who would make any newspaperman look smarter than they really are. Chief among these are Marc Berman, Les Carpenter, Jack Curry, Ian O'Connor, Joe Posnanski, Steve Politi, and Adrian Wojnarowski. Ours is a proud fraternity, even if it seems to shrink in numbers by the day, but for now and forever I wish to salute the folks who are not only my friends but continue to make this such an honorable vocation, notably: Dominic Amore, Dave Anderson, Marty Appel, Harvey Araton, Don Burke, Dave Buscema, Pete Caldera, Rich Chere, Brian Costello, Chris D'Amico, Mike Fannin, Chris Faytok, John Feinstein, Pat Forde, Kevin Gleason, Dan Graziano, Vahe Gregorian, Mark Hale, Jon Heyman, Kim Jones, George King, Bob Klapisch, Kevin Manahan, Dave Lennon, Dinn Mann, Tom Missel, Chuck Pollock, Steve Popper, Ed Price, T. J. Quinn, Lenn Robbins, Mike Rodman, Michael Rosenberg, Bob Ryan, Ben Shpigel, Tara Sullivan, Wright Thompson, Chuck Ward, Charlie Wenzelberg, Dan Wetzel, and Steve Wright. And it isn't just newspaper folks who help a guy out with a project like this, so I must also recognize Charlie Albanese, Eddie Burns, Amy Carr, Pamela Curry, Nick Cusano, John Egan, Esq., Dr. George Evans, Bill Going, John Hammersley, Bro. Robert Lahey, John Lovisolo, Scott Mackenzie, Mike Mac-Donald, Tim McMahon, Dr. Jim Martine, Tom Pecora, Kevin Quigley, Melanie Rolli, Paul Sabini, and Dr. Richard Simpson.

As I mentioned in the dedication my mother, Ann, is a constant source of strength and faith, a glass-half-full soul in a glass-half-empty world. And then there is Leigh Hursey Vaccaro, Molly to my Desmond, Diane to my Jack, Brenda to my Eddie (though I suspect she would never go for deep-pile carpets and a couple of paintings from Sears). The remarkable thing isn't that we're this happy after this many years together; it's that, if anything, the laughter is louder and longer now than it was at the start. And yes: I'll get to work cleaning the staircase now. Deadline is past. Back to the world.

Mike Vaccaro
Hillsdale, New Jersey
September 2008